THE BOLDEST DREAM

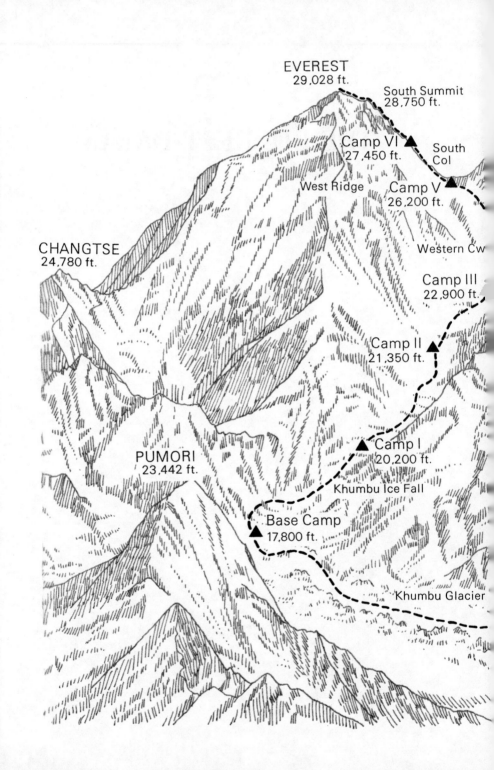

LHOTSE
27,923 ft.

neva
ur

NUPTSE
25,726 ft.

Camp1V
24,900 ft.

BARUNTSE
23,688 ft.

The Story of Twelve

THE BOLD

Harcourt Brace Jovanovich
New York and London

**RICK
RIDGEWAY**

Who Climbed Mount Everest

EST DREAM

Map by Nicholas Fasciano

Requests for permission to make copies of any part of the work should be mailed to:
Permissions, Harcourt Brace Jovanovich, Inc.
757 Third Avenue, New York, N.Y. 10017

Printed in the United States of America

Library of Congress Cataloging in Publication Data
Ridgeway, Rick.
The boldest dream.
1. Mountaineering—Everest, Mount. 2. Ridgeway, Rick. 3. Mountaineers—United States—Biography. 4. Everest, Mount—Description. I. Title.
GV199.44.E85R5   796.5'22'0954   78–11091

ISBN 0–15–113432–4

First edition
B C D E

Dedicated to
RON FEAR
and
BRUCE CARSON
two climbers who
were with us all the
way to the summit

危機 WEI-JI

A Chinese character that has no
translation into English. It is a
combination of the two characters
for danger and for opportunity.

"Whatever you can do, or dream you can,
begin it. Boldness has genius,
power, and magic in it."

—GOETHE

ACKNOWLEDGMENTS

Foremost, I would like to thank Mark Herron for helping me edit this book. I would also like to thank all the climbing members and the film crew of the expedition for their support and the loan of their diaries. I would especially like to thank Arlene Blum for the use of the hours of taped interviews she made during the climb, Dan Emmett for his invaluable help in locating an editor, Gene and Natalie Jones for locating a publisher, and Ed Goren of CBS who made available the entire collection of tapes recorded by the film crew.

The assistance of many others connected with the expedition was invaluable: officers of the U.S. embassy in Kathmandu, David Fischer and Kent Obee; employees of Mountain Travel in Kathmandu; Bernie and Nancy Hausner; Teri Storseth; Ken Sullet; Peter Klika. The final hacked, taped, and penciled draft was patiently typed by Pat Rueckert.

Finally, I want to thank my ace pal, John Kiewit, for always reminding me there is more to life than sitting in front of a typewriter.

RICK RIDGEWAY
Malibu, California
May 1978

PREFACE

The Library of Congress card catalogue lists under "Mount Everest" 121 titles; under "Mount Everest, expeditions," 48 titles. Before I finally decided to write this book, I thought it perhaps presumptuous to consider adding another title to that long list. What could I possibly have to say that hadn't already been said in dozens of other books? We were the thirteenth expedition to attempt Everest from the Nepal side; our summit climbers were something like the fifty-fourth and fifty-fifth people to reach the top; we didn't climb the mountain by a new route but used the southeast ridge route, which has been the way of ascent for nearly all previous expeditions; we weren't even the first Americans to climb Everest (that honor went to the 1963 American Everest Expedition).

Yet I had a notion that in our expedition was a story worth telling. For one thing, our team was centered around a core of three longtime friends—they had met each other years before at law school—who could only be described as weekend enthusiasts of the sport of mountain climbing. They were like thousands of other people who get out a few times a year to scale a peak in the Sierras or Rockies, sometimes finding a need for technical gear like pitons and ropes, but frequently just scrambling to a summit. They were somewhat different in that every year they liked to travel abroad for a climbing holiday, but they definitely were not the type who normally get involved in a major Himalayan expedition.

I doubt that there are many people in this country who at some time in their lives haven't daydreamed of climbing Mount Everest. Everest is more than a lump of rock and ice and snow. It is more than just the world's highest mountain. Everest is a symbol and a metaphor. It represents the ultimate goal and the ultimate achievement. While considering whether to write this book I realized that the fact that three lawyers who by normal standards of the sport were not prepared for such an undertaking but had decided to trade metaphor for reality was in itself a story that warranted writing.

When I did start this book, however, I took care not to lionize either the lawyers or the other people who eventually became involved in the expedition. After all, we were just human beings with human foibles. I've tried to tell this story as honestly as possible, documenting the strong as well as the weak aspects of the twelve people brought together for a few months on the world's highest mountain. This book is necessarily a personal account, and my point of view may differ from that of the others who were on the trip.

To each of the twelve people Everest was a personal experience, a personal lesson. While none of us would come back from the expedition and "move to Big Sur and become a Buddhist hermit meditating in a sea cliff cave," we were all in some way changed by the expedition. For me, it was the visit to an exotic and magical land, with memories like those of a childhood fairy tale; it was the camaraderie of the Sherpas and the lessons learned from them; it was the vision gained from being so intimately close for so long to such a powerful mountain. If I can succeed in sharing with the reader even a part of those memories, lessons, and visions, then I think I have justified adding another title to the card catalogue.

R.R.

Besides the obvious increase in size, the addition of the film crew also altered the complexion of the expedition. We were now "Hollywood," and we learned we had to start doing things we normally wouldn't have. Mike Hoover, hired by CBS as the director, went to Boulder to film part of the team in training. He asked Barb, Gerry, Bob, and Dee to meet him at the quarter-mile track at the University of Colorado. He wanted to film them jogging. When they showed up in gym trunks and Adidas, he immediately said that wouldn't do.

"This is Everest. You guys are training for the world's highest mountain. We have to make it *look* that way."

He then had them shoulder fully loaded backpacks and, still wearing gym trunks, lace up their huge high-altitude double boots. They then again ran around the track, cameras rolling.

"Now that looks more like guys who are training for Everest," Hoover said.

Gerry didn't say anything, but he was silently wondering if this didn't bode ill for possible conflicts with the camera crew later in the expedition. Gerry was concerned the film crew would assign him a personality for the film's sake, and he was worried they might portray all of us as mountain-climbing charlatans. For now, Gerry remained silent. "If a requirement for climbing Everest is that I must enter into the entertainment business for three months," he later wrote, "so be it."

CBS also arranged for crews to film Hans working in Holland and Frank jogging through the streets of Jakarta. Accompanied by a film team, Dan, Phil, Arlene, Chris, and I made a practice ascent of Mount Rainier. Perhaps because we weren't asked to do anything out of the ordinary, we all had a good time and came away from the Rainier climb feeling the film would add an interesting dimension to the expedition. Then, with only days remaining before our departure to Nepal, we all flew to New York City for a press conference paid for by CBS and hosted by the plush Explorers Club.

The interior of the Explorers Club could be taken from Jules

Verne's novel where Phileas Fogg, member of London's Reform Club society, is wagering the armchair adventurers that he can travel around the world in less than eighty days. We entered the club, passing under crossed elephant tusks, then were greeted by a twelve-foot-high stuffed polar bear. Other samples of taxidermy created a forest of antlers and glass eyeballs. In the back of the reception room was a five-foot solid ice carving of Mount Everest. It was sculpted to exact scale. I recognized the Lhotse Face, the South Col, even the Hillary Step. A small note said it was made by the Waldorf-Astoria. While I was staring at it, a bow-tied waiter asked me what I would like to drink. I glanced over and saw a full wet bar with an international galaxy of assorted booze. "Beer," I said. "No, make that scotch on the rocks—I mean Chivas on the rocks." Why not? This was heady stuff for a climbing bum used to scrounging pennies for beer money.

In the reception room swarms of media people from newspapers, radios, and magazines were hobnobbing with people I guessed to be the CBS honchos. I spotted a good-looking young woman standing by herself and decided to do a little hobnobbing myself.

"Are you from a newspaper?" I asked.

"No, a magazine," she said.

"Oh? Which one?"

"*McCall's.*"

"*McCall's?* What interest do they have in Mount Everest?" I thought perhaps they were considering doing a piece on the two women on our team.

"Interest? Oh, none. I just come to these press conferences for the free booze."

By then my drink had arrived, so I toasted her, saying she probably had the best reason of anyone for being there. Then Barry Frank, the president of CBS Sports, announced he would introduce the climbing team and the director of the film. We all walked forward to stand and be identified. Only Hans and

Frank, who were overseas, were absent. Dan and Phil were dressed in tailored suits. Arlene wore an attractive cotton print dress that looked incongruous against her unshaven legs. Gerry, Barb, Dee, and Bob were modestly dressed. Chris, hair neatly tied in a pony tail, had on Levi's, Adidas shoes, and a freshly laundered surgeon's shirt. I wore Levi's and a Hawaiian Aloha shirt.

After our introduction, Barry Frank explained how CBS had been impressed by eleven climbers, none well-known or famous, who believed they could climb Mount Everest. "CBS believes they can do it too," he said. "This won't be a mountain-climbing show, this will be a people show." He then introduced the director, Mike Hoover.

Hoover is an impressive man. Thirty-three years old, six foot four, lean and solid with an angular face and aquiline eyes. He looks as if he should be an army general. I'd learned a few things about him. He was respected in the film business as a very competent cameraman and director capable of working in adverse conditions. He was also the best mountain climber in the film business. His credits included Clint Eastwood's *Eiger Sanction* and several other climbing films, including an Emmy award–winning *National Geographic* special. He had a reputation as a man who got what he wanted out of his crew and his film subjects. It was going to be interesting to see how he managed with this group.

In addition to Hoover and five other climber-filmmakers hired for this job, CBS was also sending one of their regular directors to assist Hoover as far as Base Camp. His name was Ed Goren. Ed was thirty-two years old, born and raised in New York, and he had never been hiking. When Barry Frank first considered Ed for the job, Frank had instructed him to come to the Central Park Reservoir at seven in the morning. Frank told Ed to bring jogging shorts and shoes to the reservoir. Ed suspected something unusual was in the air. After they had lapped the reservoir twice—and Ed was still standing—Frank told him he had passed the test. His next assignment was to film the American Bicentennial Everest Expedition's climb of the world's highest mountain. He would have to accompany the team as far as their Base Camp. What Frank didn't tell him was that he would have to hike 170 miles through muddy, leech-infested jungles to get there.

After the introductions we all descended on the bar, except for Barb and Gerry who were on strict training programs. I was developing a dense mental fog, wandering through the crowd looking for the *McCall's* girl. I found myself standing next to a short, serious-looking man. I asked if he was from the press.

"No," he said, "I'm vice-president of CBS Sports."

"Glad to meet you," I said, shaking his hand and spilling part of my scotch on an antique Persian carpet. "That was sure great of you guys to back our expedition."

"Yes," he said, "I was surprised we decided to do it. I don't think we would have except for the tall ships."

"Tall ships?"

"You must have heard about it. Two days ago, on the Fourth of July, there was a review of old square-rigged ships down the Hudson. New York responded with a patriotic enthusiasm very rare here. Everybody was suddenly proud to be American. We were all surprised by the response."

"What's that got to do with Mount Everest?" I asked.

"We thought that if people were so enthused about celebrating the Bicentennial with a fleet of tall ships, perhaps they would respond to a group of Americans celebrating the country's two hundredth by climbing the world's highest mountain." He looked at me for a moment, then added, "I hope we didn't make a mistake."

"Oh, no, I'm sure you made the right decision," I said. I decided to leave him before I put my foot in my mouth. I walked back to the ice carving and stared at the miniature mountain, tracing the route we would follow, thinking about what I had just heard. If that stationery designer in Dan Emmett's office hadn't attached the word *Bicentennial* to our letterhead, we might not have obtained backing for the expedition. We might not have received the permit. Any of a hundred things could have gone wrong. But now, no matter what, I knew we would at least reach the mountain.

4

"So you think the team will make the summit?"

"Yes, I do. It will be tough, but I think we'll put at least two climbers on the summit. All this talk about eight or ten people getting to the top is nonsense."

"If only two climbers get up, who do you think it will most likely be?"

"Well, if I had to put money on it, I would place my bets on Roach and Ridgeway. Gerry is by far the most physically fit of all of us, and I think Rick has hidden strength that will probably surface toward the end of the expedition."

I was eavesdropping on the newspaper correspondent interviewing Dee Crouch. They apparently weren't aware that I could hear them. They were two rows of seats behind me, their voices just audible above the whir of the jet engines. In fifteen minutes we would be landing in Kathmandu.

I thought, So Dee thinks Gerry and I have the best chance and I've got hidden strengths. They're hidden all right. I still harbored doubts. For one thing, I had a vague feeling of foreboding, a presentiment. Glancing over the back of my seat, I surveyed the rest of the group. They were all cheerful, knowing we would soon arrive at our destination, that it was really going to happen. I hoped all of us would be laughing in two and a half months.

My thoughts were interrupted by someone at the rear of the plane yelling excitedly about mountains out the window. Crossing the aisle. I leaned over a disconcerted Nepali and craned my neck for a view. The horizon was crammed with huge monsoon cumulus boiling thousands of feet upward. Then I saw it, peaking out on top of the clouds, a white mass glittering with a different shine than the surrounding clouds, an incredible hulk of ice and snow—my first sighting of the great Himalaya. My excitement was like that of a young child, seeing something new, great, and wonderful. I recognized a peak from all the years of pursuing mountaineering books. It was Kanchenjunga, near Darjeeling, in India. The third-highest mountain in the world, it looked just as impressive as it had in the photo books. I followed the horizon north, then back west. Nothing but towering monsoon clouds. I knew Everest was somewhere underneath the clouds, hiding. I would see it soon enough. The "Fasten seatbelts" sign came on as we approached the Valley of Kathmandu. We would be down in a few minutes.

I knew from the travel books it was eight miles long and eight miles wide and surrounded by foothills. The valley's floor has a mean elevation of 4,500 feet above sea level. The crest of the Himalayas is about thirty-five miles north of the city. Because of the monsoon, it was covered with clouds. The Kathmandu Valley has about 500,000 inhabitants, and from the plane's window I could see that many of them lived in red brick houses. There were no high buildings—the tallest perhaps five stories—and I spotted, rising in the back of the city, like a bishop on a chessboard, a minaret several hundred feet tall. Although I didn't know it at the time, there was also a siren that at that moment was crying across the airport, warning the farmers to move their cows off the airstrip. We were coming in for a landing in a place that considered cows much more valuable than jet airplanes.

I saw Chris leave the house and run across the compound, wildly waving with his arms. He had already been in Kathmandu for four days, assisting in the preparations. I jumped out of the car and we bear-hugged, and then one by one he greeted the rest of the team.

"You won't believe this place," he said. "It's unreal. Kathmandu is right out of the Middle Ages."

Dave Fischer came out of his house and we all exchanged introductions. In his mid-thirties, light-haired, and boyish-looking, he was dressed in a khaki safari suit similar to those foreign service officers wear in the tropics. With all of us listening he said, "Everything's going according to plan. The first wave of porters left a few days ago. The second wave left yesterday. That leaves slightly less than two hundred loads to go, and those will leave with the rest of you when you start the approach march."

He pointed to stacks of cardboard boxes that I had last seen at the docks in Los Angeles. There were several men busy opening boxes and repacking equipment. They must be the Sherpas. Although I was eager to meet them, I knew it was important to listen to what Dave had to say.

"It's a lot easier staggering the departure of the porters—they have less impact on the local villages, and it makes it easier for them to find food and shelter each night." The previous American Everest expedition in 1963 had used some 900 porters who trekked in one huge group. Since the porters are expected to find their own food in the villages along the trail, that expedition had left a wake of famine as it approached Everest. By dividing our group, we hoped to avoid that problem.

Chris grabbed my arm and said, "Come on, let's go over to the garage—I want you to meet some of the Sherps." (For some reason we all started referring to the Sherpas by that abbreviated name, "Sherps.") We walked over to the staging area in front of the garage, and several of them looked up, grinning expectantly, knowing they were about to be introduced to some of the people with whom they would be spending the next three months.

About twenty of them had come to Kathmandu from their villages near Mount Everest to help pack loads. I was amazed how small they were. Some of them weighed little more than one hundred pounds. I had expected them to be short but also strongly built and compact. After all, these were the fabled Sherpas, capable of carrying huge loads at impossible altitudes, of climbing time after time to the South Col without the benefit of oxygen, and famous for heroics performed on the early Everest expeditions in the 1920s and 1930s. Rather than being barrel-chested, they were average-looking men of short stature. Some of them were downright skinny.

I was introduced to Ang Phurba, one of our sirdars. *Sirdar* is the term for the leader of the Sherpa team, and on our expedition there were to be two: one in charge of the Sherpas up to the time they left Base Camp and began the actual climbing, the other in charge while they were above Base Camp. Ang had the latter duty—high-altitude sirdar. I recognized him from photographs I'd seen in the books by Chris Bonington, the well-known British expedition leader. Ang had distinguished himself on Bonington's two attempts to climb the huge southwest face of Everest, the later of which, in 1975, was successful. He had made several carries to the highest camp, Camp 6, at

27,300 feet. Doug Scott, one of the climbers with Bonington, said, "I think Ang has all the confidence of a regular alpine climber. He is the most natural climber I have ever met among the Sherpas."

Ang was twenty-nine, although he could have passed for a teenager. He was good-looking, with Mongolian features, hair stylishly cut and carefully combed. He wore a clean yellow T-shirt neatly tucked into his modishly striped bell-bottom pants. Holding a clipboard on which he was taking inventory of several boxes, he didn't look at all like a hillsman from a land that had no roads and no written language. I noticed that his inventory notes were in English.

We shook hands. He said, "Hello," and then, "Nice to meet you" in pidgin, but clearly understandable, English. I told him I recognized him from photographs I'd seen in mountain-climbing books, and that I had read what a good climber he was. He grinned sheepishly as the other Sherpas standing nearby laughed.

Chris introduced me to the rest of the Sherpas, at least those whose names he could remember. It was hopeless to try to remember more than a couple of names upon the first introduction. They all seemed to be called by some two-word name that combined a few basic names like Tsering, Nima, Nawang, Tenzing, Pema. Like Ang, all of them were carefully dressed, with hair neatly combed.

The last Sherpa I met I had no trouble remembering. For months I had been reading his name on the Xerox copies of the Telex correspondence between Kathmandu and Washington, D.C., periodically sent by Phil to all the expedition members. He was Pasang Kami, "P.K." for short. He had been hired in late April to buy all the local provisions we would take on the approach march. During the preparation his name always popped up as the man who was buying the rice and potatoes, the tea and sugar, the cook's utensils and kitchenware, and a myriad other items big and small. Dave Fischer had originally recommended him, and Mike Cheney had reluctantly agreed to release him from his regular duties as chief sirdar for Mountain Travel, a Kathmandu trekking agency. Besides his responsibilities organizing the approach march, P.K. would also, during the actual climb, be the manager of Base Camp. Ours was the first Everest expedition on which a Sherpa would be given this important responsibility. P.K.'s wife, very much aware that most of the accidents on Everest occur in the Icefall, had agreed to his joining our expedition only if he stayed in Base Camp. He had been through the Icefall too many times on previous expeditions, and she felt he was tempting fate. He promised her he would remain below.

P.K. appeared middle-aged, about five foot six, weighing perhaps 130 pounds. He wore moderately thick glasses, and because his hair and general appearance were more unkempt than the other Sherpas', he had the slightly disheveled look of a university scholar.

He looked at me and said, "Ah, finally I get to meet all the expedition member. How did you say your name?"

"Rick," I said.

"Good. Easy name to remember. What state do you come from?"

"A place on the west side of the United States called California."

"Near what city?"

"Well, near the city of Los Angeles. I live in a little town north of there—on the ocean."

"Oh. What town is that?"

"Well, it's a little town called Malibu. Do you know where that is?"

"Oh, yes. Many rich peoples live in that area. Very nice, that part of California. I like it there very much."

"You've been there, then?"

"Oh, yes. Some time ago I make the visit to the United States.

I visit forty states altogether. You know, too much the ride in the bus, but I get to see almost everything. I stay in Los Angeles with friends for many days—they take me all over."

"That's amazing. Did you like Los Angeles?"

"Oh, very big city and some nice building, but the air come all yellow, you know, and make it choking to breathe. But my friends take me to Disneyland. That's something else, you know, we don't have anything like that in Nepal."

At his last comment, P.K. chuckled. Like Ang, P.K. also had a clipboard on which he had been adding long columns of figures. Lying next to it was a Rockwell pocket calculator. Obviously, I was dealing with an organized, intelligent man, not some back-country bumpkin.

P.K. told Phil the first two waves of porters were already off, and everything was on schedule.

Phil asked, "How many porters will we have altogether?"

P.K. replied, "Oh, I think we will have more than five hundred, maybe five hundred and fifty."

Phil whistled and raised his eyebrows. It seemed as though a lot of people were expending a lot of energy so twelve could climb a mountain.

"Not so bad," said P.K. "When the Italians climb Everest few years ago, they go up the South Col route just like you but they take two thousand porters. You still have a small expedition." It was comforting to know that, even though we considered ourselves to be a big expedition, by past Everest standards we qualified as a small group. P.K. next explained there was plenty to do before we began the approach march: buying last-minute items, repacking many of the boxes, issuing the hiking equipment we would need on the approach march, and completing some unfinished paper work with the government. Nevertheless, he said, we should be ready to start the approach in a few days.

Phil was then introduced to another man dressed in plain pants and a slightly wrinkled white business shirt who looked different from the Sherpas. He was Byanju, who would be our liaison officer. All expeditions in Nepal are required to be accompanied by an official from the government who remains with them to the end. This presence is to ensure that the expedition doesn't do anything the Nepalese don't want it to do —such as climb mountains for which they don't have permits, film places that are considered off limits, or even go so far as to be a front for a spying operation on the Chinese.

This latter possibility is not as farfetched as it might seem. There was a case in the early sixties of just such a group operating in India. Ostensibly it was an innocuous climbing expedition; in reality it was a CIA group working in conjunction with the Indian government. The operation is still classified today—although the Nepalese are very much aware of it—and it includes several of America's best-known mountaineers. The group arrived in India, where they let it be known that their intention was to climb a mountain in the Nanda Devi massif. They hired a group of Sherpas to help them porter their equipment, but among the boxes of gear and food was an item seldom found on mountaineering expeditions—a nuclear-powered monitor with a super-sensitive seismograph and a Geiger counter capable of detecting abnormal radioactive material in the atmosphere. The monitor could, if planted in the right location, detect a nuclear explosion hundreds of miles away—in other words, in China. And in this case, the right location was the summit of a 7,000-meter mountain near the border of Tibet.

The expedition reached their base camp without mishap, but then, partway up the mountain, they were devastated by a big avalanche. The result was tragic—several Sherpas were killed. They regrouped, however, and continued on. The weakened team couldn't make the summit, so they did the next best thing—they planted the monitor, positioned in the right direction, at their high point on the mountain. All seemed well until a few weeks later when another avalanche destroyed the monitor, carrying it down the mountain. The CIA was worried; there was a substantial quantity of very powerful radioactive material in the monitor which was now possibly lying crushed in the snowfield, snow that fed into the sacred Ganges River. If the Ganges were contaminated by radioactive material, it would create an international scandal. The team was sent back to the mountain, equipped with sensitive Geiger counters, to locate the missing monitor. Unable to locate any sign of the instrument, they assumed it had not been crushed in the avalanche and the radioactive material was still safely sealed in its container. Presumably, the monitor is still up there, buried in the ice, with the nuclear material decaying at the rate of a half-life as slow as the descent of a glacier.

I heard the ringing of a handlebar bell, the kind with which every bicycle in Kathmandu is equipped. A servant opened the iron gates and in rode a man in his early thirties, Caucasian, with dark hair wetted down and combed with a perfectly defined part on the side. It was Joe Reinhardt, who would be working as our interpreter and Advance Base Camp manager. Shaking hands, he joined the rest of us, Sherpas and sahibs alike, all opening boxes, checking lists, chatting and laughing, getting to know each other.

Most people, including the Sherpas, were colorfully dressed: Arlene had a flowered hat that looked like a tropical sombrero, Chris wore a rainbow shirt dyed with tribal colors he had bought in Africa, and I had on a gaudy yellow Aloha shirt with pictures of red and orange Japanese carp. So, this is it, I thought. For the first time since this thing started, all of us are gathered together at the same time in the same place. It looked more like a crowd at an outdoor rock 'n' roll concert than a team set to climb Everest.

On our arrival in Nepal we tentatively set a departure day of July 31, a Saturday, as the day we would begin the approach march. As each day passed, it seemed less likely we could make that optimistic deadline. For one thing we were having trouble getting a permit for our single side-band radio which would serve as a communication link between Base Camp and Kathmandu. It appeared we would get the permit, but it would take a few days. There were smaller problems that also took time. We discovered our foam sleeping pads didn't have covers, and that they would double as tent sponges unless we found something to cover them. Some food items were missing and had to be replaced. Still another reason why we would have difficulty leaving on Saturday had nothing to do with government permits or regulations, or with equipment and supplies. It was simply that in Nepal, Saturday is a very unlucky day to begin a journey.

To compound our problem, the Saturday of July 31, 1976, was the most inauspicious Saturday the Nepalese astrologers had seen for many years. The Royal Astrologers of the King's Court, among the highest paid and most respected government employees in Nepal, had computed that two days were missing from the lunar calendar (like our own Western calendar, theirs is not quite adequate to describe, over a period of time, the complete celestial cycle). On July 28, the day after our arrival in Nepal, the Prime Minister ruled that a twelve-day festival should begin in order to propitiate the gods and ward off evils that would surely try to take advantage of this dark period to wreak havoc. This fear was confirmed later that same day when news arrived in Kathmandu that China had been devastated by an immense earthquake (later considered to be the second most destructive earthquake in the world's history, having killed over 700,000 persons). It was commonly believed in Kathmandu that the earthquake had hit China, and not Nepal, only because the festival had been initiated in time.

Dave Fischer was worried by these events. While there was a concern we might not be able to leave on Saturday, our real worry was over the 400 loads that were already on their way to Everest. If the porters who were carrying the loads learned that the court astrologers considered the period one of extraordinarily grave crisis, they would set down their loads and refuse to go any farther until celestial conditions improved. Since the evil period would last for twelve days, it was conceivable our boxes could lie in the mud of the monsoon rain for that long. Since the boxes were only made of wax-coated cardboard, they would decompose in the rain and our gear would be scattered for miles along the trail.

There was one hope of preventing such a strike—the temple of the Hindu god Ganesha, located directly in front of Dave Fischer's house. I had noticed it the day of our arrival. It was very small, nothing more than a short pagoda, perhaps six feet high, situated in the bottom of a sunken area so that the top of the pagoda was only a few feet above ground level. Dave's house was located at the back of a short U-shaped road that connected at both ends with the main road running through the residential district, and the temple, or Ganesha-tan (*tan* means "temple"), was located in the middle of this U-shaped detour.

One day I saw several people descend the short steps to the pagoda, where they pressed their hands together in Asian obeisance to the gods. I decided to have a look and, following their example, I removed my shoes and also remembered to take off my belt, as I had been told never to wear leather in a temple— cows are sacred, and leather of itself is a sacrilege. Walking down to the pagoda, I peered in and saw a statue of Ganesha—the body of a man, with the head of an elephant. There were several brass lamps burning and a strong smell of incense. Nearby, under an awning erected adjacent to the temple, a group was singing a repetitious chant in time to cymbals and a tabla drum. It was an enchanting, hypnotic melody, and combined with the heady smell of incense, it was easy to drift in reverie. I stood for some time, listening to the singers, gazing at nothing in particular. Then I noticed that automobiles coming from one direction on the main road always turned in the U-shaped loop, drove through the detour, and continued on after regaining the thoroughfare. The cars coming from the other direction always proceeded without turning down the loop. I later learned that both Hindu and Buddhist temples, and for that matter, any sacred location, should always remain on the right side of a person. Hence, the cars from one direction drove through the loop because driving past the temple via the main thoroughfare would have resulted in the temple's being on their left side. I also learned that this temple in front of Fischer's house, despite its small size, was one of the more important in Kathmandu—impressive since there are over 2,700 temples in Kathmandu.

The god Ganesha, the son of Shiva, is an important figure in the Hindu pantheon. He is the god of good luck, among other things, and it is important to pay homage to him before undertaking any journey. The fact that the expedition had originated from Fischer's house, the site of the Ganesha-tan, was a strong omen of good fortune, and we hoped it would prevent a porter strike. It seemed unlikely to any of us that anyone would abandon a well-paid job because the moon was out of phase. We paid the porters little over a dollar a day to carry a sixty-pound load—good wages in Nepal. (In the end Ganesha came through, because there never was a porters' strike.)

On Saturday we chartered a small bus, complete with an English-speaking tour guide, to drive us to the nearby town where the principal festivities were under way. Our tour guide was accustomed to disciplined masses of Japanese. I doubt he had ever been confronted with a menagerie of unruly mountain climbers. With the bus trundling down the road on the half-hour drive, the tour guide began his usual lecture: "Ladies and gentlemen, my name is Nakia Sakia taking you on the morning tour to the historical areas of my country. As you may well know, Nepal is a mountainous terrain . . ."

From the back of the bus came a yell, "I sure as hell hope so or CBS is in for a surprise."

Peter Pilafian, the CBS sound man, who was recording the tour lecture, turned off his recorder and said, "No sense wasting tape on this one; I don't think it has much chance of being used on the show."

Nakia Sakia, obviously disconcerted, tried to continue. "Our first stop will be Baktipur. It was founded in ninth century A.D. *Baktipur* is a Sanskrit word meaning 'Bakti,' which is Buddha, and 'pur,' which is town. So we have Buddha's town. We have about ninety thousand people living in the town, and they are the farmer people, they are the tillers of the soil. This is a religious center and a city of devotees. It is a storehouse of sculpture and colossal pagodas that will hit you right in the eye . . ."

In a studied discipline that spoke of generations of cultured Asian patience, Nakia Sakia continued his lecture until the bus-load of hooting, boisterous Americans arrived at the ancient city of Baktipur, also known as Bhadgaon. We entered under the Lion's Gate, built in A.D. 1696, a monolithic arch guarded by ferocious feline statues. We stopped in the central square—Durbar Square—where the festival was under way.

The first day I was in Nepal I received a packet of tourist brochures published by His Majesty's Department of Tourism. One, titled "Nepal Festivals," started with this paragraph: "Nepal has been described in many ways—home of Gods, land of Yak and Yeti, land of Gurka's gallantry. We may add to the long list with equal appropriateness by defining it as the 'Land of Festivals.' Not a week passes without some festivals taking place in some part or the Whole of the Kingdom . . ." The brochure went on to catalogue dozens of major festivals, each month featuring five to six different ones. Only in a country used to celebrating one thing or another nearly every week of the year could an impromptu mustering of the clerics have resulted in the size of the gathering we now witnessed.

The crowds were grouped around three large canopies, placed equidistant from each other in the rectangular Central Square. From each canopy came sounds of singing and chanting, of bells and drums. I weaseled through to the nearest tent, straining to get a view. In the center I saw a beautiful woman in a gossamer sari dancing in a circular motion to the tintinnabulation of dozens of bells. She was enchanting, waving her hands with flowing, dexterous fingers. Nearby, people were queued up to pass by a large shell in which a fire burned. When they reached the shell, they put their hands through the fire and then placed their fingers on their eyes and then on their foreheads.

The other two tents housed dozens of monks chanting to the mesmerizing pulse of a tabla drum. Three priests were sitting lotus-fashion, on elevated platforms, from where they threw rice into a central fire. Behind them were row upon row of votive butter lamps that burn mustard oil, and through the whole scene filtered dense wafts of sweet incense. I passed from one tent to another and spotted several tourists huddled around a posted sign. It was an explanation, in English, of the religious significance of the ceremonies. It had no doubt been posted by the "Yak and Yeti" at the efficient Department of Tourism. One statement from the sign remained with me. The priests intended, the sign said, during the twelve days the festival was to last, to burn in offering to the gods 100,000 butter lamps.

I needed a break from the thick incense and smell of densely packed brown bodies sweating in monsoon heat. To escape, I explored down a narrow side street, where I was met by the pungent odor of shit. It brought to mind T. S. Eliot's maxim: "The first condition of right thought is right sensation—the first condition of understanding a foreign country is to smell it." If Eliot is right, I was on the path to enlightenment. I sidestepped mounds of cow shit mingled with the mud and muck of the rain-soaked dirt alley. I was thinking it was little wonder these people were so fond of incense when I found myself deposited in another square.

Like most squares, this one featured a large pagoda temple. The most interesting feature was a carved wood frieze that banded the fascia of the lower tier and depicted, in a series of scenes, a partially dressed prince making love, in every position imaginable, to a full-bosomed, roundly built maiden. One scene in particular caught my imagination and made me want to take up yoga: the maiden had her legs contorted behind her head while the prince, from an equally awkward position, penetrated her. I continued to walk around the temple, gawking at the figures. The frieze reminded me I was about to leave for the longest climbing trip of my career, and unless I was lucky enough to find a cute Sherpani along the trail, I would be without available females for the next few months. There were still a few days before starting on the approach march—maybe enough time to locate a sweetheart.

I might have a chance to meet a girl that evening. The expedition members were being honored at a cocktail party hosted by the American embassy. There were two reasons for the party. One, we were to be introduced to the foreign community of Kathmandu. Two, we were to meet many of the upper crust of Nepalese society. The U.S. embassy had reason to make the party good. As one of the few big American expeditions ever to visit Nepal, we were in the public eye of the Nepalese. We had already received sharp criticism from the Nepalese press, who considered us a group of amateur incompetents with no chance of reaching the summit. One local writer said, "It seems to me the team is not very strong, especially considering they do not have any climbing experience in the Nepalese Himalayas. None of the members have climbed over 8,000 meters and that seems to me fundamental."

There were several reasons why the Nepalese had this attitude. For one thing, we were led by a group of lawyers—something not likely to evoke an attitude of confidence in the group's strength. The Nepalese also knew we had put the expedition together in a hurry, and they were quick to point out that none of us had climbed before in the Nepalese Himalayas. On top of it all—and this, perhaps more than anything, led to our lack of credibility—we didn't *look* like a group of serious climbers. It was our air of traveling circus that raised the most eyebrows. The Nepalese press had been weaned on Hunts and Hillarys and

Boningtons. Who were these people dressed in Aloha shirts and surgeon's costumes who claimed they could get up Everest?

We arrived at the party dressed as we always dressed. The lawyers, at one end of the spectrum, were smartly attired in after-dinner clothes, while Chris Chandler, at the other end, found his stained surgeon's shirt now perfect casual wear for the tropical climes of Kathmandu. The rest of us were somewhere in the middle.

The American embassy had done a bang-up job organizing the party; the hors d'oeuvres were excellent, and the bar had a selection of booze available only in overseas commissaries. The guests were a *Who's Who* of Kathmandu—perhaps 150 people altogether.

I was fascinated by the people at the party; it was like browsing through a curio shop in some exotic port, not knowing what type of treasure I might find. Places like Kathmandu are lodestones to offbeat travelers and people who don't happen to fit in. At one point I found myself talking to an elderly American gentleman who had lived for years in Kathmandu and had taken as his avocation the study of Nepalese ornithology. He was at that time the world's authority on the subject, and his latest book—*The Birds of Nepal*—had just been released. Another elderly gentleman I met was connected with the British embassy in Kathmandu. He was one of those gray-flanneled types who stand out sharply against a colorful background like Nepal—a character from a Graham Greene novel.

I glanced around and saw a guy who looked as though he'd been raised in a beach town of southern California.

"You look like you must be one of the climbers on this expedition," he said.

"Don't hold it against me," I replied.

"No, not at all," he said, laughing. "In fact, I'm kind of envious. I've seen Everest a few times from the air, but I can't even imagine trying to climb it. Sounds far-out."

"You've been in Kathmandu awhile?"

"Off and on for several years. I come and go."

"What do you do here?"

"I export carpets back to the States: Persians, Afghans, Tibetans."

Everybody in Asia seems to have a cover story masking what he really does for a living, so I was suspicious of anyone billing himself as a carpet buyer.

"You go to quite a few of these things?"

"Yeah, these parties are great. Always lots of free booze, and once in a while an available chick."

"Well, hey, you wouldn't happen to know of any single young ladies around you might be able to introduce me to?"

"Oh, yeah, no problem. I just happen to know someone at this very party who would be perfect for you. Cute local girl. That's her, over there. The girl in the green sari."

It was hard to tell her age; maybe eighteen, maybe twenty-eight. She had short black hair, sharp features, and a bright red tika dot on her forehead. He brought her over and introduced us.

"She doesn't speak much English," he said, "but she's a great gal."

I looked in her face and caught a twinkle in her eye as she looked away, blushing slightly. She was very cute; clear, light tan-brown skin and deep black eyes, and very tiny—she couldn't have weighed over a hundred pounds. Despite her tiny size, she had large breasts. She said something in Nepali.

"She wants to know if you are one of the Everest climbers." I smiled at her and nodded affirmatively.

She spoke again. "She says she always wanted to meet someone who was going to climb Everest." Now it was my turn to blush.

"Oh, it's nothing special, you know," I said. "There's lots of us mountain climbers around." She giggled, obviously amused at my embarrassment.

She continued staring at me with that same mischievous

twinkle in her eye. Then the beach-bum-turned-carpet-buyer said, "I've got some knockout hash I just picked up in Afghanistan. Maybe you'd like to get loaded before taking off for that big mountain."

"Never touch the stuff," I said, and we both laughed. "But since this is my last supper, maybe I'll make an exception." I winked at the girl, and she puckered her lips in a suggestive kiss.

We caught a taxi and the girl and I crawled in the back. She sat very close to me, and I held her hand. We drove down narrow streets flanked by sturdy brick houses with wood windows magnificently and minutely carved with small figures. Incense displaced plumeria, with a hint of jasmine. I felt her finger lightly tracing a circle on my palm. I glanced at her and saw her staring at me seductively. Her dark eyes, combined with every sight, sound, and sensation surrounding me, suggested something deep and intriguing, foreign and unknown.

"You know, I never get tired of this place," the carpet buyer said, his voice drifting over from the front seat. "It's always something new and bizarre here; every time I come I see something I missed the last time . . ."

As he was talking, I felt her hand slip from mine and gently move down the inside of my leg.

I called up to the front seat, "I thought these upper-class Brahman girls were brought up with strict Hindu morals."

"This one's different," he said. "She was a lucky find."

"You mean she kind of goes out with you, too?"

"Oh, yeah, but I don't like to mix pleasure and business too often. Never works out."

"Yeah. I get the picture."

"She usually gets twenty dollars a gig. That's about the same going rate as Bangkok these days. Got to keep things competitive, you know." He chuckled at his own joke.

"There's just one thing I've got to tell you," he continued. "Don't tell anybody about this. I have to keep these things secret so her family doesn't find out what she's doing."

"What would they do if they found out?"

"Well, that's where this place *is* different from Bangkok. Around here they're still in the Dark Ages." There was a brief pause as he lit a cigarette and took a deep drag. "Around here," he said, "they would haul her out in the street and stone her to death."

5

"We should be preceded by handstanding jesters, sackbut, and drums," Frank Morgan wrote in his diary.

"That bloody jamboree," as Mike Cheney described us, was finally under way. Climbers, cameramen, press correspondents, thirty or forty Sherpas, 200 porters, a liaison officer, wives, friends, and the U.S. ambassador to Nepal, Marguita Maytag.

We had started our first day at Lamosangmu, a small road stop a two-hour drive out of Kathmandu. After all the loads were assigned and the porters off and on the trail, we began the trek. The first day had a 5,000-foot climb out of a river valley, and it was miserably hot. Not only were we in the middle of July heat, but we were in the middle of monsoon humidity as well. We had no choice but to begin the approach at the full height of the monsoon rains; otherwise, we wouldn't arrive at the base of Everest in time to position ourselves to take advantage of the short period of good weather that follows the monsoon. There are two periods each year during which it is possible to climb Everest: before the monsoon, March, April, and May; and after the monsoon, September and October. All things considered, the pre-monsoon period is superior for climbing, but our permit was only for the post-monsoon period. A pre-monsoon expedition begins as the winter ends—sometime in March—so that the first weeks of climbing are in cold weather, but as the climb progresses and the camps are pushed higher, the weather grows warmer when it is most needed. The summit must be reached, however, before the onset of the monsoon, which usually occurs during the first week of June. The opposite conditions exist for the post-monsoon season. As the climb progresses, winter approaches, so the climbers are at the highest camps during the coldest period. This problem is compounded by the onset of winter winds caused by the jet stream descending over the summit. There is an interim period of about three weeks following the last monsoon snows and preceding the beginning of the winds. We hoped to take advantage of this window of good weather. It hinged on whether we could position ourselves in the high camps when it occurred. That meant, in effect, that even on the approach march we were on a tight, precalculated schedule.

Before leaving Kathmandu we had each been given a printed itinerary for the approach with two columns—one marked "Day," the other marked "Camping place." The first day we were scheduled to camp in a place called Thulo Pakha. P.K. had told us before we started hiking that we could reach the campsite by early afternoon. After the long climb out of the river valley, the trail followed a broad ridge. We passed thatched huts with mud-caked kids running out to greet us, cupped hands held forward, lot of climbs it's necessary to make two goes at the summit. That's one reason my summit-to-attempt ratio is so high. On Aconcagua we had to make two attempts. On Foraker it was the same thing. It's a philosophy of mine not to turn back because of any setback. We're here for the duration, and we stay until we get to the top." Gerry's whole purpose was to summit, and it was easy to understand his frustrations at seeing so many people at Base Camp who he felt were not necessary to achieving that goal. He was being a little inattentive to reality, however, by labeling the film crew "superfluous" and ignoring the obvious fact that without their financial support we simply wouldn't have been there.

Most of the others seemed happy with the way things were going. It was encouraging to see Bob and Dan agree so readily to rope up with each other; they were probably the two most adaptable people on the trip. Even Dee seemed to be improving and said he might feel well enough in a few days to go into the Icefall. Although he still walked with a painful limp, Phil's ankle was rapidly healing, and he had managed to walk from Lobuche to Base Camp. He too thought that he might be able to go into the Icefall in a few days. Arlene was apparently very upset, however, because she wasn't chosen for either of the two teams on the first two days of Icefall exploration. She was keeping quiet about it; she hadn't spoken up at the meeting as Hans had. Ed Goren sensed Arlene's frustration, and that morning, when the first team went into the Icefall, he sat down with her at Base Camp to talk things over.

Arlene began, "I'm very unhappy, very upset. Part of it is a misunderstanding. I told Phil I wanted to climb, and he claims I told him I didn't want to, which just isn't true. Somehow he remembers just the opposite of what I said. So he sends Emmett up there who had giardiasis [a type of dysentery from which nearly all of us, at one time or another, suffered], and Morgan, who has a headache. It's totally unfair. I mean yesterday I was carrying heavy boxes around camp all day; I'm not sick; I'm the most experienced Himalayan climber here [she had been on five previous Himalayan expeditions and reached the summits of seven peaks, three of them previously unclimbed]. After all those years, after all my women's expeditions, it's totally unfair." Arlene continued, with her voice quivering, on the edge of tears, "And it's because I'm a woman, damn it, I know it.

"What really annoys me is that nobody even asked if I wanted to go—nobody said one nice word to me. I tried to talk to Gerry, but he said, 'Well, if you're in a bad mood, you shouldn't be in the Icefall anyway.' Hans is really sympathetic, and Joe understands. But I think unless people are totally unobservant, they know I'm upset. If one person would come up to me, or be sympathetic, it wouldn't be so bad. I mean you're the first person who has talked to me. If I don't have any friends here, damn it, I just don't want to be here. Everybody is so involved in his own little world. Climbing Mount Everest is neat, but the main thing is to be happy."

Goren said, "Are you serious about joining me in the helicopter out?" Because he had to return to New York, he had arranged for a helicopter to come in a few days and land near Namche.

"Hans said he'd fly home if I do, and we're both seriously thinking about it."

Arlene had disclosed to Goren feelings that apparently she was reluctant to discuss openly. At least, that is, she hadn't talked about them at our group meeting. Even though she hadn't spoken up, it was obvious to everyone that she was upset because she hadn't been chosen to go into the Icefall. Arlene often stated that she wanted everybody to like her, but as the expedition progressed she came to believe the opposite was true, and by the end of the expedition she would say that it was the first trip she had been on in which few liked her. Why this should be so remained, to her, a mystery.

She was greatly annoyed, knowing she was responsible, directly or indirectly, for the recruitment of almost half the people on the expedition, and no one seemed thankful. First, she had a tendency to voice her criticisms of people's actions, pointing out people's faults and weaknesses. She was not able to take the "people will be people" attitude. In better circumstances she doubtless would have been a fun traveling companion. She had traveled through Asia and it was interesting to hear her comments on local life and custom. She had a good sense of humor and a dry wit.

Her good points probably would have counterbalanced any problems that arose in any situation other than that of being pinned together for three months during a high-altitude climbing expedition. There is something about expeditions of this sort that tends to bring out the worst in everyone. Even the members of our expedition who in normal day-to-day life are the most mild-mannered, easy-going types imaginable sooner or later, as the expedition dragged on, launched into vituperative tirades about so-and-so doing this or that. And even the one or two people who didn't publicly display their acrimony purged themselves of this need to criticize at night, in the privacy of their tents, while writing in their journals.

Why being on an expedition should bring this out in people is hard to say. This kind of behavior can be observed among soldiers in war or, for that matter, in anybody under stress, and the expedition was a stressful situation. There was the daily toil of hard work, the constant threat of being squashed in an avalanche. The other factor that created stress, and one not found in other situations, was the lack of oxygen. Psychologists and physiologists are uncertain what are the specific results of continued hypoxia (lack of oxygen), but there was no doubt it contributed to people's tendency to be edgy, to be irritable, and to criticize others gratuitously. It was a tendency that increased as the expedition wore on and we spent more and more time at higher altitudes. What little research has been done in high-altitude physiology has shown one thing: above about 19,000 feet (the elevation varies a little with individuals) a person's red blood cells begin to be destroyed faster than they can be replaced. In other words, above 19,000 feet you are slowly dying. How long it actually takes to die is not known, but it would be many months. Most people begin to lose weight that they can't replace no matter how much they eat. Even the use of pressurized oxygen doesn't help very much, and we wouldn't start breathing it, anyway, until we were above about 24,000 feet. Under these conditions it is little wonder that people start to bother each other. Bickering and fighting, short tempers and temper tantrums, all have contributed to the early end of more than one high-altitude expedition.

It is honest to say our expedition probably had fewer problems with this than most climbs to extreme altitudes, and it should be pointed out that most of the time all of us got along well enough. However, it came as no surprise when people started picking on each other.

That first day in the Icefall Gerry and Hans made considerable progress in the lower sections, and the next day Chris and I went up to continue the lead. It was wonderful to be climbing. There were still frustrations. We encountered one crevasse that had no way around, so we waited for the Sherpas to arrive with a few ladder sections so we could span them across the chasm. The ladders arrived, but no one had remembered to bring a wrench to loosen the bolts so we could fasten together the sections. It reminded me of stories you hear about the army—our entire operation, all the dozens of people, ground to a halt for want of a nickel-and-dime spanner. Too frustrated to wait, we climbed down in the crevasse and up the opposite vertical wall. I was happy to see Ang Phurba follow us with apparent ease. From the smile on his face, it was obvious he was happy to be out and stretching his legs. We made good progress that day and were back in camp by 10:30, before the sun warmed the ice.

Gerry and Hans were back in the lead the following day, with Gerry demonstrating that his months of training had been for a purpose. In an amazing show of endurance, he spent several hours working up steep, loose snow, weaving in and out of seracs and over crevasses, pushing the route to within less than 1,000 vertical feet of the top of the Icefall. They were back in camp by early afternoon, and their blitzlike progress undid the discontent of the previous two days. Hans was enthusiastic and satisfied with the progress; Arlene had her chance to go into the Icefall and, with the help of Joe, rig ladders and fix ropes. Even Dee Crouch was feeling better, having partially recovered from his dysentery, and was considering going into the Icefall the following day. Chris and I were in the docket to take over the lead again, and there were high hopes in camp that the following day, August 31, we might be able to push to the top of the Icefall.

I awoke at 1:30 A.M., and before crawling out of my bag, I thought through the day's itinerary: get dressed, wake up Chris, make sure your gear is complete, wake up the Sherpas, eat breakfast, and leave at about 2:30. Should take two hours to get to Gerry and Hans's high point, then wait for first light and start climbing. We'll take Nawang—his opinions as to where the route should go might be useful. Be back in camp by noon.

I zipped open my bag and crawled out. I quickly put on my pants and parka and left the tent to wake up Chris. It was clear and cold. There was enough moonlight to see seracs shining in the Icefall. Dark lines, cast by moon shadows from the ice flutings, ran down the great face of Nuptse like furrows on a vertical snow field. After waking Chris and then rousing the Sherpas, I went to the cook tent and sat down to a hot brew of tea.

Nawang, Chris, and I finished breakfast and walked outside to the small altar where the juniper boughs were burning. We stopped, and while Nawang chanted, the three of us breathed deeply of the sweet smoke. Nawang said the smoke would cleanse our bodies, which, for a multitude of reasons, were impure. The snows of Everest were less likely to strike against someone who had a pure body, someone who had breathed the smoke. We put on our packs and left, just the three of us. The others—the long lines of them—were soon behind us, and we could see their

headlamps blinking in rows like torches carried by chanting der-
vishes en route to a secret ceremony. But we were alone. The
only noise was our crampons biting the crisp morning snow and
the low drone of Nawang's chanting. The stars were on fire overhead with a brightness experienced only in the rarefied atmosphere of high altitude. Seracs loomed on all sides, threatening,
as if they possessed their own will and might at any moment
decide to topple over and kill us. The possibility wasn't frightening, but it did cause a slight release of adrenaline that honed my
senses like a straightedge razor being drawn over a strop.

This is what I had for so long been awaiting; this was the
reward for months of preparation and weeks of hiking on the
approach march. In less than the two hours we had planned we
arrived at the high point, and we sat down, using our packs for
insulated seats, to await the dawn. The first hint of coming light
revealed, several valleys to the west, the summit of Cho Oyo, the
ninth highest peak in the world. Then the pyramid shape of
Pumori was revealed, turning slightly pink. As Chris led off to
begin the day's climbing, Nawang finished a cigarette, and we
both stared at the panorama.

"Much view coming now, sahib."

I looked at him and saw his face, barely visible in the morning
twilight; he was staring into the western valleys with a mesmer-
ized look, and I could tell he was as affected as I was by the
grandeur of the sight. Like most Sherpas, Nawang had a genuine
aesthetic appreciation of his homeland. While that might not
seem surprising, many mountain peoples of the world seem oblivious to the beauty of their surroundings. I remembered another
moment on the approach march when the Sherpa ahead of me
stopped to admire a panorama of huge snow peaks, forests of
spruce and pine, and wild flowers in the foreground. "Much
country here," he had said.

Soon the three of us were hiking through the forest of
seracs, the rope stretched between us in case one of us should
fall in a hidden crevasse. We tried to climb quickly, not so

much because of a rush to reach the top of the Icefall as because of a desire to stay ahead of the others and remain by ourselves. We switched leads, and I was out in front, wading through thigh-deep snow, testing for hidden crevasses. Suddenly I found one. Before I knew it I was up to my chest in a hole, my arms spread to hold me from dropping in further. My feet were dangling in the black pit. I yelled to Chris to keep the rope tight and, squirming, I worked my way out before plunging in all the way.

"Almost went in that one," I said to Chris as I peered into the black hole that then revealed the hidden crevasse. It is common when crossing glaciated ice to find crevasses completely covered by snow, and walking into such a booby trap is a major danger of glacier travel.

We next encountered a huge serac—a giant block of ice—some 300 or 400 feet long and about 50 feet high. We had to decide whether to go around it on the left or on the right. It was a difficult decision because which of the two routes was better depended on the geography of the terrain behind the serac—terrain that was partially hidden from our view. From what we could see, the left-hand side looked preferable. It appeared that there were fewer seracs and easier ramps connecting the crevasses. We asked Nawang, but he adamantly said the right-hand side was better. Now it *was* a difficult choice. Our instincts said left, but Nawang, who had been through the Icefall dozens of times, said right. We decided to follow Nawang's advice, rationalizing that at worst we would have to retrace our tracks and go the other way.

Our mistake soon became obvious: we were in a maze of seracs, circuitously wandering around the snow towers and over precarious ice bridges that spanned deep crevasses, seeking the best way to the top of the Icefall—now only a tantalizing few hundred feet above us. Both Chris and I were worn out from climbing in the mushy, thigh-deep snow, so we willingly gave the lead to Nawang. We came to a particularly nasty offset crevasse whose opposite wall stood thirty feet higher than the side where we were. The only way up was via a thin rib of snow connecting the two walls of the crevasse. There were large seracs all around us; I didn't at all like the looks of the place. Nawang crossed the bridge and set up a belay, and Chris started climbing, gingerly following Nawang's footsteps, not certain if his additional weight would collapse the fragile snow bridge. Halfway across, the crevasse suddenly gave a rifle-sharp crack, and the ground around us shook. The glacier was moving. One of those big seracs above us might collapse at any moment. Chris yelled, "Up or down?"

"Up!" I shouted, and in a few seconds I was on his heels, climbing as fast as I could at 20,000 feet. I was dizzy from lack of oxygen. I felt nausea, a familiar nausea, a feeling I had had someplace before. Where? It was Peru, a few years before. For a brief second my mind flashed back to that incident. Chris and I had been trying to make the first ascent of a 20,000-foot peak in the Andes; we were on a broken glacier section—similar to this one—surrounded by seracs, when the same rifle-crack occurred. Then, above us, a huge serac broke off and hurtled into space, coming directly toward us. We dove into a crevasse as the house-sized block broke all around; neither of us was hurt. That rifle-crack was the same sound as in Peru; it was the sound that produced the nausea, a nausea caused by thinking you might die.

Both of us climbed fast, and soon we were at Nawang's belay spot. The three of us scrambled up another fifty feet to a spot safe from seracs. I collapsed, short of oxygen, trying to breathe, but I felt as if I were drowning. None of the seracs had collapsed, but that noise was a harbinger of something soon to topple. After a few minutes I could breathe more easily, and the dizziness passed. Nawang had been chanting in his low monotone, and he stopped and said, "This road no good. We leave now, O.K.?" Chris and I nodded in agreement, and Nawang reached in his pack and pulled out a cloth sack. From it he took a handful of sacred rice and threw it toward the crevasse. "We lucky this time," he said.

Despite our obvious blunder in choosing the wrong route, we decided to carry on from where we were, rather than climb back through the hazardous area. We would go to the top of the Icefall and from there, looking down from the top, we might spot a safer passage. We also decided, even if the Sherpas had been through the Icefall dozens of times, it was better to trust the authority of our own instincts when making choices as to the best route. We climbed on, still feeling shaky, and even more apprehensive because it was getting late. The full sun would soon be on us, warming the ice and further increasing the chance of an avalanche. But we were now so close to the top of the Icefall that we couldn't resist continuing, and in less than an hour I was leading up the last fifty feet to the lip where the glacier levels out into the Western Cwm. Then we were on top. I belayed Chris and Nawang up the last section, and we were arm in arm, slapping each other on the back. We looked down at the tiny dots that were tents at Base Camp and, ice axes in hand, waved our arms. (They later told us that through the binoculars we could easily be seen from Base Camp and the television crew, with the aid of a telescopic lens, filmed the scene.) We had established a route through the Icefall in four days—a time rivaling the record of any past expedition. We were heady with accomplishment and optimistic that the climb would go fast. From our vantage on the lip we could see part way into the Western Cwm, back toward the face of Lhotse. We would have to establish Camp 1 close to where we stood, and from there continue the route into the Cwm, toward the juncture of the Lhotse Face and the Southwest Face of Everest, where we would establish Camp 2. The first few hundred yards into the Cwm looked heavily crevassed, and it was obvious that we still had our work cut out.

On September 1, the day after Chris and I led to the top of the Icefall, Gerry, Dee, and Dan went back up to see if they could find a safer passage through the broken upper sections where we had experienced problems. They were accompanied by a group of Sherpas led by fifty-six-year-old Phurkipa—the "old man of the Icefall." For years Phurkipa had been employed by Everest expeditions as the Icefall expert whose job was to rig ladders and logs, plant anchors, attach fixed ropes, and string handlines. With that done, it was his continuing job to maintain the route, which, because of shifting seracs and opening crevasses, was always in need of repair. Since Phurkipa therefore had to spend more time in the Icefall than anyone on the expedition, it was no surprise that he was also the most religious man among the Sherpas. He could frequently be seen reading from his dog-eared prayer book, and it was a rare moment that he wasn't chanting a mantra or throwing sacred rice about the Icefall.

Although Phurkipa and his team were doing a satisfactory job rigging the route, we had noticed with growing concern that they seemed oblivious to a few safety precautions we considered basic, such as keeping a tight rope between two climbers when traveling through a crevassed area. Some of them had not even bothered to rope up. We tried to convince them to be more careful by explaining the danger of falling in a hidden crevasse, but they ignored our advice. That day was no exception. Although they had at least bothered to rope up, none of them had recognized the need to keep the rope tight. They were, however, about to learn the reason for this important safety precaution.

After successfully finding a safer route through the upper section, the sahibs and some of the Sherpas reached the top of the Icefall. Tied to a Sherpa's rope was Jonathan Wright, a member of the camera crew, and it was his rope team that first started back down. They hadn't traveled more than fifty yards when Jonathan suddenly disappeared as if he had been swept down a trap door. Before the eyes of the startled Sherpa the rope paid out, but before all the slack was taken, Jonathan's plunge was stopped when his body became wedged in the narrowing V-shaped sides of the crevasse walls. He had fallen thirty feet. The Sherpa ran over and peered down the black hole where Jonathan had disappeared. Not certain what to do, he began to yell at the other sahibs who had just begun their descent. Sensing alarm, they rushed down to see what the problem was. Meanwhile Jonathan, down in the near blackness of the crevasse, remained motionless, afraid he would loosen his wedge and fall further. From his diary:

I was walking down the snow ramp in bright sunlight, and the next moment I was tumbling in a blueblack dream. Then boom! I hit a small ledge, and my legs braced against the opposite wall. I could hear one of the Sherpas far above shouting. I took stock of my body: no broken bones, a few cuts on my arms and hands. Everything else was with me except my hat. About 30 feet below me was the bottom of the crevasse—a jumble of ice blocks. I was wedged in the narrowest part, and below it again widened, so I could easily have fallen further. About 30 feet overhead the rope disappeared through a gray hole. I couldn't tell if I was looking at sky or at snow. Although I was only in a T-shirt, and surrounded by ice, I wasn't cold. I remember my first thought when I hit bottom was "welcome to the Khumbu—you're in the big leagues now." It reminded me of the story about the rookie quarterback who is decked by a huge linebacker who as he is helping him up says, "Welcome to the NFL." Then my next thought was "I hope to hell this doesn't move now, because if it does I will be crushed." Then I realized the real danger was if they didn't rescue me, I'd freeze to death. But then I heard what sounded like footsteps and a ladder plopped across the hole. What a relief when I saw Gerry's face look down.

On his arrival, Gerry had immediately taken charge of the rescue. He was the type of climber who in advance had thought out such procedures as crevasse rescues. After a quick appraisal of the situation, he ordered a Sherpa to fetch a ladder. He placed it across the exposed hole, then crawled out and yelled down to Jonathan to see if he was injured. When he learned he was O.K., Gerry next lowered a rope and told Jonathan to tie it to his pack. When the pack was retrieved, he again lowered the rope, and using mechanical clamps called jumars, Jonathan climbed up the rope. Once up, Jonathan sat beside the crevasse, panting hard, and Gerry said, "I'm glad the camera crew knows how to jumar —that would have been a bad place to teach you." Once again Gerry had shown himself to be perhaps the most valuable member of the expedition.

8

"If it had been one of the climbers, and not one of the film crew, who fell in that crevasse, I doubt seriously that the camera crew would have helped get him out. We need to make some sort of agreement now, before we have another accident, to ensure that the film crew will help and not just keep filming."

It was our usual after-dinner meeting in the mess tent, and Arlene was making a complaint. Her concern had arisen earlier that day when news first arrived in Base Camp that somebody had fallen in a crevasse. Ed Goren, who was standing next to Arlene, said, "I hope Jonathan is filming it." Then, of course, it was learned that it was Jonathan who was in the crevasse. Nevertheless, Arlene felt that had it been one of the climbers in the crevasse, the film crew would have been filming instead of helping.

"I don't think that's true," Frank Morgan said. "I really think if there was somebody in danger, and there was nobody else around to help except the film crew, they would put their cameras down and give a hand. Look, Hoover is standing right here, let's ask him."

Hoover lowered his camera and contemptuously, as if addressing a class of school kids, said, "Now just what do you *think* we would do?"

Arlene continued, "I don't know. I think it might be just like when Phil sprained his ankle, and instead of helping, you guys——"

"Ah, this is just what I need for the film," Hoover said, and he stuck his camera a few inches from Arlene's face. "O.K., let's hear some more. Rolling." Arlene had trouble finishing another sentence and, flustered, she sat down.

Although relations between the film crew and the climbers were far from perfect, in this case almost everyone agreed with Frank and sided with the film crew. It was obvious that if someone was in trouble and there were no other climbers around to help, the camera crew would put down their cameras and give a hand. It was also obvious, or at least it should have been, that if there were other climbers to help, they would continue to film. That's just what happened when Phil sprained his ankle. Most of the climbers on the team didn't fully appreciate the difficulty of the film crew's job. They not only had to climb the mountain, they also had to film it. Usually it was impossible for them to be ahead of the lead climbers, and since that is where the action is, they often asked us to re-create a certain scene. It was the only way they could possibly record the expedition's progress on film. Some of the climbers questioned the ethics of this technique, and it only added to the feeling that, as Gerry Roach put it, "we had sold out to the entertainment business."

After Hoover had quieted Arlene, we were ready to continue our meeting, but instead of discussing the plans for the next day, Phil stood and made a sad announcement. Barb Roach had been suffering several days from a toothache. Phil said she was to return to Kathmandu for the necessary dental work. She planned to leave with Ed Goren the next day from Namche. There was hope that if she could hitch a return helicopter ride back to Namche, she might be able to catch up with everyone and participate in the final stages of the expedition. We all knew, though, that as soon as she returned to lower elevations, she would lose valuable acclimatization, and there would be slim chance she could regain it in time.

Of all the people on the expedition, it seemed most unfair that Barb had to be the one with the bad luck that forced her to leave. She had spent more man-hours on the preparation of the expedition than anyone. Despite doubts she could single-handedly complete the task, Barb had never given up in her day-to-day efforts to organize the expedition's food supply. And she never complained. For many of us, for example, the announcement that she was leaving was the first we had learned that she even had a toothache. She was a quiet person, keeping her thoughts and her feelings to herself. It was obvious, though, that she was very saddened to be leaving the expedition, and especially saddened to be parting from Gerry during such a critical period in his climbing career.

Though they had climbed so much together, Barb felt that on Everest she was out of her league, and for some time, even before her tooth problem, she had inwardly known that this time Gerry was going to have to carry on alone. In her diary she wrote:

We have become such a close mountaineering team in the past ten years that it will be hard to climb without each other. I feel, however, past my peak strength, and he is just beginning to reach his. So there may be a few trips in the future where he goes with all my blessings. There is still all the love between us, but we have to do different things to fulfill each individual.

We finished the meeting by discussing the following day's plans. Gerry, Hans, and Dee had managed to scout a safer route around the dangerous area where Chris, Nawang, and I had experienced that shifting ice, and now that the route was consolidated, we could send a group of lead climbers up to establish Camp 1. We decided to send Bob, Joe, Chris, and me. From Camp 1 we would begin engineering a route through the heavily crevassed Western Cwm. We would also be accompanied through the Icefall by twenty-four Sherpas who would carry the first loads to the site of Camp 1 and then return to Base.

Reluctant and grumpy, Chris and I crawled out of our bags well before dawn the next morning and prepared to face the day. So that we wouldn't waste time getting away, we had readied our packs the previous day. All the personal gear we would need at the higher camps for the rest of the climb was in one incredible load weighing about sixty-five pounds. We were being foolish to try to haul it all in one trip, but the alternatives were either to leave part of it, even though we had culled all those items we labeled "unnecessary," or to parcel out some of it to the Sherpas. We knew that some climbers would be tempted to have the Sherpas porter most of their personal climbing gear, and since we felt strongly against that, we thought we should set an example by carrying all our own stuff. We almost killed ourselves doing it. As we struggled up the Icefall, the increasing altitude seemed to add even more weight to our backs, and we continually cursed ourselves for our stupidity. My mind was going through those "essential" items that I would jettison, and my legs, as if in a hypnotic stupor, continued to plow upward. Because of our slow pace we were in the full force of the noon sun. Finally we staggered into camp. I took off the pack and felt as if I had been levitated, as if all I had to do was flap my arms and I could fly to the summit.

The Sherpas arriving before us had already erected several tents. I dragged my pack over to the nearest one to stake my territory. Mike Hoover and one of the Sherpas, Nima Norbu, were already inside, so the three of us would be tentmates. I unpacked my belongings and stretched out, exhausted, while another Sherpa came by with a steaming pot of milk tea. Maybe the old British colonial days weren't so bad after all. Hoover and Nima also sat back and we gazed out the tent flap, enjoying the incomparable beauty of the Western Cwm. The afternoon clouds were beginning to move in, but we still had a good view up the valley. We had located Camp 1 at the last flat flank of ice before the glacier spilled over into the Icefall. It was like floating on the edge of Niagara Falls, but there was absolutely no other place to locate the campsite. We speculated how long the ice flank would remain before it was inevitably pushed into the Icefall. Fortunately, we wouldn't be long at the camp. As soon as we pushed the route to Camp 2, we would move up there. About two hours after arriving, we were napping in our tent when suddenly a sharp crack issued from somewhere deep in the ice and our tent shook as our ice flank quivered under new pressure. Hoover jumped up on both feet and squatted in a karate posture. Both Nima and I stared at him, and, realizing how ridiculous he looked, he said, "If I'm goin' over, I'm goin' over standing up." Nima said, "Don't worry, Mike-sahib, Camp One always make noise like this." Maybe so, but it was disconcerting, and as the cracking and shaking occurred every few hours, it was hard to get a good night's sleep.

Chris and I were again in the lead, and for the next three days we had a wonderful time exploring the territory past Camp 1. The final route we established was much more circuitous than we had imagined. Because the glacier was split so badly with crevasses, we had to walk from side to side searching for suitable bridges, and often our parallel trails would cover more than a quarter-mile to gain a net distance of less than fifty yards.

While Chris and I were busy, a backup team led by Bob Cormack was occupied rigging ladders over the sections we had already scouted. Though perhaps not as glamorous as lead climbing, the job of rigging the ladders took just as much, if not more, ingenuity. It was complicated work. Every ladder had to be secured rigidly, to avoid swaying, and each had to be rigged with handlines. "Somebody's got to do it," Bob said, "and I don't mind staying behind and making sure the job gets done. In fact, I kind of get satisfaction rigging a big crevasse, and I know that's just as important in getting to this mountain as anything else."

On the third day of our lead, Chris and I got a predawn start. The previous two sunrises had been the most spectacular we had thus witnessed, and that third morning was no disappointment. Low clouds mysteriously enveloped the sides of the mountains. Their tops were phantomlike, and the air was still. As the sun's rays filtered in, a million crystals suddenly twinkled in the fresh sunlight. When we stopped to rest, there was absolutely no sound other than our own breathing. I understood why the Swiss, who in 1952 were the first men to enter this sanctuary, chose to call it the Valley of Silence. It was more than quiet; it was a haunting void. If I listened carefully, I could detect noise, and I realized it was the sound of my blood pumping through my veins, the sound of my heart beating. It was sensory deprivation, and since I wasn't used to it, it was unsettling. I was reminded of a passage in Captain Robert Scott's journal from his Antarctic explorations where he wrote that the most frightening aspect of polar exploration was living in silence. It drove strong men crazy. We were happy to start moving so the sound of our crampons crushing the snow would break the silence.

Shortly after noon we reached a big crevasse that split the Cwm from wall to wall. We spotted a narrow ramp on the right side and discovered an old British ladder section buried at its base. Its presence left no doubt we were on the right route. Once up and across, we had our first glimpse into the back of the Cwm, and our first close-up view of the main pyramid of Everest.

The Southwest Face looked immense, and I could only have respect for Bonington's team who had the year before pushed a route up it. Our own way up the ridge that bordered the South-west Face looked tame in comparison, but I knew because of the altitude we had our work cut out. More immediate, however, was the discovery that we still had two more big crevasses to cross, and then it looked like easy hiking for a mile or two up the Cwm to the site of Camp 2. These next two crevasses, though, looked like difficult obstacles. There were no natural bridges, and they were too wide to span with ladders. We realized the only solution was to hug the Nuptse Wall and cross the crevasses where avalanche debris had filled the chasms. It was disconcerting to realize we had to expose ourselves to avalanche danger, but the time needed to cross the dangerous area would fortunately be short. I was reminded of advice once given by an experienced airline pilot: "Whenever you have to place yourself in a dangerous position, get out as soon as you can."

The afternoon clouds had started to build and threatened to envelop us and obscure our vision, and we knew we had only a few more minutes before further route finding would become impossible. A few hundred yards behind us we saw Hans and Arlene. After a short time the clouds did cover us, and we knew it was time to go home. We felt confident Gerry and the next lead team would have no problems pushing on to Camp 2. We were turning around when we heard the ominous sound of an avalanche bursting loose somewhere up on one of the walls. We couldn't see anything through the whiteout, but we were fright-fully close to the Nuptse Wall. The roar grew louder, and Chris and I stared at each other, fingers crossed. Then from the mist we saw the big avalanche cloud bearing down on us. I yelled, "Take cover!" and we both spread prone and covered our heads. In a few seconds a strong wind snapped at our clothes and we were covered in fine spindrift snow. But we were safe. All the solid stuff had dumped in a crevasse in front of us. We got up and dusted ourselves off, and I could hear the radio in my pack crackling with Hans's panicked voice: "Come in, Chris and Rick. Come in, Chris and Rick. Are you O.K.? Are you O.K.?" I reached down to pick up the radio and Chris, dusting snow from his hair, said, "I think this mountain is telling us something. It's time to go down to Base and have a rest."

Throughout the expedition Base Camp served as an R&R center where climbers could descend to a less debilitating altitude, eat well, sleep on rocks instead of ice, and even take a bath by standing in a makeshift shower stall while an assistant poured hot water from a large tea kettle. After our push into the Cwm, Chris and I descended for a two-day rest. The first night down I stole into the supply tent and lifted a bottle of Johnny Walker Black Label from a case Dave Fischer had sent from Kathmandu and took it down to the Sherpa mess tent. There were three big caravan-type tents in Base Camp: one for the kitchen, one for the sahib mess tent, one for the Sherpa mess tent. There was an unspoken agreement in camp that the Sherpas' tent was their territory, and we had to use some discretion when visiting. I was often envious of their tent because frequently we would be over in our tent pondering logistics and climbing strategies while across the tracks they would be partying it up, yelling, joking, laughing.

So with prudence I poked my head in the door of their tent, smiled, and said hello to everyone, and then from my coat pulled the bottle. I held it up and everyone gave a hearty cheer and beckoned me in. We filled our tin cups with straight whisky, lifted them high, and toasted to that wonderful Sherpa condition called "good luck," and belted down the throat-

as early as possible for the South Col. We would still be in a
bad position to help Bob and Chris down from much above the
Col—they would be on their own to that point—but at least we
could assist them from there. We finished our tea and in a des-
ultory way I began to cook some muck for dinner. I thought,
They must be wishing they had a cup of tea right now. Wait
until later on tonight when they're really fighting for survival.
God, I hope they pull through it O.K.

We called Hoover at the Col to see if he could see any lights
or other signs of them. "Nothing," he reported. He added that
the wind seemed to be even stronger, with gusts, he guessed, over
a hundred miles per hour. He was worried about his own safety.
He said if the tent didn't hold up through the night, he would
be in serious shape. He would look for them one more time a
little later, but he said the spindrift was so bad, and the plume
so thick, he doubted if he would see anything. We put the radio
down and prepared to go to bed. I nestled into my down and
slipped on the oxygen mask. The gas had a warming, soothing
feel as it flowed through my body. But it was hard to appreciate.
I only wished that I could share it. They must be getting cold
by now, I thought. I looked at my watch. It was 8:40. It would
be a long, long time until sunrise.

October 9. I awoke suddenly from a nightmare. I dreamed I
saw two indistinct figures in a snowstorm, groping toward me.
Their arms were outstretched, as if pleading for help. Their hair
was frozen, with icicles hanging down. Finally, when they were
close enough, I recognized them. They were Bob and Chris. The
dream faded, and I remembered where I was and what I had to
do. I took off my oxygen mask. It was sucking dry anyway, the
bottle empty. The faint morning light lit the tent walls. The
night was over, and I hoped they had survived. Reluctantly I
crawled out of my bag and reached over to start the stove and
melt water. I wanted to get some hot liquid and a quick breakfast as soon as possible so we could get an early start toward the

Col. Gerry had spent the night in a tent next to the one Hans and I were in, and on his radio I could hear Hoover calling from the Col.

"Hello, Camp Four. This is Hoover."

"Read you, Mike."

"We made it through the night O.K. but about four A.M. one side of the tent blew off. We moved to another tent but it's the last one up here. I hope it lasts. No sign of either Bob or Chris. Did you read that?"

"Yeah, go ahead."

"I looked up with my lens but could see no sign of them anywhere. The wind up here is as fierce as ever. I'm afraid if they didn't make it back to the tent last night they're probably goners. Are you still planning on coming up here this morning?"

"Yes, that's affirmative. We'll be leaving here shortly."

"Bring some fuel canisters and a little food. We're short on supplies here—just hanging on."

"O.K. See you there in a while."

We finished tea and breakfast and prepared to go. It was difficult managing all the layers of clothes and equipment while inside the tent. But it would have been impossible to dress outside. I had to bend through layers of down to reach my boots and fit my crampons. With them on, I got up, ready to leave. I stepped on the nylon tent floor, the steel spikes leaving ten evenly spaced puncture wounds. But I didn't care; we would be leaving the tent since there would be no one to carry it down. Outside I strapped an oxygen bottle in my pack, fastened the regulator to the bottle, and adjusted the flow to two liters a minute. I would turn that up when we encountered steep sections like the Yellow Band. I hefted the pack and strapped it to my back, then pulled on the oxygen mask bonnet—a tight-fitting cloth skullcap like that of a surgeon. With the mask snapped on covering my mouth and nose and the wide-lensed ski goggles across my eyes, there was no exposed skin on my body. Nearly everything was under more than one layer. With the oxygen bladder ballooned in front of my mask, I couldn't see my feet. It is very awkward to climb when you can't see your feet, and I found it necessary to concentrate on movement to avoid stumbling.

I tied into the rope, looked back to Hans and Gerry, and they gave me the thumbs-up signal, indicating they too were ready. With the oxygen masks on we couldn't talk to each other, so communication was with sign language. I led off, walked a few steps, but then stopped to look up toward the summit. The wind on top looked even worse, the plume now flying to leeward one, maybe two miles. I spotted the red dot, Camp 6, but there was no hint of movement. Nothing. If they bivouacked, I thought, they would be out moving by now. That is, if they had survived the night. I started climbing toward the South Col.

While the three of us slowly climbed the thousands of feet of fixed rope toward Camp 5, the others sat in various camps, anxiously waiting for any news of the fate of Bob and Chris. In Base Camp that morning the mood was solemn. For the first time since we had arrived nearly two months before, huge plumes were flying straight up from the Lhotse-Nuptse Ridge, carried aloft by winds blowing up the wall. The Icefall was also ominously creaking and groaning, making more noise than it had in the previous weeks. Three days before, when Dee, Frank, and Dan had descended from Camp 2, they found the route through the Icefall partially destroyed by an enormous surge of ice that had crumbled acres of ice blocks. Ladders, ropes, and anchors could be seen in the bottoms of newly formed crevasses, twisted and broken like cheap toys. Had anybody been in that part of the Icefall at the time, they certainly would have been killed. It all added to the feeling of despair in Base Camp that morning.

Everyone sat near the radio. Dan, Frank, Dee, Barb, and Chris's girlfriend, Terri. The only news was the message relayed by Phil that we at Camp 4 had received from Hoover: conditions at the Col were worse than ever, no sign of them. At 9:00 they received a call from Kathmandu on our single side-band radio.

Our contact at the U.S. embassy said he was being hounded by correspondents from the local and the international press wanting to know what was going on. Dan radioed back, "Bob Cormack and Chris Chandler made the summit yesterday about four fifteen P.M. and were last seen at six P.M. on the south summit descending. As of now there has been no further sighting of the summit pair, and their fate is still unknown." After delivering the message, Dan went down to the mess tent to join the others in a melancholy breakfast. Although no one said it, they all had the same thought. It was nearly 10:00, and if they were O.K., they should have been sighted by then.

At 10:00 Phil called from Camp 2 and said he had just received a radio call from Hoover. Hoover had said, "There is still no sign of Bob and Chris. We are all fearing the worst. Pema [the Sherpa staying with Hoover at the Col] thinks they are dead, and he wants to come down. The conditions up here are at a max. If the wind increases one more notch, I don't think we can hold on. It's impossible to go outside to take a piss. I think if you went out and pulled your pants down you would only last a few seconds. Inside the tent is nearly as bad as outside. Spindrift everywhere. Can hardly talk to each other with the noise." Phil added that the wind conditions at Camp 2 were also growing worse.

They left the mess tent and wandered to their own tents, each person quiet in his thoughts. Dan spotted Terri off by herself, sitting on a rock staring at the Icefall. He walked over to talk to her, to offer consolation.

"Hi, Terri. How're you doing?"

"Oh hi, Dan. Aw, I'm doing O.K. Just sitting, looking at the mountain, thinking."

"Listen, Terri, don't be too worried. Chris is the best downhill man we've got. When that boy smells the barn, nothing can keep him from coming home. They'll be spotting them coming down any minute now. They'll be O.K., believe me."

Terri looked up at Dan, a tear coming from her eye. It was

hard for Dan to say what he did with any conviction, because he didn't believe any of it.

"Yeah, thanks, Dan. I know he'll be O.K. He's a good climber. He's the strongest person I've ever known." She looked down, then got up and started walking toward the Icefall.

"Where you going?" Dan called.

She turned around, "Over to the base of the Icefall. I'm going to sing to the mountain. It seems like the best thing to do." Dan watched her disappear down the moraine, then he wandered back to his tent.

Dee Crouch was busy designing a jury-rigged litter to be used in case Bob and Chris had to be carried down the mountain. For the last day Dee had been like a transformed man. When he had descended to Base three days before with Dan and Frank, he had been glum, taciturn, and moody. He was feeling sorry for himself, disappointed in not being on a summit team, homesick, indifferent to the outcome of the expedition. But when Bob and Chris were finally sighted coming over the south summit, he once again came alive and rejoined the expedition. While the two inched toward the summit, Dee stayed glued to the telescope, reporting their progress to Barb, who then made the radio announcements. He continued to watch them until darkness obscured them at the south summit on descent. That night he was up late figuring medical contingency plans and calling Phil at Camp 2, us at 4, and Hoover at 5, detailing emergency procedures in case the pair were frostbitten and hypothermic. Then, the next morning, he was busy constructing the litter, and also a backpack seat similar to the one in which Phil had been carried with his sprained ankle. Dee was ready to head back up the mountain if his help was needed.

Barb was uncharacteristically inactive. Instead of busying herself sorting food boxes and planning meals, she sat quietly, pensively. She wasn't as pessimistic as the others; she felt they would probably show up, even though the hour was late. She was upset that the Sherpa with Hoover had announced that they were surely dead, and that he wanted to come down. She dismissed it as Sherpa overreaction, and she felt it unjustifiably added to the pessimism at Base Camp. But even if Barb was more sanguine than the others, she still feared for their safe return, and she was also concerned about Gerry. She knew then there was little chance the second team would have a chance for the top, and even if Bob and Chris did make it down safely, she would have to console in defeat. She knew it wouldn't be easy to repair a shattered dream.

While Barb sat thinking, the newspaper correspondent was nearby busily talking on the radio to Phil. This tension—waiting to learn the fate of the summit climbers—was terrific copy, and she wanted to make sure she was getting it right. For the last day she had been hearing everybody refer to the possibility of a "bivouac," and now she called Phil to ask exactly what that word meant. Dan sat nearby at the front of his tent, listening in disbelief. For some time many of the climbers had been growing impatient with her questioning. She was extremely dedicated, often literally burning the candle for hours in cold weather banging out her reports so that they could be carried out by a mail runner leaving the next morning. But her almost unbelievable naïveté was grating against the grain of several people. Dan, probably the most mild-tempered member of our expedition, listened with growing impatience.

"Phil, what will the expedition do with the bodies if Bob and Chris don't make it down alive?"

"O.K., goddamnit, that's enough. You've had it now!" Dan leaped up, lips closed tightly, and jumped over a boulder, heading for the correspondent. Facing the other direction, and being nearly deaf, she was unaware of Emmett's approach. Before Dan did something he would regret, Barb intercepted him halfway.

"Calm down, Dan. I know we are all on edge, but getting upset at her won't solve any problems."

"Yeah, you're right, Barb. I guess I just flew off the handle for a second." He turned to go back to his tent, and Barb walked over and calmly took the radio from the newspaper correspondent.

At 11:00 Terri came back to camp. She asked someone if there had been any further news, then she went to her tent to be alone. 11:15 passed. There was little movement in camp, little conversation. The sun was out, and with only a light breeze at the lower elevations it was a mild, pleasant day. 11:30 passed. Most people stayed in their tents, staring at the nylon walls. 11:45 passed. With each hour, it seemed, an equal quantum of hope faded. 11:55. There was a call from Phil at Camp 2. Hoover had just reported seeing two figures descending. They were about an hour or so below Camp 6, coming down very slowly, stumbling, but otherwise appearing to be O.K. He expected them to be down at the Col in perhaps an hour.

Everyone shot out of the tents and huddled around the radio. They were alive! Now, if they were in good health, with no frostbite, it seemed that there was a good chance they would be all right. They were seen below Camp 6. That meant that they must have made it down last night, climbing by moonlight. Which meant that they spent the night with both sleeping bags and oxygen. Also, they would have had fuel to melt water. They should be all right. Everyone looked at each other, smiles growing on their faces. Dan winked at Terri and gave her a nod meaning things looked promising. Her face broke into a broad grin. Base Camp, tensed with anticipation, waited for Hoover's next call.

At the South Col Hoover had zipped tight the tent flap as soon as he spotted the pair descending. Because of the blowing spindrift it had been a major effort each time he peeked outside to scan the upper slopes. The wind had seemed to increase, something he considered almost impossible. Earlier that morning he had stuck his head out to search for them and he saw a seventeen-pound aluminum oxygen cylinder blowing end over end across the Col and off into Tibet. As each hour passed, he had come to agree with the Sherpa staying with him in the tent that Bob and Chris were almost certainly dead. He was more surprised than anyone when he finally saw them.

Now he crawled back into his sleeping bag and waited for them to descend to the Col. He thought he would look out every now and again and radio down a progress report. He watched the spindrift inside the tent vibrating in time to the snapping nylon walls. The noise was almost unbearable, like some kind of Chinese torture. To occupy his mind he went over the emergency medical procedures outlined by Crouch. Don't take off their boots, one cc of morphine, two aspirins every four hours for thrombosis, full-flow oxygen, don't let Chris play doctor. He shut his eyes and waited. Surprisingly, an hour passed. It was time to have another look. He sat upright and braced himself against the coming blast of spindrift. He zipped open the flap and looked out. What he saw caused him to stare as if in shock. Spindrift streaked across the floor of the Col as if blasted from a huge cannon. There, no more than thirty feet away, was Chris Chandler. He was down down on all fours, slowly crawling toward the tent. He looked up for a moment and his eyes met Hoover's. They were sunken in his head. Both his hair and his beard were caked white with ice. Although no one could hear him above the wind, Hoover said in as loud a voice as he could muster. "Good God!"

On the Lhotse Face the three of us had been pushing upward through the wind. Above 25,000 feet it seemed as though I hit a barrier, and even with the aid of oxygen I had consciously to force myself to make each step. At the Yellow Band we had to climb over a fifteen-foot-high nearly vertical band of rock. I was aware that it was important to plan each footstep. If I chose a wrong foothold and had to search for another one, it would be wasted movement. And I had no extra movement within me to waste. By the time I got to the top of the rock section I was breathing so hard I sucked all the oxygen from the rubber bladder and in panic ripped off my mask and gasped at the thin air. I leaned on my ax, dizzy, my vision narrowing until it seemed I was gazing out of a long pipe. Then, slowly, the dizziness disappeared, my vision returned, and I continued on.

I tried to climb at an even pace, but I was forced every few steps to stop and hunker over my ice ax. Gerry and Hans were always one step behind, prodding me on. I thought perhaps my oxygen regulator wasn't working properly. (I later learned I was catching a virus and my lungs were filling with mucus, making it even harder to breathe.) We had been stopping every ten to fifteen minutes to fiddle with the regulators whose flows were erratically jumping from one to five liters a minute, often wasting precious gas. So again I took off my pack to adjust the instrument. Gerry stopped behind me and glanced up the slope. There was still no sign of Chris. He glanced at his watch. It was nearly eleven o'clock. He took off his mask and yelled above the wind, "It's really getting late. We should have seen them by now. I'm afraid they're in bad trouble." We continued upward, glancing occasionally toward Camp 6, searching for them. Then just before the Geneva Spur, Gerry started yelling through his mask. He could see two dots coming down from Camp 6. That meant they must have made it back to their tent last night.

Like everyone else on the mountain we were overjoyed to know they were still alive. But would they have frostbite? I again thought about the two Britons who had made the summit on the army expedition a few months before. And again I remembered the grim statistic: twenty toes, ten fingers. As we climbed up we watched the pair slowly descend toward Camp 5, and just before we reached the top of the Geneva Spur they disappeared from our view behind the ridge. We knew that in a few minutes they would be at the Col.

Chris stood back up and carefully made a few more steps toward Hoover's tent. He had been momentarily knocked over by the wind, and when Hoover had looked outside he was still down on all fours resting for a moment. He made the last few feet to the tent and reeled in the rope that went to Bob. When Bob had also reached the tent they crawled in together, and Hoover zipped the flap shut.

Hoover looked at both of them. He had never seen two people looking more strained. Faces gaunt, eyes sunken, hair covered with ice.

"How bad is it?" Hoover yelled.

"How bad's what?" Chris replied.

"The frostbite."

"What frostbite?"

"You mean you're O.K.?"

"Yeah, we're fine. No frostbite. Hell, we're feeling great. A little tired, but that's all."

"Then you made it back to Camp Six in the dark?"

"Yeah, we downclimbed in the moonlight. Kind of spooky, got off route a couple of times, but found our tent about seven last night."

"Well, where in the hell have you been all morning? Everybody on the mountain figured you were goners."

Chris and Bob both laughed, "We've been trying all morning to get out of our sleeping bags. We were so tired all we could do was make hot chocolate all morning. You guys really thought we were goners, huh?" Hoover smiled, shaking his head. He reached down for the radio to relay the fantastic news.

At Base Camp everyone was still huddled around the radio. It had been a long, long hour since Hoover had first reported seeing them. Dee was still busy with medical evacuation plans, and they all knew there was a chance the plans would have to be used. Then Phil's voice crackled on the radio. "We just heard from Hoover," he said. "Bob and Chris are down at Camp Five. They are totally without frostbite and otherwise in good condition. They will be descending toward Camp Two this afternoon. It's a great moment for the expedition!"

No one said anything. They simply looked at each other. Tears were coming down Terri's cheeks. Then they started cheering, hugging, slapping backs, shaking hands. In the euphoria Dee Crouch slipped away to his tent for a few moments to himself. For a guy who only a few days before had been rancorous at being preempted by a "dope-smoking hippie doctor," he had an awful big lump growing in his throat. As he reached his tent he wiped away the tears that were rolling down his face.

11

"*How can I help rejoicing in the yet
undimmed splendor, the undiminished
glory, the unconquered supremacy of
Mount Everest.*"

George Leigh Mallory, 1923

"*I walked up on it kind of thinking,
well, here it is. The summit of
Everest.*"

Bob Cormack, 1976

The decision to end the expedition came soon after Bob and
Chris returned safely to Camp 2. On the afternoon of October 9
we had met them on their way down, just as they left Camp 5.
After a bear-hugging reunion, Gerry, Hans, and I decided it made
the most sense to go down with Bob and Chris to see if there
would be a further effort to push a second assault. While we
were all descending, Phil was busy at Camp 2 trying to encourage
the Sherpas to make another carry. He called a meeting in front
of the cook tent and, to make certain they understood, had Joe
translate the speech into Nepali.

"We are very lucky. We have had a successful expedition. The two summit climbers are now on their way down the Lhotse Face. Their health is fine. No frostbite. Everything is a success, and I want to thank all of you for making it possible. We couldn't have done it without your support, and believe me, we all appreciate it."

Joe translated, and the Sherpas gave a loud, hand-clapping cheer. Phil continued:

"In the course of the expedition we have all had some disappointments. I was disappointed, and I know all of you were, that Ang Phurba's regulator malfunctioned, keeping him from going to the top. At the very beginning of the expedition one of our objectives was to put seven, eight, or nine people on top. We've not been able to do this—we can't get enough equipment to Camp Six, the weather is turning bad—and that too has been a disappointment.

"The second summit team went to the South Col today to help the two summit climbers. They too are coming down, and though I haven't yet talked to them, I think they would like to make a second attempt. But they will need help from you. What we will need is two, three, or four more carries to Camp Six. I know you don't want to do it, I know it's a grueling carry, and I know the weather doesn't look good. But if we can wait a few days for better weather, I want to ask some of you to stay and make a few more carries."

Joe translated, then gave the Sherpas' reply.

"They say it was their decision to make direct carries from Two to Five, and it was they who put the ropes up to Camp Five. They did that so that the expedition would be over quickly before the bad weather came. They feel that had some of the expedition members helped a little more in the load carrying, instead of going down to Base Camp for a rest, the expedition would have been over by now, including a second assault. If you only need two or three more carries to high camps, why don't you do it yourselves? This one attempt is going to be it. Everything is finished."

Phil still wanted to talk to Gerry, Hans, and me before giving orders to abandon the mountain. After spending the night at Camp 4, we arrived at Camp 2 the morning of the tenth. A cold wind blew through camp. It was the coldest morning yet. Higher up, plumes were coming off all the ridges, and they seemed to signal both the coming of winter and the end of our expedition. Hans and I were too tired to think immediately about another attempt. My lungs were congested, and I had little ambition to climb higher. Gerry was the only one still strong (besides Joe Reinhardt, who was trying to drum up support for another assault), but even Gerry's determination was dampened by the weather, the lack of Sherpa support, and the lack of other climbers to form another team. That night Phil made the announcement that the expedition was over, and the next morning we began our retreat. What had taken months of arduous preparation, so many miles of hiking, and weeks of climbing wound down with a dizzying speed. We evacuated the mountain in one day. Everybody carried as much as he could load. We made a mountain of unwanted food and equipment in Camp 2, and the Sherpas loaded it all. Some of them looked like Depression farmers in Model Ts fleeing the Dust Bowl. Pots and pans clanked on the sides of backpacks that were tied five feet high. But everybody was in Base Camp by nightfall. When the last person walked out of the Icefall, all gave a cheer. It meant that not only was our expedition successful—with two having reached the top—but we then knew we had done it with no deaths, no injuries, not even any serious illnesses. It had been sixty-nine days since we had left Kathmandu to start the approach march, and forty-six days since we had established Base Camp. We were all thankful to the goddess of Chomolungma for allowing us those days to trespass on her snows—and to return safely.

That night Bob and Chris gave us a detailed account of their summit experience. On October 7—the day before they made the summit—they put in an exceptionally strenuous day climbing above the South Col to establish Camp 6. Everyone—sahibs and Sherpas alike—was carrying at least a fifty-pound load. Chris narrated part of the story: "We had eight Sherpas, in addition to Ang Phurba, make carries up from the Col, but one of them dropped back, so we had seven get to Camp Six. I had never seen the Sherpas climb so slowly. We all had the same loads, more or less, but I managed to pass several of them on the way up. It was as though above twenty-six thousand feet we were all somehow equalized, all equally wiped out. When they got to the sight of Six, they all dumped their loads and shot back down to the Col. But we had enough supplies to make it: one tent, one sack of food, two stoves and a few cartridges, six full bottles and three half-bottles of oxygen.

"With the Sherpas gone, Bob, Ang, and I got busy setting up the tent. We pitched it about five feet below a rib in the ridge—actually well sheltered from the wind. There were the remnants of an old army tent—probably from the British Army. Ang also found a couple of half-full British oxygen cylinders. But the camp wasn't anything like I had pictured. It was just a small little platform on this ridge, way up in the air. You could see around you forever. Lhotse, Makalu, Kanchenjunga. Lots of clouds and lots of mountains. We could see to the horizon in Tibet—hundreds of miles away. It was really exciting to be up there."

Bob's impression was somewhat different: "I told Chris the only thing that kept me going was the knowledge that this would be the last time I was going up this mountain. I must have lost about thirty-five pounds by that point in the expedition, and I felt that maybe I was too weak to make it all the way. Just before Camp Six I ran out of oxygen and with a fifty-pound pack, it took me about a half-hour to make the last hundred feet. It took ten or fifteen breaths for each step, and I was scared because my lungs were starting to produce a little fluid. With oxygen you can't tell that it is doing anything for you until it runs out and then, Holy Christ, you just come to a stop. When I got to the camp, there were three of us for that tent and it was extremely claustrophobic. We had two stoves to melt water as fast as we could. But it was slow—the stoves don't burn hot that high. There was just not enough oxygen. It was absolutely impossible to stay in the tent without sucking on oxygen."

The lack of oxygen affected Bob and again he had the reaction he had experienced at the South Col: "It was as though I'd go into a sad, crying drunk and become very depressed. I felt so bad I even started crying. All I wanted to do was go down, but then I would be ashamed of those feelings, only making it worse. But as soon as I started breathing oxygen again the depression would go away."

The three stayed up until eight that night, eating and drinking all they could force past their diminished appetites. It was an uncomfortable night, more like a bivouac in a makeshift shelter, and they slept only sporadically.

Chris continued the narrative: "We woke up about four A.M. to start a stove and melt water. It was hard in the cramped quarters, and we knocked it over three or four times, spilling the water. We kept eating and drinking and finally about six o'clock we felt like leaving. It looked like a good early start. But it took us another hour to finish dressing. It was so cold we had to keep warming our hands over the stove while getting our crampons on, at the same time trying to breathe oxygen. Finally, about seven, we were ready to go."

Cormack continued the story: "We got about fifty feet above the tent when Ang Phurba signaled that something was wrong. He was almost collapsed, unable to move. His oxygen regulater apparently wasn't working. He got up and tried to continue, but made only about another fifty feet and collapsed. He couldn't do it. Chris and I went back and fooled with the thing for about twenty minutes. Finally I suggested hitting it with an ice ax because everything else had failed. We did that; then it started hissing and wouldn't stop—it was feeding out at a seventy psi flow. We cursed at not having brought a spare, but there was nothing we could do. Ang had to give up and go down."

Chris added, "I've never in my life seen a sadder person. The way he had counted on going to the top only to be stopped so close to the goal."

Bob said: "He was one of the strongest of the Sherpas, and I think if he could not make it without oxygen, very few people could. We continued on alone. It was then about eight fifteen. I was finally starting to gain some confidence. For the first time I thought we just might make it. It seemed like a nice day although we didn't realize at the time we were shielded from the wind by another ridge on the Southwest Face. I think part of my depression when I was in Camp Four was due to the fact that I thought if I could hardly make it to Camp Four, how was I going to make it to the summit? Well, I had gone through quite a bit since then. I didn't feel real strong, but at least I thought I had a chance. We continued up the ridge for several hours, averaging about three feet a minute—not real fast. We would go about forty minutes and then sit down and rest for about ten minutes. Finally we saw the south summit at the top of the ridge. By God, we were really going to make it. At about one we climbed to the top of the south summit, and we were immediately hit by the wind."

Chris said: "It was like running full speed into a brick wall, but the view was incredible. You could see all the Himalayas, right down to Camp Two and Base Camp. It looked like you could throw a stone and hit Camp Two. It was much steeper than I ever imagined. But the plume obscured the view into Tibet. It was like a storm on one side of the mountain. And then we saw the summit ridge, and it wasn't at all what I expected."

Bob said: "I was somewhat dismayed, too, when I saw it. It didn't look trivial at all. Had I been on a climb in Colorado and been as extended as I was there, I would have turned back at the south summit. But Chris said, 'Well, let's get on with it.' I thought of all those people who worked for months for this trip. All the money. God knows how much. And the debt, and the need to have the TV show go prime time; I hate to think about it. So I thought I owed it to all those people to trim the safety margin right to the nub, go down as close to the wire as I could gauge it. There may have been a fantastic view, but I was so preoccupied thinking about the wind, and if we had enough daylight left, that I don't even remember what it looked like. I guess that's not very romantic, is it?

"So I looked over at Chris and said, 'O.K., let's go.' But I told him we had to turn back by four o'clock no matter what. Nothing was worth getting stuck in a bivouac. We got to the bottom of the south summit and rested while we switched to fresh oxygen bottles. Then we took off. I was doing the leading at first. Then we got to the Hillary Step, which was fortunately shielded from the wind. It really didn't turn out to be much. There was probably more opportunity for disaster on the rest of the ridge than on the Hillary Step. It's not exposed; if you fall off you only go fifteen feet onto a flat part of the ridge."

Bob continued: "I got there first and started whacking my way up it. Then about a third of the way I uncovered an old fixed rope. It went up the steepest part of the Step, but I followed it anyway. Then about five feet from the top, at the steepest part, the rope went straight into the snow, presumably to its anchor. I compacted the snow with my ax, stuck it in the top, and mantled up. Chris was up a few minutes later, climbing right behind me without a belay. The Hillary Step wasn't really that bad at all. But then we had to negotiate the wind-swept, heavily corniced ridge to the summit."

Chris said: "The wind was incredible. It was blowing so hard that the rope between us arched up at forty-five degrees and never touched the snow. And it whistled as the wind held it up. I was worried that if it dropped down it might hook over a cornice on the ridge, and then we would be in trouble. We had to be careful also of not getting too close to the ridge for fear of breaking through a cornice. We continually had to plant our ice axes and hang on to them to keep from being blown away."

Bob added: "I found that just standing, balancing against the wind, I was using energy at a maximum rate. To make progress I would kneel down with my back to the wind, breathe deeply for a while to get oxygen in me, then stand up and take ten or fifteen quick steps, then kneel down again. I was feeling like I was very near the end of my ability, and that was scary. At four o'clock—the time we had arbitrarily set to turn back—I could see the summit about fifty yards ahead. We were so close we couldn't turn back, and we got there about four fifteen. I walked up on it thinking, Well, here it is, the summit of Everest. My God, who would ever have guessed that I would ever be here! I was surprised it was so small. It's just a rounded ridge, not a dome at all. I whipped out the sixteen-millimeter camera and took a couple of duty shots."

Chris said: "Bob told me to hold it while he got the camera ready. Then he signaled me to climb up to the top while he rolled the camera. I decided to make it look good, so I took five or six quick steps to the top and then waved my arm. At the same time I was yelling through my oxygen mask to turn the camera off. As soon as it stopped, I collapsed in exhaustion, hanging on to the Chinese tripod. I was gasping so desperately my head started spinning, and I was afraid I would black out. Finally the dizziness went away, and I could get up and look around. I was surprised to find the aluminum survey tripod the Chinese had placed on the summit in nineteen seventy-five still standing. Originally it had been painted bright red, but now it was polished metal—no sign of paint left. I only took three pictures at the top—it was just too cold to operate the camera. You could only take your hands out of the mittens for a few seconds before they started to freeze. I guess we stayed up there for about a half-hour, although it didn't seem that long. After Bob took some more movie footage, I said, "Let's get the hell out of here." He couldn't have agreed with me more. He had searched through his coat for an American flag he had brought up to leave on the summit, but it was buried under too much down for retrieval. You know, we were supposed to leave something on the top, right? I had a special scarf Terri had given me that had been blessed by the lama of Tengboche, so I took it off and tied it to the tripod. I felt that it was an appropriate thing to leave. Inside the scarf, tied in a small pouch, were several grains of sacred rice."

The next morning we began to desert Base Camp. Long lines of yaks loaded with surplus equipment, food, and oxygen lumbered down the ice trail on the Khumbu Glacier. If only five more of those bottles could have made Camp 6, I thought, walking behind one of the yaks. But then I knew I shouldn't have any regrets. For one thing, I was still suffering from my pleurisy, and I realized that even had the Sherpas carried more oxygen to the high camp, I probably wouldn't have been fit to make the summit. The other team members who also didn't make it seemed, at least outwardly, philosophical and satisfied that they played a role in getting Bob and Chris up there. All except Gerry and Ang Phurba. While neither was openly morose, I could sense the extent of their disappointment.

We passed dozens of Sherpas carrying empty baskets tied to their backs. Word had passed among the villages that the expedition was over, and people were coming up, hopeful of finding two or three days' employment carrying gear to Namche Bazaar. Many of them stopped us and asked the same question. They wanted to know if Ang Phurba had made the summit. The disappointment on their faces when we explained the failure of his regulator showed how much they had been hoping for his success.

I began to realize the extent of Ang's disappointment. I suggested that money, with the possible addition of prestige, was the main spur that drove Ang. I was still hoping, though, to find, if not in Ang, then at least in some of the Sherpas, that same love for Everest to which Tenzing Norgay had alluded in his autobiography. I recalled a passage in his book when he said, "I have climbed Everest . . . as a child climbs into the lap of its mother." Did none of the Sherpas these days have those feelings for the mountain? Several times I had asked Ang why he had such a desire to climb Everest, and each time he only laughed at the question, as if he didn't fully understand it. So once while we were sitting in front of the cook tent, I thought of another tactic. Why not ask him if he knows what had happened to the other Sherpas who reached the summit of Everest? Among those he named were Tenzing Norgay, Nawang Gombu, Ang Kami, Phu Dorje, Choturi, and Lapka Tenzing.

Some had won trips to foreign countries, others jobs teaching climbing to the army or working for trekking agencies. I had been surprised that some of them had received salary bonuses of up to $8,000. But then I later learned that the Sherpa who had received that particular bonus had given the money to a community trust fund for Sherpa education and medical care. And he had known what he was to do with the money even before he had made the long climb to the summit. Perhaps if Ang had made the summit, and received a bonus, he would have used it for a similar purpose. I had learned that the Sherpas have a moral sense of social justice stronger than any group of people I had ever met. It was a result of their Buddhist upbringing, of their belief that man's duty is to help relieve the world of suffering, and that what one does in his lifetime directly determines the quality of the next life.

That is not to say, of course, that the Sherpas weren't normal people with normal foibles. They had some habits that had tested our patience: their tendency to be messy and wasteful, and sometimes to act spontaneously without thinking through possible consequences. And I would not completely dismiss the possibility of self-seeking and even perhaps a pecuniary element in Ang's motives. But one consequence of the Sherpas' moral sense was that they were, with justification, a very proud people. And Ang had been given a mandate to carry that pride to the summit.

That afternoon we camped, as we had weeks before on the way up, at the summer yak herders' settlement of Lobuche. After making camp I took a short walk beyond the settlement, and in the distance I could see six chorten—Buddhist monuments made of brick-laid stones. I remembered that on the approach march a Sherpa had explained that they were memorials to the six Sherpas who had been killed in the Icefall during the filming of the Japanese ski expedition. I thought back once again to Ang's list of those who had made the summit. One of the names had been Sherpa Phu Dorje. He had been awarded a position teaching climbing to the Nepalese army, and he had also continued to work on expeditions. One of the chorten was for him; his good fortune had been short-lived.

It was about seven in the morning. Chris Chandler, Dee Crouch, and I were sitting on the second-floor balcony of Nima Norbu's International Footrest Hotel in Namche Bazaar. We were drinking our eleventh bottle of Star beer, a brew rumored to be made under German license in Kathmandu. It was the third day since we had abandoned Base Camp. Yesterday, after a long hike, most of the expedition had chosen to camp in Tengboche. But we decided to continue hiking after dark to reach Nima's hotel so we could sleep under a roof— for the first time in over two months. We planned to rendezvous with the others about noon at the deluxe Everest View

Hotel where we had been invited by the management for a celebration luncheon. We were getting an early start on the celebrating.

A little later we left to begin the steep hike up the hill behind Namche to the Everest View. We were already thinking about lunch. Besides featuring our first served-on-china meal, lunch would also represent the last time we would be together as an expedition. The next day most of the climbers were flying out to Kathmandu (with the dry season the dirt airstrip was now open), and from there they would be homeward bound. After so many weeks of ice and snow, it felt wonderful to be back in the world of living things. During our absence fall had visited the hills around Namche Bazaar, and the trees were burning with autumn color. The wild flowers were blossoming, and against the blue sky and ice peaks they created a fairyland panorama. The wind was still high in the snows, but in the valleys it was calm and the sun warmed the air to T-shirt temperature. It was the most beautiful month of the year in the Khumbu, and it was also the height of the tourist trekking season.

Although many people feel the area would be better served were the hotel not there, the Everest View is still to be admired as something of an engineering wonder. On a secluded hill behind the small village of Khumjung, surrounded by spruce and pine, the small twelve-room hotel commands a startling view of Everest and Ama Dablam. The wood and stone building is single story, pleasant in design, with notable Japanese influence. All the building materials were either flown in on a small plane or carried on the backs of porters from Kathmandu. The hotel's supplies, other than a few items of local produce, have to be flown or backpacked from Kathmandu, and even the water is hand carried from a well near Khumjung.

Inside the hotel we found the rest of the expedition lounging on soft padded seats surrounding a midroom fireplace, like those found at ski resorts. Behind the crackling logs our table was set with a linen cloth in front of a long picture window with a view of Everest. I could see a plume blowing off the summit, though it was much diminished from when we were there a few days before. I greeted everyone, then went to a bar decorated in modern Swiss Alp and ordered three Star beers from a Sherpa dressed in lederhosen.

I went back to the fire and gave a beer to Dee and one to Chris. Everyone was feeling festive, and all were dressed in the best clothes they could dig out of their backpacks. Most of the conversation was about how strange it felt to be reentering civilization.

Chris looked at Bob and said, "Little different than the accommodations at Camp Six."

Bob replied, "Had I known this was here, I would have gone down instead of up from Six. I had enough trouble going on just thinking about how nice it would have been returning to Camp Two."

The manager of the hotel came over, introduced himself, and announced that the luncheon was ready. He handed each of us an individually typed card listing that day's menu. We all glanced at the cards and Phil said, "I guess from now on we will have to call ourselves the SABEE."

"What's the S for?"

"It says here, 'Special Buffet Lunch in Honor of the *Successful* American Bicentennial Everest Expedition.' "

The food sounded extraordinary after weeks of freeze-dried dinners. Hotel Everest View Yak Steak, creamed spinach, Potatoes Khumbu, Rice Butterfly, mixed green salad, mango slices for dessert. We all quickly seated ourselves at the table with Phil at the head. With the food served and the Champagne poured, Phil stood to propose a toast.

"First, I would like to thank our host for his wonderful lunch." The manager, standing nearby, nodded his approval. "And then I'd like to toast all of you for making this a successful expedition without accident."

Still Life

It won't last,
of course. The sun

at just this angle
on the coral tulips. Even now
they're spinning away, but oh,

these open mouths reach out
on their supple stems,
revealing yellow throats, golden
pistil and black anthers wheeling.

They ride the air, louche cups of emptiness,
satin feathers, parrot-colored curtains, they billow,
they plume, dreamy sails, slack bells, they lift
and tremble at the slightest shift, even my breath
sets them nodding. For a minute,

maybe two, they
dwell and crest,
then the planet's stream
takes them with it
and the shallow pond of light is gone—

except the tip of one petal
still catching the sun.

Après Moi

is pest, is plague, is
global atrophy, desire
insipid, the single
saltine in its crumpled
sleeve. Future of
courtesy balance and
hysterical number,
markets depressed,
a bottomed-out
GDP.

       Oh yes,
it all goes up.
Kablooey! Good luck
enjoying those bonfires
with no s'mores!
       Big, BIG
mistake, to make this
life without me. So
when the horsemen
descend on your
address, ride jiggety
clop to your
empty door,
       you
can explain this mess.
I won't live here
anymore. To you,
I bequeath a world
where cupboards stick,
with nothing left
to creak for.

Dad Poem

No visitors allowed
is what the masked woman behind
the desk says only seconds
after me and your mother
arrive for the ultrasound. *But I'm the father,*
I explain, like it means something
defensible. She looks at me as if
I've just confessed to being a minotaur
in human disguise. Repeats the line. Caught
in the space between astonishment
& rage, we hold hands a minute
or so more, imagining you a final time
before our rushed goodbye,
your mother vanishing
down the corridor
to call forth a veiled vision
of you through glowing white
machines. One she will bring
to me later on, printed and slight
-ly wrinkled at its edges,
this secondhand sight
of you almost unbearable
both for its beauty and
necessary deferral.
What can I be to you now,
smallest one, across the expanse
of category & world catastrophe,
what love persists
in a time without touch

Haunt

Six months after death, my mother
has come to haunt me. Ever
the opportunist, she finds the virus
lockdown a handy time to slide
into the slot for my shadow, as if
I faced the sun at an angle of forty-
five degrees. There she is, darkening
my starboard periphery un-
smiling, reaching cold mist hands
into mine to whisk the eggs, fold
the sheets, sort the papers, choose
spools of thread for stitching
another face mask. This is her kind
of catastrophe, rife with irony and fear
and small domestic refinements
of infinite unimportance as we sail
about the house and yard, posing
for no one. I once thought
ghosts made "appearances," but she
eludes sight: dodgy, palpable,
squeezing in for one last clutch
at the stuff of my survival.

Ode

in which during a pandemic you were scarcely to be found

You once
stood patiently, heroically,

wrapped & sealed underneath
your childproof top,

lined up like a dependable
army of toy soldiers

in rows on the shelf of the pain
reliever aisle,

even the little packets
of two one might find at a newspaper
stand or airport—are gone.

The streets are empty too.
I mourn those wasteful days,

when we downed
two for a headache, a slight fever,
ache or pain, sometimes three

for a hangover, after a night out
at the bars or a crowded party,

325 mg of acetaminophen, cellulose,
cornstarch, magnesium stearate,
sodium starch glycolate

dressed in a sanitary coat of white.
Once my girlfriend chugged
20 from my mother's medicine cabinet,

heartsick over a boy.

It did not look as if it was frightened,
even while walking my hand,
which moved it through swiftness and air.

Ant, alone, without companions,
whose ant-heart I could not fathom—
how is your life, I wanted to ask.

I lifted it, took it outside.

This first day when I could do nothing,
contribute nothing
beyond staying distant from my own kind,
I did this.

April

I spend half the day in the bathtub, trying to read something,
trying to find something to latch on to.
I read a newish novel, very classy, winner
of the Prix Goncourt, now in English.
The water becomes cold, my cock becomes soft.
No real interest in the narrative. Everything's stopped. My life
in equilibrium: my love is happy, my other loves
in New York or Berlin, one in Mexico City, waiting things out;
they've forgotten about me.
I drink a can of seltzer in the tub.
Actually, there's something I like in this novel.
Something finally.
When the boys are on the beach, one of them puts his sunglasses
    inside a sneaker while he swims.

Watching the Full Moon in a Time of Pandemic

I watch the full moon's light slide like silver water through the
   silhouettes of trees
that cast long shadows over mounds and rocks, a hidden stream, and
   the expanse of lawn.
I think back to when I played hide-and-seek games with cousins at
   the shoreline,
Pūpūkea near Shark's Cove on O'ahu, dodging in and out of the
   shadows of ironwood trees.

We hid amidst the vapors of murk mixed with sea spray and wild
   laughter, sought one
another in sands under the glassy moonlight that splashed our bodies
   like surf.
We stood as though rooted, silent while sighs from the sea carried
   through cool night air.

I was four or I was five and I was not Leanne or Neal or Kerry, but
   myself,
counting my own breath, one with the dark, gazing at the silver gleam
   of heaven's road
making its path from below the moon across heaving, purple waters
   to where I stood
as I do tonight, sixty years from that first shining. I told it to my
   daughter,
who hid in moonshade, isolate and lonely, missing the welter of what
   life had been,
her father five as a child unfathomable, her slim form disappearing,
   while I stood, seeking.

Ballina

For Alice Lyons

Where an island well is helped
By the pebble on the left
So the one behind it can slip
A bit to let the water up
Now it's a bungalow
Built from grit and shells.
Hellebore growing by the door.
A granny sometimes to be there
Bent in a chair, laughter not far.
Please God so.

Ides of March, 2020

Two doves land in the moss
below the feeder,
sunbathe in the last light
of an early spring day then huddle
on the lower branch of the ancient
hackberry tree where we wait to see
them mate. By today,
the newest plague has killed
thousands in Italy,
so any life is good life.
The 2016 Viberti Dolbà
although not communion
feels sacred—
as do our crackers and cheese,
our hike under a biblically blue sky,
our fire raging in its cage
when we return home.
I have complained about so much
for so often, how now do I love
that tiny fellow chipmunk who
on hind legs checks the celestial movement
of the sun before digging what I imagine
are Christian catacombs under our foundation?
He has a mission. So should I.
No rain today fell into the open
graves of the dead, only a sunset
and life as we know it.

Order to Disperse

Tonight my children are facing live ammunition.

One holds a rock, one brought a bible, one has a phone.

The fires of the provocateurs burn so brightly.

The police put duct tape over their badges.

The soldiers are hooded; they wear no insignia.

Last night they had rubber bullets, tonight hollow-point.

In the smoke you see the outlines of a bank, a cathedral,

absent as the profiles of Presidents on coins.

A voice advances, a voice retreats, someone aims.

Have you ever died in a dream? What happened then?

Tell me what happened! There is only one life.

How long will I hold mine like water in cupped hands?

Two Days in March
from Corona Sonnets

March 18, 2020

The color of lilacs, only darker—the clouds
that cover the top of Mt. Rainier like a shroud
this evening. Another beautiful day. Disturbing
to see so many people walking the waterfront
as if the sky weren't burning. The fish market is closed.
The café is closed. The bar is closed. The daffodils
are heedless. Today, the first death in Tacoma. A woman
in her fifties. Droplets cover me, probably. My neighbor veers.
Conversation grows heavier by the word.
In clinic I don plastic face-shield and gown
of goldenrod when seeing a *person*
under investigation. The nights are growing quieter.
We no longer hear passenger trains, only freight trains,
and fewer, from our cabin.

Pandemicon

I don't want to find meaning in it. The narcissus,
I guess I see it more clearly, its crisp gold corona,
I suppose I feel more indebted to it, to flowers
in general, how entertaining they are, how they dot
the landscape in spring like the new commercials
on TV about how we're all in this together, incredible
how America can brand even a pandemic, turn it
into *a thing,* face masks printed with dragonflies and Prince
in *Purple Rain,* it's a reality series with viral bread recipes
and optimism, so this narcissus, isn't it said the gods
made the flowers for us, the grand unified field of us,
the us that is grandly unified into a me, and we are to find
a way to love them, flowers, trees, animals, bugs, most
of us don't see amphibians that often, or reptiles, except
for snakes, remember when Britney Spears danced
at the VMAs with an albino python draped over her shoulders,
that was September 6, 2001, five days before 9/11, an omen
almost, Britney didn't know what she was in for, Britney
never knows what she's in for, that was six years before
she shaved her head, she's not a person who looks good
with a shaved head, she just looked the kind of crazy
they accused her of, Aaliyah had just died, and Joey Ramone,
end of an era, and Fatboy Slim took most of the awards
for that video he did with Christopher Walken, but looking
back on that video, well, who wants to see someone they know,
like Christopher Walken, I mean, I don't know him personally
but I watched *The Deer Hunter,* those Russian roulette scenes,
terrible, who wants to see him dancing, it's like seeing your
next-door neighbor's sex tape, just please, no, but there he was,
dancing, and then there was that one part where he jumps off

the balcony and flies over the hotel lobby, flies, that was
a bit much and maybe another omen, I'm thinking everything
since the 2001 VMAs was an omen of this current situation
in which what you touch can contain a little spiked red
ball of death, you've seen the photos of the corona online,
it looks like a toy my dog would like, to be honest, but it's
microscopic so it could be anywhere and is therefore
everywhere, smeared on all the stuff we used to live for,
especially each other, we can kill who we touch, we can
be killed by who touches us, but wasn't that always true,
it was for me, it was for Pan, the only god in the pantheon
who dies, who fell in love with Echo, who fell in love
with Narcissus, who fell in love with himself and turned
into a flower with a gold corona at the center like a crown,
like it's royalty or something and we have to get down
on our knees in front of it, an omen if there ever was one,
that we almost have to stop living in order to save our lives.

Spillover

Why do I miss you, so suddenly, now? It's been
so many years. Over half my life I never thought
to miss you. Think of all that time I could've spent.

It hasn't been an hour since then. I see that now
that it's so clear. A day can be a year, a year a decade
or two, but there never was anyone else like you.

I thought there would be, later, when I was ready.
But soon it was too late; was entirely full of myself
by then. And again, a mess of my breakfast dress,

this transparent film covers recent events, stretched
between intimates. Now a little screen of your letters,
your ellipses pulse as if I'm with you, all fingers.

I screen you. It's transfixing. It's real-life Netflix,
what boxed muffin mix makes. A trail of crumbs
to let the ants take home. I used to have purpose.

That turned into leftovers. I remember a dream I
slept with, a thing I watched, a way I was. I didn't live
online and drift all day. Didn't move from room

to room to remember what I was going to say.
I had planes to catch and children to hand over.
I had bigger fish to fry. Big fish, small ponder—

smaller wonder, hooked. When I had nothing nothing
looked half bad. I had what it took but it took what I had.
Now I just try not to die, confused. To quote Prince:

"It's June." What's next and how soon? Did you get
my text? Full moon can't spill like the new. I can get
there closer to noon, stay till maybe half past two.

Danielle Chapman is the author of a collection of poems, *Delinquent Palaces*. Her recent essays can be found in *The Oxford American* and *Commonweal*. She teaches literature and creative writing at Yale.

Nicholas Christopher is the author of nine books of poems, most recently *Crossing the Equator* and *On Jupiter Place;* seven novels, including *Veronica* and *A Trip to the Stars;* and a book about film noir. He lives in New York City.

Ama Codjoe is the author of the chapbook *Blood of the Air* and the recipient of honors including a 2017 Rona Jaffe Writers' Award, a 2018 Loraine Williams Poetry Prize, and a 2019 NEA Creative Writing Fellowship.

Catherine Cohen is a comedian and actress based in New York City. She has a weekly residency at Alan Cumming's East Village cabaret, Club Cumming, and cohosts the popular podcast *Seek Treatment with Cat and Pat*. Follow her @catccohen while you're young!

Elizabeth J. Coleman is the editor of *HERE: Poems for the Planet* (Copper Canyon Press, 2019). She is the author of two collections, *The Fifth Generation* (Spuyten Duyvil Press, 2016) and *Proof* (Spuyten Duyvil Press, 2014), and two chapbooks.

Billy Collins's latest book is *The Rain in Portugal*. A new collection, *Whale Day*, is forthcoming in September 2020. He is a member of the American Academy of Arts and Letters.

Nicole Cooley is the author of six books of poems, most recently *Of Marriage* (Alice James Books, 2018). She is the director of the MFA Program in Creative Writing and Literary Translation at Queens College–The City University of New York.

Peter Cooley is a professor emeritus at Tulane University in New Orleans, where he was Director of Creative Writing from 1975 to 2018. His eleventh book of poetry, *The One Certain Thing,* will appear in 2021.

Cooley is poetry editor of *Christianity and Literature* and was Louisiana's poet laureate from 2015 to 2017.

Timothy Donnelly's most recent books include *The Problem of the Many* and *The Cloud Corporation,* winner of the 2012 Kingsley Tufts Poetry Award. He teaches in the writing program at Columbia University School of the Arts and lives in Brooklyn with his family.

Cornelius Eady's seven poetry collections include *Victims of the Latest Dance Craze,* winner of the 1985 Lamont Prize, and *Hardheaded Weather* (Putnam, 2008). He is cofounder of the Cave Canem Foundation and a professor of English at SUNY Stony Brook Southampton.

John Freeman edits the literary annual *Freeman's* and is author and editor of eight books, including *Maps, Tales of Two Americas,* and *Dictionary of the Undoing. The Park* is his most recent collection of poetry. His work has been translated into more than twenty languages.

Forrest Gander's *Twice Alive* is forthcoming from New Directions in 2021. A poet and translator, Gander lives in California. His book *Be With* won the 2019 Pulitzer Prize.

Suzanne Gardinier is the author of five poetry collections, most recently *Iridium & Selected Poems 1986–2009* (2010) and *Atlas* (2015). She lives in Manhattan.

Deborah Garrison lives in Montclair, New Jersey. "Leaving Evanston" is dedicated to Daisy, to Ellie and her women who will measure the universe, to Delia, Harley, Jane Emma, Louisa, and all the Northwestern class of 2020.

Tammy Melody Gomez is a Texas-based poet and performing artist who lost track of the number of Zoom meetups and webinars she attended during the COVID-19 pandemic, but she is certain that she sheltered in place with precisely seven cats.

Rigoberto González is the author of twelve books of prose and five collections of poetry, most recently *The Book of Ruin.* He is director of the MFA program in creative writing at Rutgers–Newark.

George Green resides in Manhattan. His book, *Lord Byron's Foot,* won the New Criterion Poetry Prize and the Poets' Prize. His poems appear in ten anthologies; in 2014 he received an award for literature from the American Academy of Arts and Letters.

Linda Gregerson's most recent book is *Prodigal: New and Selected Poems.* She is the Caroline Walker Bynum Distinguished University Professor of English at the University of Michigan and a chancellor of the Academy of American Poets.

Rachel Eliza Griffiths is a poet and visual artist. Her most recent collection of poetry and photography is *Seeing the Body* (W. W. Norton, 2020).

Eliza Griswold, whose most recent book of poems, *If Men, Then,* was published in 2020 by Farrar, Straus and Giroux, was awarded the 2019 Pulitzer Prize for her nonfiction book *Amity and Prosperity.*

Julia Guez is the author of *In an Invisible Glass Case Which Is Also a Frame* (Four Way Books). She teaches creative writing at Rutgers University and works at Teach for America New York. Guez lives in Brooklyn and online at www.juliaguez.net.

Nathalie Handal is the author of seven poetry collections, most recently *Life in a Country Album* (2019). She is the recipient of awards from the PEN Foundation, the Lannan Foundation, and Fondazione di Venezia, among others.

Brooks Haxton and his wife see migratory waterfowl on Snooks Pond in Manlius, New York.

Aleksandar Hemon's most recent book is *My Parents: An Introduction/ This Does Not Belong to You* (Farrar, Straus and Giroux, 2019). He teaches at Princeton University.

Brenda Hillman is the author of ten collections of poetry, the most recent of which is *Extra Hidden Life, Among the Days.* She currently serves as a chancellor for the Academy of American Poets and teaches at Saint Mary's College of California.

Soldiers of Anatin's Mercenary Deck

	SUN	STARS	BLOOD	SNOW	TEMPEST
PRINCE	ANATIN		TOIL		
17	Foren				
16	Sonnersyn				
KNIGHT	PAYL	~~OLUT~~	REFT	SAFIR	TESHEN
14	Karra	Dortrinas	Silm	Layir	Finc
13	Fashail	Arut	Brellis	Aspegrin	
DIVINER		ESTAL	HIMBEL		LLAITH
11	Haphori	Rubesh	Crast		Flinth
10					
STRANGER	VARAIN		ULAX		LYNX
8	Darm		Toam	Sandath	
7	Brols		Sethail	Ylor	
MADMAN	CRAIS	KAS		BURNEL	
5	Fael	Hald		Shoal	
4				Ismont	
JESTER	SITAIN	~~ASHIS~~	DEERN	~~TYN~~	BRAQE
2			Hule		Tunnest
1					

What Has Gone Before

Stranger of Tempest –
Book 1 of the God Fragments

Once, Lynx was a soldier – an idealistic young man in the warrior state of So Han. As a commando lieutenant he was at the spearhead of So Han's war of conquest, but refused to engage in the atrocities being committed. After killing his commanding officer in a duel he was sent to the brutal To Lort prison and forced to labour in the mines there.

Eventually the Hanese conquest imploded and To Lort prison was taken over by a foreign governor called Lorfen, who saw something of himself in Lynx. He taught the damaged young man the philosophy of the Vagrim brotherhood – a nebulous group of war veterans who had found renewed purpose in helping and protecting others – and released him.

Years later, an older, wiser and slightly more rotund Lynx arrives in the town of Jangarai. Hoping to find more work as a bodyguard, he meets Kas, a woman of Anatin's Mercenary Deck, and with his welcome in town fast running out Lynx agrees to join her company for a rescue mission.

On the way the company encounters a group of Knights-Charnel of the Long Dusk – one of the most powerful of the militant religious orders on the continent. They are escorting a young half-Hanese woman who appeals to Lynx for help and when he confronts them, Lynx learns she is a mage. The power of the Militant Orders stems from their control of mages and fragments of the five shattered gods, which they use to create magical cartridges that every gun across the known world uses.

When the smoke clears, the Knights-Charnel lie dead and Lynx has a new ward, Sitain. Matters become further complicated when the rescue mission turns out to be covering the escape of an assassin called Toil from the city of Grasiel. Their flight turns into a street battle after Lynx and Sitain are betrayed to the Knights-Charnel by one of the Cards, Deern, and they are pursued from the city by the Knights-Charnel's elite Torquen regiment.

Toil persuades Anatin to leave the road and head across the wilds surrounding Shadows Deep, an ancient Duegar city-ruin where elementals and monsters reign. Forced underground, the outnumbered Cards are beaten to the only bridges that cross a miles-deep canyon blocking their path. To even up the odds Toil awakens a huge dragon-like creature and in the ensuing chaos Lynx ends up luring the monster out on to the main bridge where he and his comrades manage to bring it down. Leaving any surviving Charnelers lost in the darkness, the Cards escape to the surface and don't look back.

Honour Under Moonlight –
a novella of the God Fragments

Midwinter in Su Dregir brings a festival of costumed revelry and Lynx arrives at Toil's apartments to escort her to the Archelect's ball. There he discovers two corpses in strange costumes instead of one living Toil. Before he can work out what's going on, a watchman appears and an assassin attacks. The watchman dies and Lynx flees.

Following a clue left by Toil, Lynx goes in search of her. More costumed assassins ambush him and despite the efforts of his comrades, he is captured by Toil's enemies. Toil meanwhile has discovered a plot to upturn the balance of power in the criminal gangs of Su Dregir. After preventing a massacre she goes to rescue Lynx and, with the assistance of her employer's bodyguard, turns the tables on the remaining assassins before killing the traitor.

Interlude 1
(Now)

'So a pederast, an assassin and a convict walk into a palace.'

'Shut up.'

Lynx sighed. 'What? I'm bored.'

'I don't care.'

'No one's listening.'

Toil's voice lowered to the whisper of a razor being sharpened. 'What part of "I don't care" confuses you?'

'What's the harm in passing the time with a joke?'

'Because if you don't shut up I'll rip your kneecaps off and use them for earmuffs to block out your bloody whining. You're not standing here for your health, we've got a job to do, remember?'

Lynx shut up and looked around at the grand hall of Jarrazir's Bridge Palace once more. It was magnificent, he had to admit. Jewelled light shone through a long bank of stained glass windows running almost the entire length of the hall. Dancing motes of emerald, blazing orange and glittering sapphire washed over the assembled crowd of Jarrazir's nobility. A spray of red carpet surrounded the pair of thrones at one end, all canopied by pristine white cloth bearing the symbols of the city and prayers stitched in red. Flanking them was a battered pair of stone urns that bore only fragments of faded glazing. They looked strangely out of place there until Lynx realised they were Duegar artefacts.

4

After an hour of the sight Lynx felt it was all very pretty, but lunch was fast intruding on his thoughts as the scents of spices and roasted meats hung thick in the air. As a portly and tattooed ex-soldier of a nation everyone hated, he was very aware how noticeable he was at the best of times and right then the great and the good were out in their finery to notice and be noticed. Unobtrusively sidling over to the buffet probably wasn't an option.

Swan-necked maidens with bare shoulders stood like serene statues, or perhaps well-behaved cattle, while watchful matrons in silk headscarves fussed at their side. Prowling around the girls displayed like goods were knots of young noblemen, searching out both marriageable flesh and offence. Several had more than one glove tucked into their belt that did not match their clothes, proof of a duel to come.

Official delegations studded the throng, obvious by their matching clothing and uniforms, while members of the priesthood stood out even more clearly. Just ahead of Lynx were the starkly austere priests of Insar, in plain white robes with heads cleanly shaved, while red and grey figures displaying the intricate braiding and geometric patterns of Catrac's cult loitered near the far wall. Lynx looked down at his own clothes. Fortunately the grey and green of Su Dregir's Lighthouse Guard was as understated as he could have reasonably hoped for. The fact he was in any form of uniform was a detail he remained unhappy about, but now wasn't the time for *that* discussion so he contented himself with not looking like an utter tit. This was Toil's business and he was just window-dressing for the hour.

Lynx felt a nudge from the man beside him.

'Tell me the joke instead,' Teshen said. 'Distract me from the urge to fire a burner into the roof.'

Lynx glanced up at the huge pale beams, so high the grain of the wood was invisible. Flags of every colour fluttered in the slight breeze, representing each of the city-state's several hundred noble families, while the beast emblems of Jarrazir hung over the empty thrones.

'It'd stop the boredom,' he conceded. 'Maybe even cook a dove or two if one is lurking up in the rafters.'

'You're not still bloody hungry are you?'

'I could eat.'

Toil turned around, eyes flashing with anger. Ahead of her stood the Su Dregir Envoy himself, chatting to a doughy old lady wrapped in purple silk like a child's sweet. The captain of his personal guard stood just behind them, but if either man had heard the conversation over the general hubbub they chose to ignore it. Lynx doubted it, given the pederast comment was aimed at one of them.

'Both of you, shut your traps right now,' she hissed. 'At least try to look like real guards.'

'Sounds like *someone's* a little on edge,' Teshen whispered primly once Toil had turned back. The tone didn't exactly match the man's dead-eyed killer look, but joining a mercenary company had forced Teshen to develop a light-hearted side, even if he remained firmly in the alarmingly lethal category.

'It's the dress,' Lynx said. 'Maybe the heels. They don't look comfy.'

'Oh, I like the heels,' joined in Payl from the other side of Teshen. 'The poor bugger who had to buff her feet to make them presentable, however – now *they* have cause for complaint.'

Lynx smirked over at Payl. The woman was usually calm and professional – as second-in-command to a lazy, roguish drunk she had to be. That she'd joined in was a testament to the sheer boredom of standing amid that crowd and waiting for the city's ruler to finish whatever was taking so long.

'Was it you, Lynx?' Teshen asked. He was a burly man with long pale hair and under normal circumstances wore the Knight of Tempest as his badge – Lynx's direct superior – but today he was just another Su Dregir guardsman.

'Well, I don't like to brag,' Lynx said. 'But I reckon I've a certain deftness with a pumice stone.'

It was just possible he could see the tips of Toil's ears turning scarlet with fury, but he knew she wouldn't give them the satisfaction of turning around again. Toil – ruin-raider, assassin, agent of Su Dregir, plus half a dozen other unsavoury things – had scrubbed up remarkably well, he had to admit. A layered silk dress of the Archelect's green and grey ran from calf to neck, following the Jarraziran form of leaving arms and feet on show, with her dark red hair in a complex triple braid down her back.

'Almost fell over with shock when I saw her,' Teshen said. 'Who'd have thought under those hobnailed boots was a pair of feet like that? Probably best Anatin didn't come with us; man's got a thing for a well-turned ankle. I know I'm new to this, but I'm guessing elite guardsmen shouldn't have a hard-on.'

Lynx had to agree, the feet really had been a surprise. Toil wore thin sandals – straps of grey silk exposing neat, uncallused heels and pristinely groomed, painted toenails.

'Are all you fighting women like this?' he whispered to Payl. 'All with your little beauty secrets?'

Payl snorted. 'My feet look like they got chewed on by feral dogs. Just as well I'm tall. No man ever bothers to look that far down.'

'I'll tell Fashail to report back next time he's hard at work down there,' Teshen said.

'The boy knows he'll get his nuts cut off,' Payl said confidently. 'As scary as you are, Teshen, he ain't that stupid.'

'It's the arms that get me, I reckon,' Lynx said after a moment's reflection. 'So she's secretly a delicate little princess when it comes to her feet, now we all know, but it takes real skill to pull off the arms.'

'Not so much,' Teshen said dismissively. 'I've seen Reft do it easy enough.'

'I meant, pull off that concealment.'

'Ah.'

While almost every woman not in fighting dress had bare arms, none sported the number of scars Toil did. A lifetime of fighting and clambering about the pitch-black caverns of Duegar city-ruins had done little to support today's role of bookish secretary to Su Dregir's official Envoy.

It had required a complex variety of ribbons, torcs, bracelets, painted charms and rings to distract from the battering Toil's arms had received over the years. Close scrutiny would catch her out still, but with luck few would be getting that close. Toil was a distractingly beautiful woman for those who would be distracted and physically imposing for those who wouldn't.

'How about you, Aben?' Teshen asked the last of the group serving as guards to the Envoy. 'Anything you'd like to add?'

Aben was new to their number, a bigger man even than Lynx, with tanned skin, an easy smile and neat black curls spilling out from under his official cap. Currently his face was scarlet and he seemed to be having some sort of silent shaking episode, possibly a coronary.

'You okay there, friend?' Lynx said with a nudge. 'Looks like something in your head just burst. Was it the feet? Does a well-turned ankle do it for you too?'

Aben's eyes swivelled in their sockets as though seeking an escape. He'd worked for Toil for several years now. She was *the boss* to him, a ruthless and remorseless figure within the Su Dregir underworld. She *wasn't* a person to be joked about in her earshot and *was* someone with a long and enthusiastically vengeful memory.

'Hey, look, more people come to join the vigil,' Payl commented. 'And of fucking course it's the last bastards we want to see here, there or anywhere else.'

Lynx turned as Teshen voiced the words they were all thinking.

'Bastard shitting Charnelers.'

'Least all those who chased us will be dead by now,' Payl added quietly. 'Don't fancy getting recognised by anyone after Grasiel.'

'So – an assassin, a convict and a whole boatload of pederast shites walk into a palace,' Lynx muttered.

Toil spun right round, cheeks now spotted pink with anger. 'If they're here, you lot keep your mouths shut, understand? No jokes, no witty asides, no . . .' Her eyes narrowed as she focused on the Charnelers and Lynx saw anger turn to murder in her eyes. 'Godspit and the shitting deepest black!'

Without warning she started off, shoving Payl out of her way. In his surprise Lynx barely noticed her slip a dagger from Payl's belt as she stalked forward.

'What? So it's all right for her to swear?' Teshen commented in a mock-hurt voice.

'I'm going to fucking gut you like a fish!' Toil roared across the great hall.

Lynx and Teshen exchanged looks while Payl and Aben started off after the spirit of vengeance. Ahead of Toil the crowd erupted into chaos.

'Well, that's the boredom part sorted out,' Lynx said.

'Should we . . . ?' Teshen nodded after the others.

'If you like, but they can handle it I'm sure. And I'm damn sure Toil can handle herself. Not like I'm keen for her to win friends here anyway, given what she wants to volunteer us for. More importantly I've just spotted a roast pheasant that no one's watching. Reckon it's near enough lunchtime.'

'Is there beer?'

'Round here? Fat chance.'

Teshen shrugged as shouts filled the air. 'The sacrifices we must make . . . Lead on, my friend.'

Chapter 1
(Three Weeks Earlier)

A dusting of snow lay on the ancient city of Jarrazir as five figures hurried through the still hours of night. Every stone and tile sparkled in the silver glow of the Skyriver, every curl and twist of the bay's waters was limned in white moonlight. Statues of heroes and rulers watched from the great arc of the Senate wall, beneath which the Deep Market nestled. The market itself was a sweeping warren of walkways and arches, arcades and canopies, spread over three storeys in parts and bewildering in the detail and intricacy of its design.

The five figures kept silent as they wound their way towards the market's heart, the three who led moving with the confidence of familiarity. Jarrazir was a city of old names and older customs, one of which was a prohibition on alcohol so the night-time streets were empty and silent. The Deep Market in particular was deserted – the cold of winter and its unsettling, unearthly design of both Duegar and human magery meaning even vagrants kept clear at night.

Had she been alone, Lastani would have been apprehensive at best. She had lived her whole life in Jarrazir; a childhood of tales and superstitions not so long left behind for more academic pursuits. Only the reassuring purpose of Mistress Ishienne ahead kept her focused on the task in hand.

No, not quite. Not just that. She suppressed a nervous giggle. There was something more bringing her here, to the oldest part of an ancient city where even the light of the Skyriver strug-gled to reach. *There is the possibility of something quite wonderful too – a place in history perhaps, should we be successful.*

Lastani bit her lip and kept on walking. She would not be the one to draw Ishienne Matarin's ire this night, not at the culmination of all her teacher's work.

Let Castiere do that. He's incapable of keeping his mouth shut. Let him be the fool who sullies this night with some idiocy, I will be the perfect pupil at least this once.

As they rounded a corner and entered a small square cut through with jagged shadows, she glanced once at Castiere as the slender young man drew level in his haste to get to the market's heart. He saw her looking and flashed Lastani a grin, his excitement bubbling close to the surface.

'Almost there,' whispered Mistress Ishienne, her voice carrying clearly in the hush despite the scarf across her face.

The words were unnecessary, perhaps an indication of Ishienne's own anticipation. This might prove a breakthrough in her work, the fruits of years of translating and deciphering a script thousands of years old. Lastani could not fault this one crack in the detached calm that had been a constant of Lastani's four years tutelage.

She looked around as they neared the Fountain, as it was called, though in truth it was the entrance to a labyrinth built before human civilisation. A mystery lurking beneath the city streets that had never been opened in recorded history, but was mentioned in texts from across the continent. Lastani had spent so many days here amid the bustle of humanity as wares were sold and all manner of services offered from dawn until dusk. Day after day of transcribing and sketching, measuring and dreaming – losing her purse twice, her heart once and her maidenhood along with it. But now it was alien and frightening here, scoured of life and the things of men. The stone mages who had built the Deep Market, hundreds of years before, had chosen the fountain itself as inspiration for their otherworldly craft and, by custom, only stone remained here at night.

There, where the stall of kind Uslien normally stood, only bare and empty stone. Here, dear Lefaqe's tent of silks would be strung each morning – to see the space empty was to feel a curious hole in her heart though their affair had ended months ago. But no one would leave their belongings here, certainly not so close to the Fountain that was at the heart of it all. The Fountain which was no fountain and no crafting of a stone mage – at least, no human one.

They turned the corner and stopped, Lastani almost running into Mistress Ishienne as the Fountain itself came into view. It was a forbidding, squat lump of stone almost invisible in the darkness of shadow, but somehow all the more chilling for it. In the light of day she found it fascinating – the intricacy and otherworldly beauty of the ancient artefact breathtaking to behold – but now it was profoundly disquieting.

A nine-sided stone block the height of a man was set within a trio of fat, sinuous serpents of some unknown metal. The Fountain was Duegar-made and the finest example of that race's artistry within a hundred miles. Every flat surface was covered with wind-scoured carvings of remarkable intricacy and complexity – a puzzle of knots and patterns that incorporated every face and facet of the Fountain into one vast mathematical pattern. A domed stone canopy stood over it, perhaps twelve feet above, and it was this that restored Lastani's courage.

The Duegar script that covered the inner face of the dome was just as intricate as the decoration below, worked into a three-branched spiral that wound into the centre. And now, amid the blackness of night, the curling metal script was faintly glowing.

Lastani had always half-believed that to be nothing more than embellishment – a lie told in the assumption that no sensible person would visit at night to refute it. But there it was; the star-script of the Duegar now shining bright, almost as perfect and complete as the day that long-dead race had set it there. Two small pieces were missing. She had read the accounts of the enterprising thieves a dozen times or more, and the gruesome deaths that had found them before they could escape the market. Lastani was still staring when a figure stepped out from behind the Fountain and gave her such a fright that she squeaked in terror, breaking the reverential hush.

Mistresss Ishienne turned and fixed her with a stern look, unperturbed by the stranger's sudden appearance. Lastani covered her mouth and ducked her head, cheeks flushed with embarrassment. They were there on an errand of momentous and grave scholarly import, not to jump at ghosts. Lastani felt Castiere's patronising hand on her shoulder, the youth suppressing a laugh before he followed their mistress's lead and bowed to the newcomer.

'Master Atienolentra,' Ishienne called through the still night, 'you are well met again.'

'Let's hope so,' the man replied in a deep, rumbling voice. 'You, Mistress, continue to be a delight on the eyes.' He paused. 'Your pronunciation less so, however. Perhaps best just call me Atieno.'

'My apologies,' Ishienne said, inclining her head. 'It seems I have spent too much time favouring dead languages over existing ones.'

With a start, Lastani realised she had seen this man before, or glimpsed him at any rate. At a meeting Ishienne had taken, just a week before. Lastani had been returning to the house when she saw Master Atieno leaving. Hidden from the faint shine of the Skyriver by his hood, she had only glimpsed the white threads of his neat, pointed beard, but it was enough.

With piercing light brown eyes against a dark face of crow's feet and prominent cheekbones, Atieno would have been a handsome man but for the glowering severity he wore. His greying black hair was long and tied back, his worn clothes kept clean and neat. In his fifth decade at least, he remained tall and strong-looking – a marked improvement on the handful of suitors who had attempted to woo Mistress Ishienne during the time Lastani had lived in her house. Judging by Atieno's words, the idea had crossed his mind too.

The last two figures of Ishienne's group stepped out from behind Castiere and eyed the man suspiciously.

'Who's he?' Bokrel demanded.

The mercenary fingered the rounded butt of his holstered mage-pistol as he stared at Master Atieno. Bokrel was a monkey-faced wretch with grubby cheeks, a scrappy beard and wandering hands. Right now there was a livid pink frost-burn down the back of his left hand, a testament to how slow the mercenary was to take a hint, but he was the brains of the operation compared to his rotund comrade, Ybryl.

'He, Master Bokrel, is a key component of what we attempt tonight,' Ishienne said sharply. 'Try not to shoot him please. I doubt it would end well for you.'

Atieno pushed back his hood and gave the two mercenaries a stern look then seemed to mentally dismiss them. He carried a large walking staff that looked like a weapon in his hands, but like the mercenaries he also had a mage-pistol in his belt. With stiff movements that spoke of a lame leg, he walked around to the face of the Fountain that was, by common agreement, the front.

'You believe you can do this?' Master Atieno called.

Ishienne gestured to the swirls of script glowing above them. 'I have seen it in the stars,' she said with a small smile.

'That, I have heard before. Rarely has it inspired confidence.'

'The difference, I suspect, is that I've had to understand enough to teach my pupils.'

Lastani took a step forward. 'Mistress Ishienne translated the Duegar script, but the riddle within has been something we have all devoted our lives to unpicking.'

'The young say such things so easily,' Atieno said with gentle mocking. 'They've had less to devote thus far.'

'I have given it enough years for all three of us,' Ishienne declared, 'and my assistants contributed several of their own on top. The sacrifice has been shared, and now we must see if it was in vain or not.'

'Where do you want us?' Bokrel asked abruptly.

'At the edge of the dome,' she replied, pointing to the arched gaps between the dome's stone supports.

'And then what?'

'Keep guard,' Ishienne said simply. 'We must not be disturbed. Most likely you need do nothing to earn your pay, gods grant. I require you only to be awake and ready in case anything . . . unexpected occurs.'

'Like what?'

'If I knew that, it would hardly be unexpected. Come now, Master Bokrel, you led me to believe you were an experienced soldier and had explored Duegar city-ruins.'

Ybryl snorted at Bokrel's side, causing the man to glare at her. 'We ain't explored the damn things.' Ybryl chuckled, not noticing the look Bokrel gave her. 'We ain't that stupid.'

'What then?'

'Guard duty, escort,' Bokrel explained reluctantly. 'Let the other damn fools go underground an' play with monsters.'

Ishienne hissed in irritation. 'You have combat experience at least?'

'Yeah, we've been in a few fights.'

'Good – in that case keep your eyes open and your guns loaded, your mouths shut and your wits primed.'

Before Bokrel had a chance to object, Ishienne turned away and gestured to her two charges. 'Come, take your places.'

Lastani and Castiere ducked their heads in acknowledgement and went to stand beneath the nearest two snake mouths, peering up into the dark, toothless maws that looked down on them.

'And I?'

'Just as you are, Master Atieno,' Ishienne said, making her way around to the last of the snake mouths. 'Yours is the most complicated of tasks I'm afraid.'

'It always is,' he said. 'Firstly, your powers, though. What are they?'

'Does it matter?'

'It does.'

Ishienne frowned. 'Very well, but I will be doing the sculpting of magic – you need but be the key around which I will fit the lock. I am a stone mage, Lastani an ice mage, and Castiere fire. Does that meet with your approval?'

'It does,' Atieno said with a nod. 'There are powers that my kind will not work with. The risk is too great.'

'And those are?'

'Not stone, fire or ice.'

After a moment it was clear he would say no more on the subject so Ishienne gave a cluck of the tongue and went back about her task.

'For the first stage, you are not required, Master Atieno,' she informed him. 'The job is ours alone.'

At her nod, Lastani stretched up to the mouth of the metal serpent above her and opened herself to her magic. A faint white haze appeared around her hand then she felt the bite of cold on her skin – not painful to her, just different, for all

16

that it would freeze the skin off any other human in a matter of seconds.

A soft crackle from the far side told her that Castiere was doing the same, sending magic up into the mouth of the serpent with all the control he could muster. Ishienne was silent, but Lastani could just see her out of the corner of her eye and the woman was reaching up also. She concentrated on the task at hand, allowing the magic inside her to flow out through her fingers and coil up into the snake.

All this they had expected. The months of deciphering and research meant she could quote the words above by rote, but still Lastani felt a thrill at it working. The Fountain was drawing her magic, not greedily leeching off her but gathering all that she released to flow down the bodies of the serpents. Mistress Ishienne had described it as a votive offering, something that had made poor pious Castiere wince, but Lastani saw now how right she was. They were giving the Fountain something of themselves, a trace of their power, to prepare the way for what would come next – what they would ask of it.

The flow of magic steadily grew and Lastani began to be able to sense the others, the heat of Castiere's magic and the cool weight of Ishienne's. There was a balance in what they were offering and Lastani knew not to overtax herself in this initial stage, but still she freed a little more of the clean, cold bite in her bones to more closely match Castiere.

Their powers were to be most obviously in balance, as they often had been in Ishienne's library while debating the grand puzzle of the Fountain, the labyrinth beneath and whatever was hidden at the heart of that. Whether by chance or consequence of their magic, the two thought in entirely different ways. Sometimes Castiere's dancing focus would alight on the path, sometimes Lastani's careful method would instead.

'Enough,' Ishienne called and the trio cut the flow of their magic.

Lastani stepped back so she could see her teacher's face. Though the woman's expression was hidden in the shadows, years in her company told Lastani that Ishienne was satisfied with the first step.

'Now we wait,' Ishienne added for the benefit of Atieno. 'There is a precise order to this ritual that must be followed.'

'You are confident in your interpretation?' Atieno replied in a voice that betrayed neither scepticism nor belief. 'Many have attempted to best this puzzle over the centuries.'

'And many have got this far,' Ishienne said. 'This pause is the first test, your presence another, the details of the crafting a third. A plain translation of the text above your head will get you no further than this.'

'And a mistranslation would see Lastani dead,' Castiere added drily.

'Now it is your confidence that concerns me,' Atieno declared. The man leaned heavily on his staff as he spoke, but made no effort to move away from the Fountain.

'Our confidence is well founded,' Lastani found herself saying. 'Otherwise I would not be so willing! The work is a puzzle, understanding that is the crux of Mistress Ishienne's breakthrough. By mirroring the decoration on the Fountain—'

'I'm sure Master Atieno isn't interested in the details of our research,' Ishienne broke in. Lastani couldn't tell whether that was through a desire to preserve her secrets or impatience to be getting on, but she shut her mouth with a snap and tried not to picture Castiere's smirk.

'Research is not where I excel,' Atieno agreed sombrely, 'so I will take your word as though it were scripture.'

'Would that the Book of the First Sun could stand up to such rigour,' Castiere muttered.

'This is not the time, Castiere,' Ishienne reminded him. 'Now, are you both ready for the second phase?'

Lastani nodded and stepped forward, opening herself again as Castiere did the same. This time they let their magic only gently bleed out and Ishienne, controlling something within the Fountain itself, regulated the magic in a precise pattern before both assistants threw one long, sustained burst of raw power in. When Lastani stepped back again, she was light-headed and suddenly weary, but there had been no apparent effect on the Fountain.

'Now you, Master Atieno,' Ishienne said, stepping to the side until she could see the man. 'Palm against the middle panel, please. Let the stone draw your hand in and take your magic. I will guide you, a core of tempest magic that will ensure the stone is responsive to me.'

'Have a care,' Atieno warned her as he stepped forward and placed a hand against the stone. 'Tempest is unlike your magic. There is cost and wildness other mages do not know.'

Despite everything, Lastani felt a shiver down her spine as he said the word. The mages of tempest were so rare most considered them a myth, their magic not of elements but of change. The Militant Orders had no use for them and struggled to control them, so they demonised Atieno's kind and killed them when they could. It had taken Ishienne's extensive contacts and several bribes before she had found Atieno and convinced him to come.

'I understand,' Ishienne said calmly. 'A trace of tempest is required, nothing more. It is the key, not the shoulder to the door, and I know you pay for every drawing.'

'Not only me,' he said. 'It would twist every strand of magic it touched, if you tried to draw much, and turn your power against you. It cannot be controlled – refusing to accept that has killed more of my brethren than the Militant Orders ever managed.'

'Your warning is appreciated, then,' she replied. 'Should anything more than the tiniest amount prove inadequate, we will break off and reassess.'

A grunt was all Atieno replied with, but he set to work without hesitation. Lastani resumed her place, hand stretched up to offer a steady, modest flow of power. The mingling she had sensed within the Fountain remained, but she could not feel any of the tempest magic within that blend. Only by the sound could she tell the carved surface under Atieno's hand had opened under Ishienne's stone magery and closed again around it.

At first there was nothing, no indication that the magic was affecting the Fountain at all, but eventually she began to feel the ground faintly tremble. Carefully regulating herself to match Castiere, she touched one finger to the metal snake. It was doing the same, a tiny shudder running through the entire Fountain and deep underground.

Off to her right there was a slight gasp from Ishienne, then a sound of satisfaction. Lastani could not tell that anything had changed until she heard a telltale grind and the whisper of stone on stone – Ishienne forming and shaping the very structure of the Fountain. It was a Duegar construction, designed with magic in mind and made to respond, but still Ishienne moved slowly.

Lastani saw the brief flourish of surprise on Atieno's reserved face as the stone abruptly split and opened like a double door, freeing his arm and allowing the man to take a laboured step back. That face of the Fountain continued to open, petals of stone peeling organically back under Ishienne's deft touch until the stone had folded right back to the metal snake-shapes on either side.

'There,' Ishienne declared, releasing her magic and stepping back. 'It is done.'

Lastani smiled and moved to do the same when with a jolt she realised she couldn't cut the flow of magic.

'Ah, mistress?' called Castiere from the other side. 'I've got a—'

Either he didn't get any further or Lastani didn't hear him. The mouth of the snake snapped shut on her fingertips and for a moment there was only the white-hot pain of crushing. From the howl that broke through it, Castiere had experienced the same. Lastani had time for one brief flash of fear before the snake began to feed savagely on her magic and all rational thought vanished from her mind.

She wailed and hauled at her trapped fingers but her muscles had turned to jelly, her mind a cold void as the trickle of magic was turned to a raging torrent. The air whitened before her eyes as her ice magic turned the chill night freezing. Within moments she couldn't feel her body except the unremitting pressure on her fingers, everything else subordinate to the wild plunder of magic.

Her eyes blurred and a veil of darkness started to descend. Lastani barely noticed hands on her body, the shouting voices. Even when the hands began to pull then frantically haul at her, it was distant and unreal. The pain receded, the world around her darkened and contracted to a single, diminishing point of light before everything snapped back with terrible force.

Lastani took one ragged breath then screamed with all her might as something popped in her fingers and she was dragged away. Shrieking, she curled over her injury but strong hands unpeeled her fingers and roughly stretched them out.

'The other one! Go!' roared a man above her, just a dark blur through her tumbling tears.

She fought him but could do nothing against the man's strength and with perfunctory jerks he yanked one finger then the next straight. Each movement sparked another shriek from Lastani, but afterwards the pain dampened and her wits returned. Her vision cleared a fraction to see Atieno and Mistress Ishienne staring down at her bleeding, pinched but no longer dislocated fingers.

'He's on fire!' Bokrel yelled, prompting Atieno to turn with a snarl on his face.

'Cut the hand!' he bellowed, rising. 'Get him away or he'll die!'

An orange corona lit the inscribed canopy above and haloed the Fountain. Lastani couldn't see Castiere from where she lay, but she knew how the fire mage would be looking if he was trapped as she had been – surrounded by the unchecked ferocity of his magic.

There was a grunt and a wet crunch. The light vanished and she heard a weight fall to the ground, but not the screams of a man whose limb had just been severed.

'Castiere!' Ishienne yelled, running past the open face of the fountain towards her pupil, but never reaching him.

A flash of pale grey light darted out towards her, as fast as a striking snake, and snatched the woman up like she was a toy. Lastani screamed in terror, Ishienne's cry cut off in the same instant it began. Impaled on blades of shining mist, she hung helpless – her mouth open in a silent scream – as an indistinct nightmare hauled itself out of the darkness inside the Fountain.

Long, slender limbs unfolded, two, six, eight – the ghostly creature seemed all limbs and no body, just a knot where the joints met, but it moved with fearsome purpose and speed.

A great detonation crashed against Lastani's ears. She reeled, eyes watering and barely registering the taste of ice magic in the air. Atieno had fired his mage-pistol, but though the horror flinched there was no damage Lastani could see.

Wailing in terror, the two mercenaries backed away. Bokrel had his gun out, wavering uncertainly in the apparition's

Leaving Teshen behind, they rounded one more corner and headed down the side of the great hall, towards the inner door that led to the throne room. More curious and startled faces turned their way, Toil ignoring them while Lynx did his best to look apologetic and helpless. Toil made it all the way into the great hall before a guard sought to forcibly bar her progress, whereupon she deftly wrong-footed the man and was around and past him in the next instant.

Lynx put himself between the two of them and then it was only the pair of personal bodyguards at the great door to the throne room she had to negotiate. With the Monarch inside, however, they were less open to Toil's act, but again surprise came to her aid. The first guard didn't take the threat of an unarmed woman as seriously as he might and just grabbed her by the arm to arrest her progress.

Toil headbutted him. As he staggered she stepped inside the reach of the other's gun and slammed him bodily into the jamb of the closed door. A swift knee and a punch felled him while Lynx put the first guard down, then she was through the door.

Inside there were squawks of alarm and the rush of bodies – a roar of surprise from Envoy Ammen, a shout for the guards from someone else. Lynx followed close behind and saw Toil punch some richly dressed nobleman full in the face and put him flat on his back. The Envoy charged towards her, waving his arms as he bellowed furiously, but Toil simply grabbed him and manoeuvred the big man around as a shield while one final guard levelled his gun.

From the throne there was a shout as the Monarch called for the guard to hold his fire, while the Crown-Prince leaped from his seat to put himself between Toil and his wife. The Crown-Prince drew his sword and mage-pistol in the same movement so Toil barely avoided impaling herself on the tip of his sword as she abruptly yanked the Envoy aside. She dropped to her knees, now bellowing her request to the Monarch.

'Crown-Princess Stilanna!' she called above the clamour. 'I come to beg your forgiveness—'

Toil broke off as the Crown-Prince's rapier touched her throat, a thin line of blood welling up where the razor-sharp edge kissed her skin. Lynx had ground to a halt just a few steps inside the room, not wanting to appear any more of a threat, and didn't see the blow from behind that knocked him down.

'I beg your forgiveness, Monarch,' Toil continued in a more subdued voice, 'both for the incident with your guest and this intrusion, but I have a letter I must deliver upon forfeit of my life. Such actions as I took earlier, I swear it was in the interests of your city – let your husband's blade take my life if I am mad or a liar.'

She looked up straight into the Monarch's eyes as she said that last before slowly raising the pouch she carried.

'Envoy Ammen has already begged my forgiveness,' Crown-Princess Stilanna said coldly. 'Your master is already engaged in his job and attempting to undo all that you have done.'

'I understand, Monarch,' Toil said, lowering her eyes, 'but my mission is not only in his service. The letter, I implore you.'

'What letter is this?' Ammen demanded from behind her. 'There was no further letter in the official correspondence.'

'Your Envoy disagrees with you,' the Monarch said to Toil.

'The Envoy does not know of it,' Toil said. 'The Envoy's function here is already fulfilled. The letter, Monarch, is for royal eyes only.'

Stilanna glanced up at her husband and gave the tiniest of nods. Without a pause the man struck down at Toil's head with his mage-pistol. She was thrown to the ground under the blow and went limp. Lynx shouted and tried to scrabble forward but was pounced upon by black-uniformed soldiers. He stopped struggling, realising they would kill him if he fought, and watched the Crown-Prince retrieve the pouch, ignoring Ammen's protests. The man slipped a letter free, then Lynx's vision was full of mosaic tile floor and little else as he was dragged away.

Chapter 5
(Two weeks earlier)

The lamplight seems to barely touch the walls. Rough, undecorated stone surrounded them – as much a cave as ancient crypt.

'There's nothing here!' whispered Staul, turning with his lamp raised. The yellow light trembled as he moved and his gun was no more steady.

Asolist snorted, the sound echoing loud enough to make the others jump. Two of them anyway, Staul and Lirish. His Hanese manservant, Yel Dan, was unmoved and appeared unimpressed with the underground room. Asolist hadn't intended to make that much noise but his blood was still fizzing with a combination of Wisp Dust and firedrake leaf. The mixture of drugs, excitement and childhood terror meant he couldn't keep still.

'What were you expecting? Piles of gold and God Fragments? The bodies of Duegar kings?' Asolist shook his head. 'That'll be far below the surface, this is just a back door.'

The youngest of the group, Staul had gone white when Asolist announced they were off to explore the labyrinth after a spirited evening in a local alchemist parlour. He'd not argued, though, he never did. His family were minor vassals of Asolist's father, the Lessar-Prince, and knew when suggestions were really orders.

'Still not safe,' Lirish said in a breathless voice. He was a skinny, unlovely third son of a count, but a loyal friend to Asolist. 'Weren't just that academic got killed, she had guards.

Then the brown-jackets that never came back up, folk say they screamed for hours.'

'Fucking mercenaries and watchmen with cudgels?' Asolist spat. 'Useless scum the lot of them.' He brandished his mage-pistol, one of a pair with beautiful polished brass inlay. 'Now keep your eyes open.'

The stone room was an uneven, kidney-shaped space about twenty yards long. At the foot of the stair they'd descended was the only flat wall. One stretch at waist height had been polished smooth, but no amount of prodding or inspection had yielded the reason for it. Round behind that, at the far end of the room, was a tunnel mouth leading further down, but the sobering effect of stepping into the labyrinth had tempered Asolist's usual bravado.

'What was that?' Staul hissed, whirling around.

They all turned their guns that way, but Asolist could see nothing. He kept quiet, though, he'd heard some sort of scratching noise too.

'There!' Lirish gasped.

The blond youth fired on instinct and the deafening report of an icer crashed against Asolist's ears. Despite everything he winced at the noise, magnified by the enclosed space. In the dim light Asolist could see nothing but the trail of the icer and shards of stone bursting out from the wall.

'Godspit and curses!' Asolist yelled. 'Don't do that!'

'I saw something!'

'You jumped at bloody—'

Yel Dan cut him off with a gesture, stepping across Asolist towards the nearer wall. Before Asolist could summon words he saw a thin wisp of white dart out from the grey stone. It flickered forward then pulled back and vanished, but they had all seen it.

'We go,' Yel Dan commanded.

With his free hand the Hanese urged Asolist back towards the stair but he barely had time to move before the room exploded into movement. More wisps of white flashed out from the wall – long spider-legs probing delicately at the ground. Staul fired at one and the icer passed straight through the ghostly limb without effect. He cried out and stumbled as the legs reached towards him, falling on his backside and spilling a cartridge as he tried to reload.

More legs darted out with shocking speed, then a monstrous blurring body obscured the entire wall. Yel Dan fired in the same moment as Asolist, but the Hanese had loaded an earther. A dark mass seemed to smash into the ghostly creature and hammer it back against the wall behind. Stone exploded behind it and shards lashed Asolist's face. The creature reeled and its long legs thrashed madly for a few moments, but before any of them could load another cartridge it struck.

One leg caught Staul in the back of the calf and dragged him off his feet. Another slapped across Lirish's belly and he collapsed with a shriek. Asolist watched, frozen in horror, as Staul was hauled towards the huge spider-like ghost. The youth had time for one scream of terror then the legs rose and fell, three stabbing down as one and tearing his chest open.

'Run!' Yel Dan roared, shoving Asolist back.

He dropped the pistol he was loading and pulled his second. The icer had no effect, seemingly passing through its misty body without touching it.

Yel Dan thumped Asolist in the shoulder with the butt of his mage-gun and sent him stumbling towards the entrance. There was a crazed wordless roar from the Hanese then a blinding flash of light.

Asolist turned tail and ran, one arm across his eyes to shield them from the light of the burner. Behind him Yel Dan continued to shout and Lirish's screams took on a new, awful intensity. Asolist didn't look back – even when Yel Dan's yells turned to pain. He scrambled up the steps and out into the cool dark of night, running as fast as he could to the open. Only then did he even glance behind. The voices behind had fallen silent and a ghostly shape reached up out of the ground. A jolt of terror ran through his body and turned Asolist's muscles to jelly. He tripped and fell.

*

In the cold light of morning, there was no avoiding the silent scream on the corpse's face. He lay on his back in the street, arms splayed wide and green velvet coat spread beneath like wings. The ruin of his chest was displayed for the world to see, as though he had been left purposely on display, but Crown-Princess Stilanna, Monarch of Jarrazir, thought not.

There was no trail of blood leading here, only the blood that had spread evenly underneath him. The young man had run and tripped, rolled over on to his back and then . . . Well, she doubted his heart had actually been taken, but things were such a mess in there it was difficult to tell.

She looked up toward her husband as the Crown-Prince conversed quietly with Colonel Pilter, commander of the city regiment. The men could hardly have been less alike; one tall, dark of hair and complexion, handsome to boot, the other portly and bald with sandy mutton-chop whiskers and some sort of stain down the sleeve of his grey uniform.

'My love?'

Tylom glanced up and nodded, breaking off his conversation to join her. His face was grim as he passed the corpse. For all his skill with rapier and pistol, the man had never been comfortable around the sight of blood.

Just as well he's not the one who's going to give birth, she told herself, one hand rubbing her swollen belly in what had almost become an unconscious action to her these days.

A ring of soldiers in the austere black and silver of her personal Bridge Watch kept onlookers back both from her and the fat stub of a pillar a few yards away. For all her life it had stood there, the height of a child and unremarkable in every way except for a single glyph inscribed on its flat top. Until the night some foolish scholar had gone into the Deep Market, a mile west of here, and performed a feat of magic everyone had always assumed was impossible.

Stilanna was still coming to terms with the shock of that. She'd paid the legends of the labyrinth no great regard in her life, but it was literally the bedrock of her city – an enduring fact that predated Jarrazir itself, unchanging and unknowable. Except now it had changed and now it had killed people. The bedrock shifted beneath them all and the prospect of what might come next worried her.

'I know him, don't I?' she said, almost in a whisper. 'I'm sure I recognise his face.'

Tylom nodded. 'Lesser-Prince Besh's second son, Deuxain Asolist. We've met him a few times, a foolish boy who could never stay still, if memory serves.'

Stilanna nodded slowly. 'Of course. Merciful Insar, he was little more than a child.'

'I suppose we must count ourselves lucky,' Tylom said. 'Besh never seemed to like the Deuxain. If the Primain was lying there, we'd have an armed expedition about to charge down into the labyrinth.'

'A scant mercy that. This brings the total to what? Nine dead in three days? Probably more, some of the casualties must have been part of groups who went inside and were just the only ones to actually get out again. Killed by gods-cursed spectres

86

rising from underground as though all the silly stories we were told as children were true. And if it wasn't for those stories, how many more might have attempted it?'

The Crown-Prince scowled. 'Eleven dead,' he corrected. 'Veraimin embrace them all. It turns out there were two people in the house in East Armoury Street when it collapsed.'

She grimaced. 'And still we've no idea how to stop it. Colonel, join us.'

As Pilter approached he beckoned forward a young woman she didn't know wearing the uniform of a lieutenant, albeit one of a far better cut to most.

'Monarch,' Pilter and the lieutenant said together, bowing low before the woman did so again to Tylom, muttering, 'Crown-Prince,' in an aristocratic accent.

'This is Lieutenant Gerail,' Pilter said, 'she has specific command over the Fountain investigation.'

'What is your progress?'

'We are looking for a pupil of Matarin's, Monarch, one Lastani Ufre. Her body was not found at the Fountain so we believe she escaped and is in hiding. She was a mage and would have been part of the ritual that opened the entrance.'

'*The* entrance?' Tylom corrected. 'Try all of the bloody entrances.'

'My apologies, yes. *All* of the entrances. She must bear some blame for this situation given she's fled, but most importantly she may know how to close them again.'

'We've gone beyond that point!' he snapped. 'Word's out already, in a few days half of Parthain will know of this.'

'And half the continent by next week,' Stilanna agreed. 'Colonel, I want a detatchment of guards at every entrance – admit no one without my personal warrant, understand?'

'Yes, Monarch.'

'Good. The city's already nervous and these deaths will only worsen that, but I know our noble youth. They'll bribe or browbeat their way inside, seeking fortune and glory. It appears these spirits only attack once someone goes inside, but who knows how far they will roam once disturbed?'

'How many entrances have we found?' Tylom asked Gerail.

'Six others thus far, Crown-Prince. Most like this, stairways opening up around blocks that have done nothing in centuries. It's lucky more people hadn't used them as foundation stones for their houses really.'

'What do the glyphs say?'

Lieutenant Gerail fumbled for a piece of paper in her jacket. She wore grey like the colonel, but better tailored and subtly picked out in red and white. A noble daughter clearly trying to make a name for herself in the city guard. Such things hadn't been so fashionable when Stilanna had been her age, but apparently the young men of the city all went mad over a girl in uniform now.

'They incorporate numbers and a complex form I'm told could be a name. We've found entrances numbered one, two, four and six; if they follow the pattern suggested, three will be in the north of the city and five near the university so I'm arranging a search of streets and cellars.'

'And the others?'

'No numbers, but other engravings from what can be seen. The Fountain of course, what appeared to be a doorway that's opened behind a stone wall in the North Keep—'

'The North Keep?' Tylom and Stilanna gasped together. That wasn't just news of ghostly monsters walking the city streets, but a threat to the whole of Jarrazir. The bombardment spheres stored there were mage-built weapons of such power, each could obliterate a half-dozen streets.

'Yes, Monarch – we've just been informed. I'm sorry, I assumed word had reached you by now.'

'Shattered gods,' Stilanna said in a stunned voice. 'This changes

88

everything.' She shook her head then glared around at the others. 'Who knows? Is it common knowledge?'

'I, ah, I don't know, Monarch,' Colonel Pilter broke in. 'I received word from the armoury commander not an hour ago. There is no damage to the keep, but I cannot say how many know of it.'

'Well damn well find out, man!' the Crown-Prince snapped. 'Go now – secure it and contain the news for as long as possible!'

'Wait,' Stilanna said. 'First, I want a search party sent down. We cannot continue in ignorance if our defences might be vulnerable.'

'I will order an expedition party,' Gerail replied hesitantly.

'Do so,' Stilanna snapped. 'Armed troops – burn out these spirits if you have to, but we must know what lies down there. All it would take was one fanatic from the Militant Orders to destroy half the city if they got into the armoury!'

'Yes, Monarch, I will lead the party myself.'

'Why so many entrances?' wondered Tylom. 'If it really is a damn labyrinth protecting a tomb, why not just one?'

'If I may, Crown-Prince?' Lieutenant Gerail said. 'According to the writings in Ishienne Matarin's house, it was not always believed to be a tomb. She was *the* authority on the labyrinth I'm told, obsessed with the Fountain but a scholar held in the highest esteem rather than some crazed eccentric. She seemed to think it may have had a different function.'

'A vault for God Fragments like in the stories we used to tell as children?'

'There is mention of a cache or a treasure within, but Matarin seemed to have her doubts as to whether its intended purpose was to house God Fragments. She thinks mistranslation or fabrication by a writer during the Revival age was just as likely, believing the labyrinth older than the Fall, though some great cache is the most common belief. She knew there were multiple entrances and suggested it might have served as some sort of contest ground or a temple complex.'

'Marvellous,' Tylom growled. 'We're risking siege by the Militant Orders over something a bloody scholar might have made up hundreds of years ago?'

'Right now, that's not my concern,' Stilanna said. 'Colonel Pilter, our priority is the security of the deep armouries. Seal the entrance that's opened up in the North Keep. Move most of the bomb-spheres to the other armouries, just make damn sure those are fully checked over first. Gerail, I want more information about what's down each stairway, markings, anything. We need to know what tunnels there are and where they go – before we even get to the question of what is really at the heart of the labyrinth. We've always known that the Militant Orders will have a better idea than us, but until now that's been a mere academic detail. Now it could be the city's downfall. Take a squad in – shoot anything that moves and have scribes on hand to detail it all. "It's dark and there are ghosts that can kill" isn't enough information, understand? I also want every text and translation that mentions the labyrinth, every scholar in the city scouring their libraries. Find the pupil too; I want her standing before me when I start handing out blame for this mess.'

'And once we send a full expedition all the way inside, she'll be part of it,' Tylom added. 'We can't trust bloody relic hunters to read and write their own names, let alone the ancient Duegar script. Whatever blame there is to apportion, her expertise may take precedence.'

'Oh Blessed Catrac and all his workings!' Stilanna sighed. 'You're right – relic hunters. We'll have an army of those unwashed madmen flocking to the city. Pilter, that'll be another problem for you. Anyone who wants to get in needs to go to you first; weed out the obviously stupid or insane and let us know if there's anyone likely to be useful. I don't like it but we may need their expertise.'

'Keeping fools away is paramount,' Tylom agreed. 'We need to know what's down there, but the rest of the city must be kept away.'

Stilanna looked over at the body once more, taking note of the distance between it and the stairway that led down into the labyrinth. Not far, but far enough to be a concern.

'If these ghosts aren't confined to the labyrinth itself, how long before entire neighbouring households are killed too? How long before the city is in chaos? The relic hunters and Orders are welcome to compete among themselves so long as they don't go down without my authorisation. Pray gods we find answers soon.'

*

The afternoon found Lastani in the Deep Market against her better instincts and watching the Fountain with a growing sense of trepidation. The soldiers of the Monarch had set up a cordon that took up a third of the market, but despite the current of fear in Jarrazir some traders were still doing wary business beyond that. The Fountain – or stairway, or entrance or whatever it was now – stood on the low ground. Two walkways overlooked it and a curved shelf of stone, normally covered with carts selling glassware and cheap jewellery, ran down the eastern side. That was where Lastani stood, wrapped tight against the morning chill in a dark woollen cloak.

She hadn't wanted to come, for all that she refused to flee the city. In a city of ancient names and dynastic wealth, she wasn't so foolish as to think her account of events would hold any more water than the Monarch or her ministers wanted it to. She had been present and was of no consequence to the city. If a quick execution calmed the simmering panic that might be exactly what she got. But at the same time she felt a duty to be present – a twofold obligation. This was Mistress Ishienne's legacy and this was Lastani's city. She would not flee while the former was ruined, nor did she want to abandon her home when her knowledge might help.

And that brought her back to the Fountain this cold afternoon, despite Atieno hearing a survivor was being sought.

Part of her just wanted to run home to her family, to scream and wail at the deaths of her friends from behind familiar walls. Nothing in their research had suggested other entrances would open by what they'd done, nor that others would die as a result. Still – people she'd loved had died, and strangers too. As she lay in bed at night, praying for a dreamless sleep, she felt the weight of those deaths while the nightmares stalked her.

Flashes of movement, shining inhuman shapes and blood in the light of the Skyriver. None of the writings had warned them of this, but perhaps they should have known. The guilt gnawed at her in her fitful sleep, their world of books and transcribed tablets now forever marked by the blood of innocent lives.

A knot of brown-jackets loitered uneasily near the Fountain. With collars turned up high, cudgels hanging from their belts and wearing battered brown hats, they looked a criminal lot. Half were nervously smoking as they watched the briskly efficient soldiers arrive with a laden mule.

Oh gods, they're really going inside.

Lastani felt a shudder run through her as the soldiers began to unload pitch-soaked torches and oil lamps that could be hung off long poles. They carried guns too of course, no matter that it wouldn't help and might only serve to damage whatever vital writings were inside.

Her instincts screaming for her to run, Lastani took a deep breath and pushed her way through the small crowd, back down to the floor of the Deep Market. As she approached the

Fountain a soldier spotted her and moved to block her path, mage-gun not quite dropping to point at her but being shifted in readiness nonetheless.

'That's as far as you can go, miss,' the man declared, walking right up to Lastani and forcing her to stop. He was a thin young man with a wispy beard and a long grey coat over his uniform, a cartridge box and bayonet visible on his belt.

'You're not going inside, are you?' she found herself asking in a nervous squeak.

He cocked his head. 'Who's asking?'

The words caught in her throat for a moment. 'I – no one. I mean, I just saw what happened. At one of the other entrances. I work a stall in the market normally.'

'Your name?'

'It doesn't matter. I'm sorry, I'll go.'

'Just wait right there,' he said sharply. 'You saw what happened where?'

'At one of the other entrances.'

'Which one?'

Lastani blinked at him, too flustered to think for a moment. 'Why does it matter?'

His response was to slide his mage-gun off his shoulder and hold it levelled. 'We've got orders to be looking for a woman, a pupil of the one who did this. Tell me your name now.'

'My name? You don't . . . Catrac's mercy! I've done nothing wrong! My name is Seniel. I told you, I work a stall here, or I did until this happened. I work for a textiles merchant, we'd normally set up over there.'

She pointed and the young soldier turned in that direction on instinct. It only took him a moment to realise his mistake but by then Lastani's magic filled the air. The sharp snap of cold flew from her fingers, cast widely and without focus so that the soldier vanished from sight behind a cloud of white mist.

Lastani turned without a second thought, knowing the mist would soon disperse. Her heart pounded as she sprinted away through the ragged crowd and gave a sudden, violent jolt as a great crash rang out behind her. The gunshot echoed around off the stone formations of the Deep Market, soon joined by screams. She didn't see the icer's trail flash past, but she heard the panic erupt like a volcano.

Soon she was being barged as people ran blindly then more soldiers began to fire in their alarm – the flash of icers darting left and right. Screams and shouts rang out from across the Deep Market as Lastani fought to keep upright. Someone fell nearby, blood spraying from an icer wound, but she didn't stop – couldn't stop running now the tide of Jarrazir's fear had swept her up. The screams echoed in her head, her own mingling with those of people around her, and still she ran, tears of shame and terror streaming down her cheeks.

Chapter 6

Lieutenant Gerail took a long breath and looked over her small command. The day's dull grey light seemed to barely reach down to the Deep Market floor, while the chill breeze had made the place its own. Distantly she heard the sounds of life continue in the furthest parts of the market. The stampede of earlier had left three dead, all because of some jumpy idiot. This whole side of the market was now deserted but for the debris left behind by those fleeing and spots of blood. A jangle of fears rang in her head and in that quiet corner of the city she could find no peace. Those deaths were on her head, the failure hers as senior officer, and they added to the weight on her shoulders.

The remaining stallholders on the far fringes were barely audible, the distilled panic of that stampede still flowing through their veins. The usual babble of background sound was absent, a pall hanging over the entire market and the city beyond it. The longer she stood there, the more Gerail experienced a sense of the world contracting around her, the air of uncertainty and fear in the city condensing to this bare patch of stone. Time seemed to have slowed, her soul feeling untethered in the breeze as even the gods themselves held their breath and waited for what was to come.

Twelve soldiers from the City Regiment stood ready in front of her, faces almost as grey as their uniforms and clutching their mage-guns tightly. Six brown-jackets from the civilian watch loitered beside them, carrying cudgels and oil lamps hung from the end of short poles. She shook her head to try and dispel her mood. A pair of young scribes stood with them, hugging sheaves of paper to their chests.

Nineteen armed men and women, nineteen! All to walk down one bloody staircase and still I'm frightened.

The sweat was icy cold against her skin as she glanced back at the bare stone steps just a few yards away. There was no sign of life down there, no movement or anything else, but she'd grown up in Jarrazir, as had the rest of them. The labyrinth was the dark heart of the city and the tales told in it – stories handed down generation to generation. The children whispered them to each other at night, the elders folded warnings and morals into their more austere retellings.

Gerail's fingers went to the charm around her neck, tucked out of sight behind the high, rounded collar of her uniform. A simple sun device, the emblem of Veraimin.

Embrace me with your light, Lord, she said in the privacy of her mind, knowing most of her soldiers would be doing the same. *Walk with me in the deepest heathen dark. Cast your radiance over all those around me and scourge these profane creatures from the land.*

Had they been going into battle a priest would be there, speaking similar words over them while they knelt, but this was just a staircase. Just a few plain steps down into some sort of room, most likely. She would have looked foolish if she'd requested a priest, though, despite her desperate desire for a blessing, and no doubt word of it would get back to her family soon enough.

'Move out. Veraimin be with us.'

It sounded like a stranger speaking in her own voice. Gerail waved forward the oldest of the brown-jackets, a tall white-haired man who looked like the bravest of the lot. He nodded and twisted a knob on the side of his lamp to increase the flame before pulling his cudgel from his belt. Gerail unbuttoned her coat and slipped her mage-pistol from its holster, checking first it was loaded and then that she had spare cartridges on her belt.

The two of them led the way to the stair and paused at the top. Only a few yards away, the darkness down there was profound. Gerail forced herself not to look at her company and took the first step down.

There was a collective exhalation as nothing happened. The lieutenant herself gasped with relief, only then realising fear had looped tight bands around her chest. She raised her gun and continued down, waving forward the brown-jacket. He kept a step behind her, lamp lowered like a lance to light the way. The stairs were plain and smoothly cut, awkwardly shallow by human standards, but she went slowly and placed each foot with great care as she watched the darkness reluctantly recede.

It didn't take Gerail long to cover the two dozen steps visible from the ground above. The walls were plain too, cut stone quickly giving way to bare, mage-worked rock. There were faint veins and colours in the rock, barely visible in the weak light. A few grooves had been cut into it – one long undulating line with shorter ones branching off from it at random. She could make no sense of it so she kept her eyes ahead – copying it down would be the job of the scribes.

Another dozen steps and the floor levelled out into a small, almost disappointingly bare chamber even if the lack of ghosts was a profound relief. A wall stood just a few yards in front of the foot of the stair, curving away in both directions as though it was a broad pillar. Looking right, Gerail could see the roof sloped down to meet the ground not far behind, while off to the left the chamber opened up. It extended about twenty yards and contained a six-sided pillar standing slightly off-centre and a wide tunnel leading away at the rear.

'Spread out,' Gerail whispered, her voice carrying easily through the empty stone room.

Her troops filed down, keeping to their assigned trios – two soldiers and a brown-jacket moving in tight knots until they were spread around the room and the walls were fully illuminated.

There was nothing there. The ceiling rose to a slight peak where the pillar stood, but beyond that there was nothing more than a musty, faintly unpleasant smell that Gerail couldn't help but imagine as that of a tomb.

'What now?' one of the scribes said, scuttling up to Gerail's side as the other finished sketching the groove down the side of the steps.

'Look around,' Gerail snapped, her anger only amplified by the apparent foolishness of the statement.

It was bare and empty – nothing she could see, at any rate, and very little room for anything to be hidden. The rock was typical mage-working; nearly flat with an almost organic flow to the mineral. Unfortunately that also meant a lack of decoration, detailing or anything else the Monarch was looking for.

'There's nothing here, should we go down the tunnel?'

'Check the walls more closely, look at the pillar, do something!'

The scribe, through fear or natural obedience, didn't question her command and went first to the pillar, his nose almost touching the stone as he ran his fingers over its surface.

'Wait, what's that?'

Gerail's head whipped around. It wasn't a scribe who'd spoken, it was one of the brown-jackets. He raised his lantern and peered forward, then touched something on the wall with his finger before Gerail could stop him. She saw nothing but heard him yelp an instant later and jerk his hand away.

'What is it?'

'Cut misself!' he whined, inspecting his finger then sucking at the tip.

'What did you see?' she insisted.

'Thought I saw a, ah . . .'

He tailed off as it suddenly became obvious – a wavering thread of light that drifted forward from the rock like some sort of plant on a sea current. The brown-jacket backed off, finger still in his mouth, then made a strange choking sound. He dropped his lantern and clutched at his throat, wheezing frantically, but no one moved to help him as more fronds emerged from the wall. There was a judder of light as the lantern struck the ground and almost went out before the spilled oil caught light and flared yellow.

Gerail felt her guts turn cold as some sort of shape was illuminated on the bare blank rock. A whimper behind told her she wasn't the only one to see it – the shape was a creature, unlike anything she'd ever come across, with long, angular limbs and legs detailed in a blink of shadow.

Without warning, the fronds twisted and jerked forward. An indistinct mass of glowing mist pulled itself free of the wall and ran the nearest soldier through. The impact was real enough; a gout of blood and a shriek erupted across the room. Gerail raised her mage-pistol and fired. The icer's crisp shaft of white slammed dead-centre into the apparition, briefly arresting its movement but doing no obvious damage even as a chunk of stone burst from the wall behind it.

The apparition scuttled forward, as bulky as a lion in the low room but with long bladed limbs. Two soldiers died in the next instant, another a few seconds later. Then those who remained were all firing. Staccato flashes of light and booms assailed Gerail as the demon was thrown jerkily back. But still it would not stop; still it was not hurt; still it threw itself across the room. Through the chaos of noise and movement it eviscerated a scribe in one deft stroke before killing again and again. Gerail's head filled with the hammer blow of gunshots and the screams of her troops, running feet and the wet chop of flesh.

She never even saw her death, just a blur of white amid the whirl of lantern-light and shadows that danced around the chamber. Then the noise and clutter and light receded and there was only the cool deepest black as it enveloped her.

Chapter 7

It took ten days to travel the length of Parthain and reach the narrow bay where Jarrazir lay. Perched on the foredeck, Lynx watched the city unfold from the morning mist. This wasn't his first visit to Jarrazir. In the years since he turned his back on his homeland, Lynx had been many things – mostly a mercenary in the messy little skirmishes that passed for war in the little republics and principalities that dotted the five inland seas. He'd travelled south too, all the way to the ocean coast there, but found the heat and scouring winds too much for him.

There was little work for him there anyway. The raging ocean tossed away human lives like a feckless, careless god and was treated as such by the locals, their efforts focused more on survival than war. While few there knew of So Han and its violent efforts at conquest, and even fewer cared, he had stayed only a few months. Enough time to turn nut-brown in the sun, contract an illness that had lingered for a year in one form or another, and find employment on a slow spice barge that traded with the tribes inhabiting the scorched deltas.

Trade on Urden kept to the interior, centred on the calmer inland seas and huge Duegar canals that crossed the continent. Lynx had been a canal-barge guard several times in the last decade. It was a good job for rootless, drifting men of violence such as himself, their sedate travels taking them across the continent, and few raiders were so bold as to try and raid the barge-trains that plied the canals.

While he'd never managed to keep to any job for long, there had been some remarkable sights that had stayed with him long after he'd moved on. Arriving in Jarrazir on the Ongir Canal was one of those, most particularly when it reached the Bridge Palace.

In his mind he recalled the surging whisper that seemed to draw the barge into the vast echoing tunnel beneath the walls of the palace. A susurrus of breath as the barge was swallowed into the red-glazed maw and dark gullet that ran for almost two hundred yards before finally opening out on to the lagoon beyond.

In his dreams that journey had evolved into the shrouded veil between this life and the next. The red tiled walls and forbidding black pillars; the centuries-old mosaic that covered the arched belly of the palace and flocks of white-winged bats that roosted there.

The scent of night jasmine brought him out of his reverie. Lynx didn't need to turn to realise Toil was standing behind him. The faint scent she wore was an affectation perhaps, but one he'd found himself craving since the day they met. It seemed incongruous for this fearless, muscular relic hunter and assassin that she might wear a delicate scent even when covered with the grime of travel, but Lynx was starting to understand it.

We've all got our own ways of handling this strange life we lead, he realised, *and hers is to cover the stink of travel, of animals and dirt and fear.* A small smile crossed his face. He'd just remembered something else about Jarrazir – smoked eels stuffed with garlic, fished from the canal and the supposedly bottomless lagoon that served to connect canal and bay in the centre of the city.

Yeah, we've all got our ways, Lynx reminded himself.

He looked up at Toil, the woman scrutinising the city as though trying to pick out a single figure on the docks beyond.

'Going to tell us any more about what we're doing here?'

'Might be there's nothing for you to do,' she replied.

'Not much of an answer.'

Toil shrugged. 'I'm no seer, I can't say what's going to happen. Ask Estal if you want a reading.'

'I'm not asking that,' he said, swallowing his irritation, 'but there's a plan. There's stuff you know and aren't sharing.'

'It's too early for sharing anything.' She shook her head. 'Want me to tell you a few things that may end up not having any significance at all? How would that make me look then?'

'Human?'

'Hah.'

'Tell me the lot then.'

'You're not my boss, remember? To him you're the hired help, one of the guns I might need to call on and not even a very senior one of those.'

'To him,' Lynx repeated. 'And to you?'

Toil sighed. 'Really? You want to have that conversation now?'

'Nope.'

'What, then?'

'If things go to shit, chances are I'll be one of those standing right beside you. Prefer not to be in the dark when I do that.'

She smiled at that. 'You handled it pretty well last time things went to shit down in the dark.'

That brought Lynx up short. 'There going to be more of that?'

'Maybe.' She looked back up at the city ahead. 'That much I'll tell you. There might be some light petting with the deepest black, sure. Best you decide ahead of time if you want to hang back in that case. Of course, hanging back may not be the easier option if it really does go to shit.'

'Aren't you little Miss Sunshine today?' Lynx sighed.

She grinned unexpectedly. 'Ah, Lynx, this is the fun bit! That first step into the dark, the jolt of excitement and fear because you don't know what's coming next. Isn't this what you're really here for?'

'No, that'd be the smoked, stuffed eel they eat here.'

'Eel?' She screwed up her face. 'You're a madman, my Hanese friend.'

*

The bulk of Jarrazir city occupied the eastern shore of the bay. To reach that they had to pass through an inlet less than a hundred yards wide and defended by a pair of huge mage-carved towers. The outer faces of the towers were rounded and had arched openings all the way up for ballistae – while huge trebuchets stood at the very top within a perimeter wall.

Lynx was more interested in the carved inner faces of the towers, however, which depicted the ancient pagan gods that had been the patron deities of Jarrazir until the five gods had been recognised. Now they were beloved emblems of the city. Despite centuries of fierce piety the Monarchs of Jarrazir kept those heads prominent on the city's flag that hung from each statue before him, each halved red and white with a beast on each side. On his left, looking down at the ship as it passed between the towers, roared the face of the Urlain, a mythical bear-like creature with stone scales for skin, while on the right the great serpent Holoh watched, fangs half-unveiled.

The former signified unwavering power and fortitude, Lynx recalled reading once, while the latter represented elegance and intellect. It was the serpent that filled him with faint trepidation – reminding Lynx far too much of the golantha they had faced while trying to cross the great rift in Shadows Deep.

Three miles in length and half a mile at its widest, the narrow shelf of land on Lynx's left nestled in the lee of three steep-sided hills and boasted the mansions of the oldest and richest families of Jarrazir. The sprawl of great houses was overlooked by the three palaces of the Lesser-Royals on the waterfront, while a squat fort atop the largest hill behind surveyed them all.

Ahead of him was the mouth of the lagoon and the peaked towers of the Bridge Palace straddling the Ongir Canal, but their ship veered right, towards the merchant districts instead. There was no challenge as they crossed the bay, just fishing coracles fleeing ahead of them. The ship had been scrutinised as they passed the towers and Lynx guessed it had done this route many times before, for all that it would rarely fly the state flag of Su Dregir.

The city's deepest docks stood to the right of the lagoon, naturally leading to the merchant's district of Sentrell behind. Eateries and teahouses studded a dockfront of limewashed merchant offices, cobbled alleys leading to goods yards behind. Smoke rose from every house, the scents of baking mingling with mud and refuse on the air. The people were little different to any dock on Parthain, mostly tanned white faces and hair ranging from blazing orange to black. The tribes of the inland sea had intermingled for more centuries than anyone could count, but trade was such that the black faces of some of the Cards wouldn't be noteworthy anywhere.

They were received with all courtesy, the dockmaster coming to greet the captain himself and bowing to the Envoy when introduced. On the dock behind waited six soldiers in grey, likely from the dock armoury. While ships were permitted to keep their weaponry on board, after a careful inspection, armed mercenary companies were rarely allowed to keep theirs. Normally their weapons would be impounded and stored there until the company chose to leave, but Envoy Ammen apparently had other ideas.

'I require a Crown dispensation and bonding, for my personal troops and their equipment,' the man called out as the ship was being tied up and the gangplank secured.

'In which case you will have to remain on board, Envoy,' the dockmaster replied. 'I will send word to the palace and make the request for you.'

'My escort will remain,' he countered. 'I'll be over there having a cup of something warm and spiced with the captain of my guard, awaiting the Monarch's pleasure.'

Once a messenger had been sent, the Envoy and Captain Onerist headed to the teahouse he'd indicated, while the rest settled in for a wait. As the armoury soldiers catalogued the weapon stores, the mercenaries sat around playing cards and by the time a writ had been brought from the Bridge Palace, most of the cartridges were ready for transport to a fortified building down the street.

Anatin lingered for a short while then beckoned Toil over before bellowing across the deck. 'Payl, Teshen, Reft, Lynx, Varain, Safir – get down here.'

Lynx hurried forward with the others, realising that the Envoy's dispensation must have included him for some reason. He knew he was one of the more experienced fighters in the company, but still it was a small surprise until Anatin explained.

'The Envoy is permitted a small personal guard beyond the handful he's got. Given the rest of the company is to go unarmed, best you're the ones holding on to your guns.' He smirked at Varain and Lynx. 'O' course, in case there's any actual guarding to be done, seniority counts.'

Ah, that's why. Great.

As the weapons were distributed Captain Onerist marched over with a greying man in a tall hat and severe frock coat.

'Commander, this is Master Tipore – he serves as a factor for several prominent Su Dregir interests and has secured accommodation for the Envoy and your company.'

Tipore bowed to Anatin, all the while casting nervous glances at the giant, Reft.

'Commander Anatin,' he said hesitantly. 'The, ah, the blessing of the gods be upon you all. As instructed I've secured an inn close to the Envoy's residence for your company. I will conduct the Envoy to his house and then return for you once the ship is unloaded.'

'Instructed, eh?' Anatin said, glancing at Toil.

'An Envoy doesn't arrive unannounced, or without somewhere to stay,' she said. 'No point having the Cards too far away, either. Do try to keep your pets off the furniture,' she added with a smile. 'Some of them aren't housetrained and it'll be a better area of the city than your usual lodgings.'

'Hear that, Reft?' Anatin cackled. 'No letting Deern sleep on your bed, it's his basket or he's out in the yard.'

Reft had nothing to say to that of course, but Anatin had spoken loudly enough that there came a muffled string of curses from the ship behind them.

'We've taken an inn?' Varain said in a hopeful voice.

'Bed and board,' Tipore said gravely. 'No alcohol.'

'I hate this place already.'

Interlude 3
(Now)

Toil opened her eyes and had to blink twice to make sure she'd really done so. It wasn't just dark. She found herself surrounded by the palpable, utter darkness of underground – blacker than night and twice as terrifying.

She groaned and tried to move; rolling on to her side and almost falling off the narrow wooden frame she'd been dumped on. Her right arm was numb to the point of being immobile. She lay back and looked up at the blackness above while a cold tingle started to spread through her fingers as the blood returned. There was a blanket underneath her, old but clean with a rough, scratchy quality to it.

Touching her fingers to her face Toil winced and the memory of being struck by the butt of a gun loomed large. The journey here was mostly a blur, movement and pain. The whisper of carpet under her heels, then wood, then rough stone and steps.

I'm alive, she acknowledged, reaching out to find the wall with shaky fingers in an attempt to get her bearings, *so that pretty much went according to plan.*

By feeling around she could tell there was a wall just inches to her left, another up past her head and a third near her feet. A small stone box with rough-hewn walls then, but lacking the stink of waste, bodies or much else at all. Not even the scent of water, the air was dry and chill for all that the blackness felt like a living thing. Somewhere outside the cell she heard a sound break the profound quiet, the clink of metal in a lock. *And that's the only sound there is – I'm alone down here. This isn't a regular gaol, but is that a good sign or really, really bad?*

Footsteps echoed in the corridor beyond, several pairs of feet – some in soft soles, some in heavy boots. She guessed at two of each approaching the cell door. Toil resisted the urge to roll over and face it as a key was turned and bolts drawn back. Light spilled into the room, but no one entered.

'Good afternoon, Monarch.'

There was a pause behind her. 'Good guess.'

'Not really,' Toil said. 'Easy enough even before I smelled your perfume. This ain't a regular cell and the city's ruler doesn't need to dump me somewhere out of the way if she wants to have me killed. But if she wants to talk away from prying eyes and ears, some hole underneath the Palace Armoury is as good as any.'

Again there was a pause.

'Nap's over,' said a man eventually, an aristocrat by his accent and one more overtly hostile than the Monarch was. 'On your feet when you address the Monarch.'

'Well now,' Toil croaked, rolling over so she could squint at them in the weak lamplight, 'that all depends, doesn't it?'

'No,' he said in a cold tone. 'Whatever her opinion on your letter, you stand in her presence or you'll get another enforced nap.'

Toil groaned and heaved her feet on to the floor, but as she did so her head spun so she remained sitting on the side of the bed. Nearest to her was a grey-haired guard carrying a lamp and a cudgel, smelling of sweat and nervousness. He stood slightly to one side to afford the Monarch a better view of the prisoner. Behind Crown-Princess Stilanna were two figures too dark to properly make out, but guessing their identities wasn't hard.

'I might need to take that bit slowly, Crown-Prince,' she said. 'Seems like someone caught me a small blow on the head earlier.'

'Be glad that is all you got.'

'Oh I am,' she admitted. 'Could have gone a whole lot worse, I'm aware.'

'And yet you took the risk,' the Monarch said before her husband could say anything more. 'That interests me.'

'Aye well, as your friend at the back can testify, I've been known to be a mite impulsive in the past. It was a risk I needed to take to get the letter to you, given I wasn't getting inside the palace again.'

She saw the ruling couple of Jarrazir turn at her words to where the fourth of their party stood, carefully back from the expensively dressed nobles. He was a large man, broad and bearded, wearing a dark frock coat and a red scarf around his neck. The light only hinted at the lines in his face, but they hadn't changed much since she last saw him.

'Impulsive is one way to put it,' said the man at last.

'Is she the one who hired you?'

'No, but she's good for the money.'

The Monarch turned back to Toil. 'So how did your employer know about the labyrinth opening? You couldn't have heard in time to get here this quickly.'

Toil forced a grin. 'I told him it was going to happen.'

'And how did you know?'

'Academics talk to each other.' She shrugged. 'I know a few who're aware the Duegar are of interest to me, they told me what Ishienne Matarin was trying to do. More importantly, they said she was making real progress. More than I'd realised; I was going to offer my services to her originally, I just had that letter for you as contingency.'

'Yet what am I to make of such an offer?' the Monarch mused. 'Given your employer is a foreign state, one that is no ally to Jarrazir and rarely generous. Or should I simply trust I have your skills and experience at my disposal with no question of reward – all based on the innate, unblemished nobility of that renowned brotherhood, the relic hunters?'

'Firm assurances are rather tricky to offer,' Toil admitted. 'All I've got is that we predicted you'd need help and that helping you serves our own purposes. Su Dregir is no friend of Jarrazir it's true, but you've always been fiercely independent and the Archelect prefers that to continue. Whatever sympathies there may be for the Militant Orders here, Jarrazir's noble families would never accept Order rule unless there was no other option. Better for the Archelect if he helps you find another option.'

'And you think sending mercenaries into my city will help that? How can I trust them?'

'Ask the Red Scarves to leave and they'll do so,' Toil said. 'They've been paid a retainer to come and offer their services, obey your instructions, make themselves available to you until summer. We could only plan for possibilities – namely that if the labyrinth gets opened, you'd likely need an experienced relic hunter to investigate it and reliable troops available to bolster your armies. It's your choice what to do with them.'

Again the Crown-Princess and Prince turned back to the large man behind them. He just grunted and inclined his head.

'And your own relic hunter company?'

'Too small to be a threat,' she said with a dismissive wave, 'just large enough to be useful for my modest purposes.'

'One might be sceptical that the woman who wants to lead our expedition into the labyrinth disrupted the announcement of said expedition.'

'There's lots to be sceptical about. Blackest rift – if you're feeling suspicious that whole confrontation could've been a way to establish my credentials!'

'Indeed.'

'If it helps,' Toil added, 'bring Sotorian Bade here to me. Picking a fake fight is one thing, ripping the man's windpipe out with my bare hands another.'

'Bade?' the mercenary at the back rumbled.

'In the flesh,' Toil confirmed. 'The one and only.'

'That explains that, then.'

The Monarch turned slightly, expecting a further comment, but the mercenary commander behind her merely looked impassive.

'The Knights-Charnel have already withdrawn to the general's barge amid protests and threats,' Crown-Prince Tylom said. 'I think the damage you've done there is enough for everyone's liking. As it is, you've given them ample reason to lay siege to the city rather than negotiate with us over entry to the labyrinth.'

'I gave them the excuse, I'll admit, but they'd have found another if I'd not been the fool to hand it to them. Or they'd have given up looking and tried some other way. With those fuckers it's always the same. "Give us what we want or we'll burn the whole world until we get it."'

'That may well be true, but still you made matters all the easier in a city that is not your own,' the Monarch pointed out. 'Robbing me of even the chance to negotiate a more peaceful outcome for my home. Would you have been so reckless in Su Dregir?'

'I do what needs to be done,' Toil growled. 'I might've made a mistake, but a Jarraziran life's worth the same as any other – whatever our indignant Charneler friends might claim.'

'Not enough reason to trust you, however.'

She shrugged. 'Got anyone else who can lead this expedition into the labyrinth?'

'Three noted crews of relic hunters have petitioned the court thus far, in addition to whatever the Knights-Charnel might have offered.'

Toil cocked her head at the Monarch, a crooked smile on her face. 'Yet you're still talking to me.'

'You claim to be a representative of Su Dregir – certainly you are in the employ of the city's official envoy, though he says you are nothing more than an educated mercenary.'

'You doubt the Archelect's seal on my letter?'

'I remain suspicious on a whole variety of levels.'

'Who're the captains of the crews?'

'Their names are Gorotadin, Fini and, ah, Rubil.'

Toil snorted. 'Rubil can't read Duegar – or even the language she speaks, for that matter. As for Hales Fini, he's just a bounty hunter and not even a very good one at that, a chancer who thinks blowing the crap out of a ruin is the way to explore it. I'm amazed either is still alive, frankly, and neither of them would make it past the guardian spirits most likely.'

'But you can?'

'Any decent relic hunter could – all you need is experience and a Duegar lamp.'

'What about Gorotadin?'

'Don't know him,' Toil admitted, 'but I've heard he's no fool.'

The Monarch looked at her husband. 'It seems we share an assessment of all three,' she said. 'We also asked who the best relic hunter they knew was. Rubil, ahem, doesn't like you very much – *really* doesn't like you – but didn't say you were bad at your job. Fini just looked frightened and started to make excuses—'

'To be fair, I did say that next time I saw him I was going to tear his ribs out of his chest and choke him with them,' Toil broke in.

'Quite. Gorotadin didn't know you, but said somewhat gnomically that your reputation spoke volumes. He did, however, name Sotorian Bade as the best – presumably the

Knights-Charnel would have offered us Bade's services had you not attempted to gut him like a fish first.'

Despite her best efforts, Toil knew the Monarch spotted her tense and she took a moment to phrase her reply rather than let her animosity win out again.

'Bade's good at his job,' she said slowly, 'but his job is doing what the Knights-Charnel want. Bounty hunter, saboteur, tomb raider, bandit, it's all the same to him and leaving witnesses isn't his style. You hire him and he'll forget that little disagreement soon enough, but you won't get anything out of the labyrinth either.'

There wasn't a twitch on the faces of either the Crown-Princess or her husband. Toil realised they'd come to the same conclusion too even before the Monarch said, 'Hence why I'm here.'

A sharp pair then, to assess all four correctly straight off. 'I've got at least one advantage over Bade, though.'

'And that is?'

'The mage – Matarin's pupil. I've got her.'

The Monarch indicated the doorway. 'That's a good start. Get up; you can continue to persuade me somewhere a little more civilised.'

Toil did as she was told, moving slowly to keep her head from pounding too hard, past the Monarch and the tunnel. She paused as she reached the mercenary, however, his stony expression not even twitching as their eyes met. Hard grey eyes and scars half concealed by his thick beard, the man could stare down a rabid dog but Toil merely sighed and kissed the man on one cheek.

'Hello, Vigilance. Miss me?'

At first there only came an indeterminate rumble from deep in his chest, but eventually Vigilance spoke. 'Always. Even mother says life is dull when our little hellcat isn't around.'

'We all have our roles in this life.' Toil smiled and headed off down the corridor with the silent guard carrying the torch right behind her. 'She wishes you'd write more, by the way.'

'I'm sure she does.'

As Toil shuffled through the dark tunnel, a face continued to intrude on her thoughts. It dragged her back to a place five hundred miles and fifteen years distant – an unnamed animal track to the south-east where, whenever she recalled her life before all *this*, it had all began. Not when she first met Master Oper nor got on his cart in the grey gloom of dawn. Not when she took her first step underground, nor even when she almost died, but sitting in the back of a cart looking at a cave in the distance.

*

'Some folk call 'emselves seafaring men,' the bearded man driving the cart had declared, throwing an arm out wide. 'Married to the waves so they are, ever drawn to the sparkle of water and cry of the gull.'

He cocked his head and gave them a small, dangerous smile. 'We're no different, not really. We just heed a different call. The deepest black, that's our mistress and oh by the shattered gods is she a hard one to please. Sailors like to curse their love for being a fickle bitch and I'm sure the sea is, but our black queen is all that and more.'

'It's just a damned cave,' the largest recruit muttered, a square-jawed lump called Hoyst.

Toil thought for a moment the bearded man would explode at that, but he did no such thing. There was murder in his green eyes, that much she could see – that much she'd learned to see in her short span of years – but no weapon was drawn.

'Just a cave,' the bearded man whispered. 'Well now, that's a thing to say.'

Sotorian Bade, Toil reminded herself. *That was his name.*

She looked around the crew Master Oper had assembled – three old hands, Bade the oldest of the three, and four wide-eyed recruits, herself included.

'That's no simple cave,' Bade continued, sidling towards Hoyst. 'You'll see my boy, you'll see.'

Toil had to admit it looked like a cave, and not much of one at that, but she wasn't such a fool as to speak up. An attractive young woman in the company of men couldn't afford to look stupid or thoughtless – and this was her first adventure away from home. She knew there'd be more than enough opportunity to look naive without bringing it on herself.

'There's a scent in the air,' Bade continued, affecting a wistful air. 'A lover's perfume, for those of you who take the black queen as your mistress.'

'Probably just Toil,' Hoyst said, prompting a barking laugh from the man beside them, a spotty youth of Toil's age called Fittil.

Toil leaned forward in the wagon and took hold of the big man's earlobe, giving it a sharp tug. Hoyst growled and drew his fist back, intending to cow her into an apology, but Toil just raised an eyebrow.

'Put it away,' she advised him, 'or you'll get more'n an ear-twist.'

'Touch me again and I'll break those pretty lips, little girl.'

Toil gave him her best smile and lazily reached for his ear again. Hoyst made to grab her hand but she snatched forward like a striking snake with the other. She pinched his top lip between strong fingers and twisted hard. Hoyst yelped and swatted her hand away with a stinging swipe, but howled as he did so – Toil not giving up her prize easily.

A sheltered upbringing had its advantages, Toil reflected as Hoyst clamped his hands around his mouth, a trickle of blood running down his teeth, *if when you're stuck in the one place, some o' the dirtiest fighters on the continent are welcomed in like family.*

'Ladies and gentlemen,' called their employer in a deep baritone from the cart behind them, 'I don't recall paying any of you to brawl among yourselves. Master Bade, please shoot the next person to step out of line.'

'With pleasure, Master Oper,' Bade said with an evil glint and a pat of his holster. 'Now then, where was I?'

'Something about me taking a mistress,' Toil said before she could stop herself. *Dammit, what happened to keeping quiet? Anyone'd think I was my father's child.*

'Ah, yes, so I was.' Bade beckoned them forward as though they were walking rather than riding in a cart loaded with supplies. 'There's no arguing with love, Toil – but we're not sailors, are we, girl?'

She made a show of looking around at the tall grasses skirting the track and long bank of willows on their left, then the cart they rode in.

'Nope, doesn't look like we are.'

'Very good, girl, you'll go far with observation like that. No we ain't, boys and girls – a sailor falls in love with the sea or he doesn't. But the deepest dark, it don't care for your love – it's a hungry mistress and it ain't one to take no. It falls in love with *you*, my boys and girls, it sinks its shadow teeth into you and either chews you up or leaves its mark for ever. Fickle she ain't, but a monster she is.

'The sailor may read the wind, see the rise and fall of waves, and know his time has come. He may know his fickle love affair is over and his sea-wife has cast him aside, but our black queen don't play that way. There's no warning with our mistress, no sign nor whisper. One moment she loves you and the next she don't.'

'And what happens then?' Fittil asked.

Toil eyed him. The youth was lapping Bade's bluster up. Sheltered she might be, but she'd seen his sort – every colour and cast.

Shattered gods, my own da spins a tale this way. I've heard it since before I could walk – turns out there was a lesson in it for me too.

'Then?' Bade asked slowly, as though only now hearing the question. 'Oh, my boy, then . . .' He let out a deep sigh. 'Then if you're lucky, there's just a click and a snap.'

As though to demonstrate, Bade slapped his palms together and Fittil jumped at the sharp sound.

They rode on in silence, but after that Toil noticed Bade paid no attention to the youth, not even to look at him or give instructions. As the carts crested the rise and the cave mouth unveiled – as the recruits gasped, the veterans chuckled and Oper let out a rumble of approval and opened the next flask of wine – Fittil had ceased to exist in the eyes of Sotorian Bade.

They set up camp well short of the cave mouth – the entrance, Toil realised. A great, hooded arch of stone rose up from the ground to invite them down, but Master Oper ignored it as he set his camp and waited for morning. In the distance behind there was a tower, slender and vast – ten times higher than any tree Toil had seen, but the riches were to be found deep underground, Bade told them around a campfire that night. The tower had been scaled in generations past; there would be no wonders to be found there now.

Toil still wanted to climb it, still wanted to feel the mage-worked stone beneath her hands and look out on the world from the place of birds, but the adventure she craved was underground. Deep down, where the darkness was a living thing according to Bade, and horrors stalked the unwary.

'Fortunes are made there, in the black,' Bade said, eyes glittering darkly in the firelight. 'A tavern of your own perhaps, Toil, an army commission for you, Hoyst?'

Hoyst grinned at the prospect. 'I'd go east,' he said in a hungry voice, 'sign with the Knight-Artificers, Knights-Charnel mebbe – fight the heathens of Ikir or Ei Det.'

'Might be I could give you a nod in that direction,' Bade commented, pulling at a pipe as he spoke. 'If you show the right stuff.'

He looked from Hoyst to Toil but she said nothing. She had no grand plan for her life. Her brother had joined her father's company and acquitted himself well, by all accounts. There would be a place for her at the Red Banner for sure – that grand sprawling way-station on the road to Su Dregir which the Red Scarves called home – but right now she wanted adventure. A life away from her great-hearted tyrant of a father and implacable, imperturbable mother. A life where she was child of neither, but Toil Deshar herself.

'Me, I'll be a barge-master,' Fittil piped up, 'see every corner of Sinabel.'

'Sure, sure,' Bade murmured, never taking his eyes from Toil.

She glanced at Fittil. The youth's gaze was distant, lost in dreams of his future. A future that Toil knew he'd never have, as though Sotorian Bade had looked into the young man's soul and seen some crack or flaw that his mistress, his black queen, would reject.

He's dead already, Toil realised, unable to find the words to tell Fittil and warn him off, but ever more certain with every passing moment that Bade was correct.

The deepest black will take him. He's dead already.

Chapter 8
(One week earlier)

'Fancy taking a walk? I want to see one for myself.'

Lynx paused and looked up at Toil. The newly appointed Princess of Blood stood in the doorway, wearing a long leather coat and hat. She had a gun-belt in her hand, freshly oiled by the smell, and another around her waist. Toil wore it so the buckle sat on her hip, the holster behind her back – hardly practical for fighting, but better than being stopped by every passing watchman.

'One what? Oh, the entrances. Aren't we supposed to be on guard duty?'

Toil shrugged and handed the gun-belt to Lynx. He looked it over briefly before nodding. There were eight unobtrusive pouches with icers cradled inside steel tubes.

'The Monarch's busy, what with entrances to the underworld opened up. She's presented her compliments to Envoy Ammen and offered an audience tomorrow.'

'So we're free to wander the city?'

'Best we take the opportunity while we can.' She brandished a rolled slip of paper. 'The Monarch's writ – permission to be armed in the city so long as we behave ourselves.'

Lynx nodded and stood. 'You believe the rumours about this labyrinth then?' he asked, putting on the gun-belt before hauling his coat over his shoulders.

'Depends which rumours you're talking about,' Toil said. 'Mostly they'll be so much shit, but there's certainly something

The door was a slab of mage-carved rock easily fifteen feet high and more than a foot thick, but it led nowhere as the doorway beyond had been walled up. Touching his fingers to his lips, Bade crept forward and inspected the obstacle. It was human-built, brick and mortar and hastily done from what he could tell. How thick was anyone's guess, but a test probe with his knife told him that the mortar was still slightly soft.

Patiently he worked one brick loose and slid it out. There were more behind of course, but it gave him an idea of what he was dealing with and, after waiting a short while to see if he could hear anything from the other side, they returned to the others.

'The intelligence is good, just as we were told,' Bade said at Chotel's inquisitive look. 'The entrance is open and the doorway's bricked up. You stay here with a couple of men and the big lamp, start the process of unpicking the wall, just be slow and silent. I'll send the supplies down so we're ready to move as soon as possible.'

'You're not going to explore the rest?'

Bade grinned. 'Work first,' he said, nodding at Kastelian. 'We can wait a day to play.'

*

A thump on his foot jerked Lynx awake. Before he could even focus he was reaching for his sword, but found nothing and after a few moments of blindly flapping, he looked up to see Toil. She had a small smile on her face and her leather coat on her back.

'Still a bit twitchy when you wake, eh?'

'Aye, looks like it,' he muttered. Lynx looked around and saw the back of Lastani heading through the door to the stairs. 'Giving her a break then?'

'The girl could do with a rest,' Toil confirmed, 'and I need to run an errand. Want to stretch your legs?'

He blinked at her for a moment then nodded and heaved himself up. 'Reckon I do, where are we going?'

'We're going dress shopping.' Toil beamed. 'You'll love it.'

'A dress? For you?'

'Of course for bloody me, who else?'

He shrugged. 'Dunno, just never seen you in a dress.'

'Here's your chance then.'

They headed out into the grey afternoon light and down the main avenue running south through the district. The streets were busy, people and horses packing the avenue, so they were forced to weave a path through slow-moving traffic until the green-sheathed roofs of guild-houses came into view. Surrounding each of those was a tight network of streets where the shops were mostly devoted to the trade of the guild-house. The Tailors' Guild was an imposing red-brick structure with fifty or more small flags flying above the pair of double doors that served as entrance to the great building. On the doors themselves was a brass crest, an eight-pointed star made of sewing needles.

'What're those?' Lynx asked, pointing at the flags.

'Guildsmen crests,' Toil said. 'Means they're accredited members and can charge more, sign of quality, see?' She pointed to one of the nearby shops where the great crest of the guild was reproduced above the door while a flag bearing the guild crest of that shop twitched in the afternoon breeze.

'But we're not going in there?'

She shook her head. 'Given I'm not looking for a soldier's uniform, no. Over there, that'll do.'

She led him across the street to an almost identical shop, but in the window of that one he saw a wooden headless mannequin wearing a green sleeveless dress. Lynx raised an eyebrow at the low-cut front as much as the bands of ribbon and crystal decoration, but Toil just snorted and shook her head as she reached for the door.

'Don't get any ideas, it ain't going to be that fancy.'

'Still, I'm liking the general thrust.'

Inside it smelled of expensive leather and dried flowers, scrubbed floors and cedar wood. They were met by a pair of hatchet-faced women who could have been sisters, both with their hair severely pinned back and wearing silk shawls over the sleeveless dresses that Lynx had realised was the fashion for civillian women of a certain status. One wore black, the other brown, but both sported the shop's crest worked into the decoration around their waist.

'May we help you, ah, madam?' asked one dubiously.

'I need a dress and I need it fast,' Toil snapped, marching inside like a duchess and turning her back on the pair as she scanned the boles of fabric lining the left-hand wall. 'Plain silk, high neck, in green and grey. To be completed by this evening.'

She shucked off her leather coat and tossed it to Lynx before sweeping back her dark red hair and giving the women an imperious look.

'Well?'

'I regret—'

Toil made an angry little sound and stepped forward, the shrewish tailor's platitudes tailing quickly off as the imposing mercenary loomed over her.

'No, no regrets.' She pulled a purse from her belt and hefted it to make the coins inside chink. 'I want quality work and I was told I could get it here. If you're not up to the challenge I will take my money elsewhere and refer the others accordingly.'

'Others?' said brown dress.

'Others,' Toil confirmed without bothering to explain further. 'Now, shouldn't you be taking measurements?'

The pair scuttled to work and Toil nodded approvingly. She removed her scarf and began to unbutton her tunic, flashing Lynx a mischievous smile before turning away. Underneath she wore only a thin linen shirt that showed the lines of her body to great effect, if Lynx was any judge.

'Don't worry, Lynx,' Toil called over her shoulder as she tossed him the tunic and submitted to measurement. 'I've not forgotten you and your friends.'

'Oh, great, the last suit you got me was such a success,' he replied gloomily.

'At least you got a few hours use out of yours,' Toil said, frowning. 'I never even put mine on!'

For the Skyriver Festival in Su Dregir, Toil had invited Lynx to the Archelect's ball and all festivities on that night were conducted in costume. Lynx had arrived at Toil's home dressed as the Knight of Blood only to discover two dead assassins inside. Sadly that had been only the start of the excitement. By the end of the night, even by Lynx's travel-worn standards his costume was less than pristine.

'So what do I get this time?'

'Nothing so dramatic, just a uniform. It occurred to me that having extras made for those of you assigned to guard duty would be prudent, so I had some made before we left just in case.'

'Not just for me then?'

'Me, Payl, Varain and Teshen too. I hadn't planned on using them quite like this, but that's the best laid plans for you.'

'Good luck getting Payl in after that public bust-up she had. This is for the announcement tomorrow, right?'

'It is. Payl's my problem, and frankly that face of yours may prove as much of one. However, if it's a case of forgoing his due dignity because of diminished numbers, I think the Envoy will agree in a pinch.'

Lynx was quiet a while, his thoughts following the path of Toil's plans to an unsavoury conclusion. 'And afterwards?'

'What about afterwards?'

'If you get your way,' he said in a tight voice. 'You'll be wanting me to volunteer?'

'Ah, that.' Toil nodded in understanding.

Lynx had found it hard to enter Shadows Deep even with a company of Knights-Charnel cavalry pursuing them. Even the thought of doing so again made his heart beat faster. His time in a So Han military prison camp was almost a decade behind him, but the misery and hardship of working in the mines there had left an indelible impression.

'Yes and no,' Toil said finally. 'I'll want you to volunteer, I won't ask you to. The choice is yours,' she added in a softer voice. 'You're good in a tight spot, but if you don't want to be there, no sense in dragging you.'

Lynx grunted, acknowledging her point. 'But you'll need Sitain,' he said at last.

'She's a big girl, doesn't need you watching over her all the time.'

'Aye,' he said dubiously.

Toil laughed. 'Shattered gods, you and the old man really are two peas in a diamond-shaped pod, aren't you?'

'Atieno?' Lynx was taken aback before realising she was just taking a friendly dig, not revealing that she knew anything more about the Vagrim. Even after months around the mercenaries, he sometimes still had to remind himself not to take everything said so seriously. 'Aye, I s'pose you could say that.'

He gave a wry smile, glad Toil's back was still turned. 'Some of us don't get wiser as we age, we just keep doing the same old thing.'

'Aye, might be you're the fool who's met the old fool he's going to turn into one day.' Toil glanced back. 'But Atieno's a handsome enough old fool, so things could be worse.'

'That's a relief, been trading on my looks for so long I wouldn't know what to do with myself.'

She nodded. 'Explains the state of your clothes at least. Jewellery too, mebbe.'

He glanced down at the silver ring on his middle finger, almost identical to the one Atieno wore.

'You could say that.'

'Want to tell me about it?'

'Not much,' he admitted. 'If you don't know, I'd prefer to keep it that way.'

'Aha, I like a man of mystery,' she said, making a clear effort to keep the conversation light.

'No great mystery, but folk read a whole lot into nothing sometimes.'

'Nothing likely to bite you in the arse?'

Lynx laughed at that. It might not be easy to follow the Vagrim path, but when it caused a problem you tended to know pretty damn quick. Saving Sitain had been one instance of that – he'd pulled a gun on a group of Charnelers without really expecting his new comrades to back him up.

'You don't need worry on that front,' he said as Toil shot him a quizzical look.

'Good,' she said after a moment. 'How are we doing, ladies, almost finished?'

'We've barely started, madam,' protested the one in the black dress. 'Your measurements are done, but there is cut and material to consider next.'

'Bah, I'm not planning on being the belle of the ball, just need to not look out of place as an aide. Your guild training should mean you can guess well enough, it's speed I'm interested in. I'll be back this evening for fitting.'

'Ahem, there is one further detail, madam.'

'What?'

'Your arms.' She plucked at Toil's sleeves with a fastidious disapproval. 'As you know, the custom of bare arms is an established tradition in Jarrazir.' She gestured to her colleague who let her shawl slip back and revealed the neat braiding around the shoulder of her dress which was as far as it went.

Toil pulled her own sleeve up. Her arms were corded with muscle and more than pleasing to Lynx's eye, but he wasn't blind to the fact she had a good variety of scars and blemishes, especially on her forearms. One long, jagged scar ran up the inside of her right arm while a smear of pinkish burned skin covered her left wrist.

As much anything, however, it was the haphazard direction of the scarring that was as noticeable as the largest injuries. Some Lynx could tell were knife cuts, other more irregular ones had to be the result of clambering around caverns and city-ruins.

'They might not help me blend in, true,' she admitted before brightening. 'However, you two seem like women of great resource. I've no doubt that by this evening you'll have come up with a solution.'

With that she stepped between the two and went to the neat desk off to the side. Emptying a dozen silver coins on to it she gestured for Lynx to pass her tunic and headed for the door.

'That should tide you over, we can discuss the rest later.'

Lynx lingered a moment longer, enjoying the stunned looks on the two women's faces. Finally they focused on him, where-upon he tipped his hat to them.

'See you at the fitting, ladies.'

Chapter 15

'I could kill you for this.'

Aben grinned. 'You can't buy authenticity, my friend.'

'Fucking can,' Barra groaned, 'it's called talent – acting, damn you!'

'Ah, it wouldn't be the same.'

'Go shove a burner up your arse, bastard. How fu— Oh, hells!'

The slim woman froze for a moment then turned and ran back to the privy, looking stricken. Aben's grin became wider. It was all he could do not to laugh out loud despite the fact he was going to suffer some sort of retribution. Barra would no doubt make him pay for weeks, but it had been a hugely entertaining sight to watch all of the Envoy's staff emerge from their rooms one by one, faces pale – embarrassment mingling with alarm as a great gust of stink accompanied them.

'Private!' snapped an angry voice from behind him. 'What's going on?'

Aben smothered the look of amusement on his face and turned to salute Captain Onerist as crisply as he could. 'Illness, sir.'

'Merciful Ulfer!' Onerist exclaimed as the smell reached him. He reeled back for a moment then pulled a handkerchief from one pocket to cover his mouth. 'What's happened to them?'

'Something they ate, sir, so I'm guessing. All the staff are down with it, they're, ah, not in a good way.'

'Something they ate?'

'Last night, sir – I was fortunate to be absent when the cook served the evening meal to the staff, and you, of course, ate with the Envoy.'

'Gods man, *all* of the staff? Is it as bad as the smell suggests?'

'Oh yes, sir, shitting like their lives depended on it,' Aben said with all the cheer of a man who'd supplied the laxative instead of swallowed it. 'Evacuating their bowels like rats off a sinking ship.'

Onerist paused, frowning. 'I'm not sure that's quite the correct analogy.'

'Don't know that word, sir,' Aben continued, trying not to enjoy himself too obviously, 'but it sounds right given what Corporal Paranil's saying about his backside.'

'Fetch them a doctor then, quick about it. Senator Ammen must have a staff attending him this afternoon – an Envoy of Su Dregir can't be seen at a foreign court with just two guards and no aides at all!'

'Begging your pardon, sir, but I've seen this before,' Aben replied, throwing in another salute for good measure as Onerist's ears were starting to turn red with fury. 'Out on campaign once, consignment of mutton some thieving shitestick of a merchant padded out with rat meat. Rotten it was, every man in the squad spent a day with the shits and couldn't move. A day at least, sir, any doctor'll tell you the same, I'd wager my beer rations on it. Nothing to be done but drink all the tea you can then watch it run out just as fast. These poor bastards ain't going nowhere.'

The captain went very quiet and for a moment Aben thought he was going to explode with fury, but when he eventually spoke it was in a quiet, worried voice. 'Private, we must have attendants, do you understand? The Envoy is calling for his private secretary right now, but later we will be in public! We are still waiting for final meetings with the Monarch's staff. The Envoy cannot arrive alone like some pauper.'

'Onerist!' roared a voice from elsewhere in the house, unmistakably the booming presence of the Envoy. 'Dammit, captain, where are you?'

Onerist closed his eyes briefly, wilting at the prospect of the Envoy's rage, but Aben just had to fight the urge to grin even more. Given he wasn't really a Lighthouse Guardsman and only playing the role, being bawled out didn't matter a jot to him. As a man used to besting most people he met in size and strength, he didn't intimidate easily. His greatest concern was laughing in the face of his betters, given they tended to dislike that.

'Come on, sir, let's give him the bad news together. Never good to do that alone, they tend to focus all their rage then, eh?'

Onerist made a choking sound, no doubt as confused by the sudden comradely manner as anything else, but he let himself be caught up in the big man's wake as Aben strode upstairs to where Senator Ammen stood, hands on hips and still bellowing as they came into view.

'Where in the living piss is everyone, man? You, private – what's going on?'

'Apologies, milord,' Aben replied, 'your staff's got the shits, if you'll pardon my language, sir.'

'What? Onerist, what's he talking about?' Ammen demanded. 'All of them? All at once?'

Onerist began to splutter more apologies and was well on his way to grovelling when Aben got bored and talked over the man instead.

'All of them, sir, rotten meat in last night's meal is my guess. I've seen it before, sits on the stomach badly overnight and as soon as you move in the morning, well, things start to move. Don't stop all day neither.'

'Every single member of my staff?' Ammen repeated, purpling with rage. 'Unacceptable, get them out of bed or the privy – I

216

don't care where, they're no use to me there. And string that damn chef up before you do, no wait. Bring him here. I'll do it my damn self! I'm invited to the Monarch's court for a special function this afternoon; they're not allowed to be ill!'

'Fired the cook myself, sir,' Aben claimed cheerfully. 'Man didn't even put up a fight or argue his case. Knew he'd been caught the moment the first of 'em got up and left a trail to the privy. Wasn't sick himself neither, bastard knew what he was doing that's for sure. I gave 'im a kick in the nuts on behalf of my mates and told 'im if he came back he'd get worse. We'll not see the bugger again, even once he does prise 'is balls out o' his gut.'

'Private!' roared Onerist, finally recovering his senses. 'Guard your tone and hold that language in front of your betters! My apologies, Senator Ammen, the man will be reprimanded for forgetting his place.'

Ammen, no stranger to a military campaign, looked far from perturbed by Aben's tone. He was already lost in thought and waved his hand dismissively.

'As you choose, captain, but it can wait. This man is the only soldier we have left at present.'

'Still got the mercenaries, sir,' Aben added, unperturbed by imaginary punishments. 'Think I recall we brought a few spare uniforms too, in case you needed a larger honour guard anywhere.'

'Did we indeed?' Ammen said thoughtfully. 'The mercenaries, eh? You said my secretary would be ill all day? You're certain of this?'

'At least a day sir, spilling out everything they put in. It's ah . . . It's a mess back there already, if I'm honest. Reckon I'll need to see if any of those mercenaries is handy with a mop too, like a troupe o' monkeys have just been flinging the stuff about!'

'Thank you, that's quite enough, private,' Ammen said sharply. 'Go to the mercenaries, bring Commander Anatin and his lieutenant, that Toil woman, here directly. If there's anyone else in that gaggle of thieves with some manners, have them come too and find out where those spare uniforms are kept.'

'Right away, milord,' Aben said, saluting once more. 'Sure they'll be delighted to oblige you in any way you require.'

*

The city wall of Jarrazir cut a long arc through the landscape from the hills on the west all the way around to the craggy cliffs of Parthain's shore on the eastern flank. Three huge towers rose from a great ridge of earth backed against the wall of stone and brick. Coupled with smaller emplacements and the fort atop the hills, they presented as fearsome an approach as the two monstrous towers guarding the bay.

The city had long ago grown up to the very perimeter of this great wall, but the buildings were low in this newer part and the great blade of the Ongir Canal cut through both. From the western shore of the canal, Exalted Kastelian could see all the way to the wall. He had been there an hour, just one dragoon for company, though of course neither of them was in uniform. To any interested onlookers, of which there seemed to be none, the pair appeared to consist of a merchant of modest means and his bodyguard.

When boredom started to intrude, Kastelian pulled a cigar and a packet of matches from his pocket. He knelt and struck a match on one of the great blocks of granite that comprised the canal bank, the match's dirty yellow smoke billowing across the water as he lit his cigar and tossed the match away. He'd chosen this spot because it afforded him a clear view of all traffic on the canal, but there was also one more sight of note.

The North Keep rose between roofs on the far bank of the canal, half a mile away.

At this distance there was little to see, but the great portcullis-covered gate had remained closed the entire time. The keep was isolated from the rest of the wall with only one entrance and supplies enough to withstand a modest siege. With the deep armoury of bombardment spheres somewhere beneath it, he doubted the standing guard changed often. It was a massive structure, a blend of stone and brick that no doubt had layers of earth encased within to absorb the power of mage-spheres hitting it.

The outer wall was rounded with a squared-off back, seventy feet high with a wall protecting the great trebuchet stationed on the top. It was a formidable building, all the more so for the fact these defences were mostly a precaution. The trebuchet ensured that threats to the tower would come in the form of sneak attack – its range was so long and the power of the bombardment spheres so great, no army could march up to Jarrazir without being obliterated.

Yet that's exactly what we intend to do, Kastelian reminded himself. *It would be the perfect time to indulge my theory about a barge-mounted catapult, but we're already considered mavericks by the rest of the Knights-Charnel. No need to give them further reason to think so.*

Finally the sight he'd been waiting for came into view. A long barge, two-decked and flying the flag of the Knights-Charnel of the Long Dusk. It was an easy one to notice, not least because of the consternation it was already provoking among the citizenry here. The barge had waited a long time where the canal met the wall, the great-horns pulling it lowing gently as Jarraziran soldiers kept a close watch without being too threatening.

No doubt a message had been sent back to the palace and the number of armed men on board carefully noted, but this was an official delegation from the Knights-Charnel of the Long Dusk. They would have little to hide and the soldiers on the wall would be careful not to give offence to the powerful Militant Order.

'Fetch Bade,' Kastelian called to the dragoon behind him. 'Tell him we're going to a party.'

'Sir.'

The man scampered off and Kastelian puffed thoughtfully on his cigar as he watched the barge advance. As it came close he walked forward about ten yards to where a swing boom was standing idle and kicked it into movement. The barge's great-horn team was still twenty yards away and had plenty of time to slow as Kastelian signalled for the helmsman to heave to.

The helmsman rang a bell and the teamster waved back to show he'd heard before coaxing his four huge beasts to a halt. Even the smallest of the four was as tall as a carthorse and far broader, with a great curved horn that ran down the centre of its head. As the monstrous creatures ground to a stop Kastelian nodded to the teamster, a scarecrow-ragged figure who ignored him entirely, before ducking under the tow-rope and stepping down on to the barge's side-rail so he could announce himself to the nearest soldier.

'Take me to your leader,' Kastelian called as he moved nimbly forward to the central deck of the barge.

'Your name, sir?' replied the soldier in an immaculate dress uniform.

'Isn't for your hearing, trooper,' Kastelian said. 'But I'm an officer of the Torquen and I need to speak to the general.' He nodded towards a small flag that fluttered behind the large sun and spear device of the Knights-Charnel. The smaller flag depicted a pair of ravens, the personal crest of General Derjain Faril.

'You're out of uniform, sir,' the soldier correctly pointed out. Clearly he'd served in the general's retinue for a while and wasn't intimidated even by the elite Torquen branch. Kastelian had heard General Faril was a stickler for rules and as he looked around he realised all the soldiers were perfectly turned out, the white quarters of their uniforms pristine. Even officers of the Torquen were required to be correctly dressed in the presence of a lord or general.

'That I am, soldier, but I'm attached to the Pentaketh regiment. If the general don't like how I'm dressed . . . Well, that's my problem, eh?'

The soldier bowed his head in understanding. The Pentaketh were irregulars even within the Torquen; auxiliary specialists like Sotorian Bade and worse who couldn't fit within the rigid structure of the Order but were useful nonetheless.

'This way, sir.'

The soldier led him to the rear of the main deck where there were two armed soldiers guarding a door. Through that and a cramped antechamber where several clerks were hard at work, then into a low captain's room. The near half was taken up by a long dining table, complete with butler polishing the silver cutlery, while the far end had a wide desk and four armchairs arranged before it. Three officers stood to one side; a pair of captains and a commander. They parted without a word to reveal a small woman no bigger than a child: General Faril.

Kastelian bowed to the general. She was older than his mother with grey hair and thin spidery fingers, pale parchment skin, and eyes like the pitiless black of far underground where not even maspids dared go. Kastelian bowed low and stayed there, waiting for her to speak.

'Exalted?' the general said at last, having noticed the studs on his collar. It wasn't an official mark of rank, of course, but it was considered polite within the Order for officers of the Torquen to give an indication of their rank when meeting others.

'General Faril, good morning.'

Kastelian straightened and did his best not to flinch under Faril's scowl.

'Name?'

'Exalted Kastelian Ubris, Pentaketh regiment liaison.'

'Good, I've been expecting you. Report.'

He nodded. 'First of all, I ask that you wait here a while longer before continuing to the palace. I've summoned a few of my men, they should be along presently.'

'See to it,' she said to one of the captains, who scuttled out. 'Right, where are we?'

'In an excellent position – an informer has confirmed one of the labyrinth entrances has opened into the North Keep. Our specialist is preparing the ground so we can breach it at our leisure, should that prove necessary. He will then scout his way into the labyrinth proper – however, an opportunity presents itself.'

'Which is?'

'The Monarch is addressing the guild leaders and noble families today, announcing the city's response to the situation. I'm sure you'll be invited to attend forthwith. To act effectively they will be in particular need of specialists such as ours. I believe your influence could win us a presence on the city's official incursion, perhaps even to lead it. The choice would be yours as to whether we send a covert group ahead and delay the Monarch's troops, of course.'

'Your man's a renowned relic hunter, no? That's what the Lord-Exalted informed me.'

'Indeed, general. More than qualified to lead the incursion. Your oncoming troops will have been noticed and reported back by now. I'm sure the Monarch will not want to give you a reason to take offence.'

'All this will not stretch you too thin?'

'No, sir. My team is ready to move with an hour's notice even without Bade and his crew on hand.'

General Faril sniffed and looked Kastelian up and down.

'Very well, but get yourself into uniform. You'll not be part of my delegation looking like that.'

'Of course, sir.'

Chapter 16
(Now)

'Toil!'

Lynx started forward on instinct, only to have the butt of a gun thumped against his chest to drive him back. They really were under arrest now, there was no confusion about it this time and no one was getting out without being shot.

'Keep back,' the other soldier snapped, levelling his mage-gun.

Away down the corridor, Toil looked up and smiled slightly. She was under escort too, limping slightly and the right-hand side of her face looked swollen. Her silk dress was torn and stained, her feet bare – though she had been given a man's coat to drape around her shoulders. It was plain and dark but clearly made for someone with money. Puzzled, Lynx looked past Toil and spotted a large bearded man with a red scarf around his neck and white shirtsleeves showing.

Who's this one? Friend of Toil's I'd guess if he's given her his coat.

Aside from the stranger, Toil was accompanied by a pair of guards and an officer in the same black uniform, burly and balding with a magnificent dark moustache and muttonchops. As they came closer the strange man reached out and touched Toil on the shoulder. He said something to her and gestured off down another corridor, whereupon she nodded and slipped the coat off her shoulders. She returned it to him and gave his hand a squeeze before he set off and disappeared from view.

Despite the events of the day and the threat of flogging that gnawed at the back of Lynx's mind like a rat, for that one moment jealousy eclipsed all. He soon got a grip of himself, but it remained in the darkness of his head even as he forced himself to focus – a mouse as dark and determined as the rat, nibbling away.

He made to start forward again, but Payl hauled him back.

'You'll keep still if you know what's good for you,' warned a second guard, levelling his gun.

Lynx snarled and pointed at the large tattoo on his cheek. 'Do I fucking look like I know what's good for me?'

'Lynx!' Payl said, putting herself between them with one hand resting lightly on his shoulder. 'Reel it in, you hear me?'

He glared at her, for a moment the spark of anger inside him blotting out all rational thought, but at last he remembered to breathe and his wits came back to him.

'That's better,' she said firmly, increasing the pressure on his shoulder. 'Now step back and let's just wait to see what's going on, eh?'

'Fine,' he muttered, looking away.

They had been dumped in a small room with barred windows that wasn't quite a cell, not with chairs and a table, but without any of the finery of the last place they'd been confined to. From the table Teshen looked lazily up at Lynx, clearly less worried than Payl about his comrade getting a beating. Aben was with him but watching them all warily, Toil included.

'Evening, boys and girls,' Toil called with forced cheer as she entered.

The guards moved aside to let her and the officer through, but she stopped short of the chair Aben offered.

'We all having fun in here?'

'Loads,' Teshen said with a yawn. He stretched and got lazily up. 'It's been a madcap few hours of getting threatened,

225

sitting down, standing up, sitting down again. If it wasn't for the witty repartee from our hosts I don't know how I'd have coped with all the fun.'

'Sorry to break up the party then, but there's work to be done.'

'What sort?'

Toil paused for a moment before replying. 'That rather depends on the Monarch,' she admitted, 'and what she wants.'

'*That*,' interjected the Bridge Watch officer, 'rather depends on how the Knights-Charnel react to your little stunt.'

Toil turned to look at the squat, moustachioed man. 'Ah yeah, this ray of furry-faced sunshine's called . . . um. No, I forgot it again.'

The man fumed quietly but was careful not to shout in reply to her needling. 'If you cannot even remember that, I doubt you'll prove much use to the Monarch.'

'How about I crack your skull and you try to remember my name?'

'Have at it,' he said, not backing off an inch. 'The Monarch does not need you wasting her time, best for all concerned if you take a swing at me and my men shoot you.'

'How about you both calm down?' Payl sighed. 'Gods, how much more am I going to have to say that by the end of the day? You, captain, what's your name then?'

'Cothkern,' the man said slowly.

'Ah, I was going for cock-something, so close,' Toil said.

'Enough, Toil!' Payl snapped. 'Captain Cothkern, may I ask what your orders are now?'

'To escort you and your comrades back to your lodgings. Apparently this one thinks she can be of more use out of her dress than in it – broadly the conclusion my men have come to.'

'That surprises me in a city of pederasts,' Toil growled. She turned her back on the man and Lynx saw her take a moment to focus on the matter at hand rather than starting another fight. 'We've got kit to pick up; the Monarch's got officers fetching our weapons to bring them here.'

'Here?'

'We're foreign mercenaries, she doesn't want us wandering the streets armed. I need to prove I can lead an expedition underground before I ask her to arm the Cards. Right now I just need a few people to volunteer for the scouting mission, not the whole Mercenary Deck.'

'I can think of someone who might not volunteer for relic hunting duty,' Lynx said pointedly. 'Other than me that is.'

'Her with the white hair?' Toil nodded. 'Tough shit for her then, I need an expert and she's not a Card so I didn't promise Anatin anything about her.'

'You gave her your word!' he said, dismayed.

'What a scamp I am then.' She caught the look on his face and scowled. 'Oh don't give me the kicked puppy routine, I'll persuade her.'

'And if you can't?'

'I'll just have to succeed, I'll use charm and everything.'

Teshen laughed. 'Been working well for you so far today.'

'I'll take a long run up at it.'

'And if she doesn't agree?' Lynx pressed, ignoring Cothkern as the man cleared his throat to interject.

'Then it's *my* problem,' Toil said, before offering up one of her best winning smiles. 'Do we need to have this argument now, honey, in front of the kids?'

As Teshen chuckled, Lynx tried to react angrily but found his temper melting away in the face of that smile. With a disgusted sound he turned away. 'Fine, let's go.'

Before anyone could take a step towards the door there was a roar in the corridor beyond. 'Where is she?' bellowed a voice, followed by the heavy stamp of feet.

'Oh goody,' Toil muttered just before Envoy Ammen rounded the corner – face purple with anger.

'There you are, you damned idiot woman! What in the name of the blessed gods do you think you're doing?' Ammen stormed up to her until his face was mere inches away from hers and the spittle flew as he continued to yell.

'I'll have you hanged the moment we set foot on Su Dregir soil, you hot-headed little whore! Have you any idea of the damage you've done to relations between our cities?'

Lynx found himself tensing, mostly getting ready to pull Toil back. Ammen was a large and well-built man, but somehow he didn't think Toil was the one at risk there. Her temper was fiery, she'd already proved that well enough today and he'd seen her fight – hard, dirty and without relent.

Of course, I could be wrong there, he thought to himself, *let's not test the theory.*

To Lynx's astonishment, Toil just stood and took the abuse, even ignoring Ammen prodding her in the chest. Out of the corner of his eye Lynx saw Aben edge forward, nothing too provocative but closing the distance between his boss and the man working himself into a lather. Captain Cothkern just smirked, apparently not intending to interrupt a foreign diplomat – especially one who was insulting a woman he didn't like himself.

Behind the Envoy Lynx saw the pale face of Captain Onerist, looking more confused than anything else. Clearly he'd been thrown by the whole thing and wasn't much for thinking under pressure. Instead of getting involved like he should be, the man was just watching and vacillating about what to do. Lynx couldn't help but suspect his superiors had passed a high-born weakling off on to escort duty where he wouldn't command troops under pressure. Given Toil's *other* mission, that seemed likely.

'What do you have to say for yourself, woman?' continued Ammen. 'Speak! Get that idiot tongue moving and explain yourself!'

In response Toil closed her eyes. Ammen paused momentarily, clearly thrown by her action, and she gently reached up and wiped the spit from her face before looking back up at the Envoy.

'Best you take a step back now,' Toil said mildly. 'Before you get hurt.'

'Don't even think about threatening me, you low-born cunt!' Ammen raged. 'I've half a mind to—'

A whip-crack sound echoed around the room and Toil slapped him full across the face. Ammen was driven back as much by shock and insult as the force of her blow, but the rage quickly returned to boiling point on his face. Before he could respond Cothkern stepped forward and the Bridge Watch soldiers levelled their weapons at the pair.

'Enough,' Captain Cothkern said in an irritated voice. 'You two want to kill each other, you do it outside of the Monarch's palace. There'll be no brawling here, anyone tries otherwise and they get a warning shot in the knee. Understand?'

'To lay a finger on me is to assault the Republic of Su Dregir,' Ammen snarled.

'To the seven hells with the Republic of Su Dregir,' Cothkern said with a shrug. 'Never liked any o' your people anyway, even before an official delegation tried to commit murder in my Monarch's hall and insulted her name. Your Archelect isn't renowned for being sentimental, certainly for those who screw up in public, and he's keen on improving trade relations.'

'You make an excellent point,' Toil said with an unnecessarily polite nod of the head, apparently happy to afford the man all possible respect now she was in the presence of someone she disliked more. 'Perhaps you would now escort me and my comrades to our lodgings so I can begin to make amends?'

'No, wait!' interjected Onerist. 'They're official guards of the Envoy – they're coming with us.'

Toil grinned. 'Not so much,' she said. 'You're both free to come with us, but there's an evens chance you'll get nailed to the wall as soon as you open that fat mouth of yours, Envoy. I suggest you scuttle back to your own lodgings and pray to whichever god you favour that I forget your words to me before I see you next.'

'I'll do no such thing – you don't even know what you've done, do you?'

'What would that be then?'

'An army has been sighted from the city walls!' Ammen declared triumphantly. 'Getting ready to march on the city; a war is coming all because of your stupidity.'

Toil ignored the gasps from those around her and adopted a carefully nonchalant voice. 'The rest have arrived already? Well, that moves things up a little. Best we get a wriggle on.'

Lynx could see her knuckles whitening, down by her waist, and recognised the rage she was holding back. Toil wasn't a woman of restraint at the best of times from what he'd seen and certainly a man screaming in her face was normally provocation enough, but she'd lost control once today already. To slap a man like that was a socially acceptable response, but he knew she was itching to open the Envoy from groin to gullet.

'You're confined to your lodgings until I say otherwise – Captain, arrest her and bind her hands!'

Toil shook her head, forced amusement on her face as she gestured to the door. 'Come on, we've got some preparations to make before I can make good on my promises to the Monarch.'

'You'll—'

Captain Cothkern pulled his mage-pistol from a holster and brandished it in the Envoy's face as he made to grab Toil's arm. 'No more of that, sir. I've got my orders and they involve her. Your domestic issues don't interest me, but I'll shoot you if you try and impede me in the execution of my duties.'

Ammen was left speechless by that and the mercenaries simply walked around him, out into the corridor and back the way they'd come. Aben raised an eyebrow to Toil and she gave him a small shake of the head so he kept his place.

Cothkern leaned closer to Lynx as they went. 'Hanese, eh?'

'Yeah.'

'Right. So are all Su Dregir folk so fucking troublesome or is it just these two?'

Lynx cast his mind back to the time he'd spent there. 'Mebbe not *all* the ones I ever met, I guess,' he conceded. 'But then I'm only a Hanese ex-convict turned mercenary, so I always try to find the good in people I meet.'

'Aye, I hear that about you lot.'

'One of our many fine qualities.'

*

Five hundred miles away and fifteen years in the distant past, a group of four people broke through a great stone doorway and had their breath taken away. Even Sotorian Bade had nothing more to say, there at the end of their quest, though words had rarely failed him during the intervening time. It had taken three days and four lives, but finally success lay before them and Toil found the fatigue in her arms and legs fading away. The climb down here had been draining, but now it was all worth it.

Not to Master Oper, she reminded herself. The sight of him tumbling out of sight and into the black was one that replayed over and over in her mind.

The hurrying man hurries straight to his death. Oper had said that the night they camped outside the cave entrance, had made a point of stressing it to all his new recruits.

And he'd tried to keep to it, Toil realised. The man had been moving slowly and cautiously along a high ledge that looked over a vast, deep pit criss-crossed with bridges and stone projections. It wasn't his fault the section of rock had tumbled away underneath him, but Bade's dark mistress had taken him all the same.

I didn't even hear him hit anything. He just kept falling and screaming until he ran out of breath.

Toil shivered. It had been a better death than Fittil had managed. Bitten by some angular monstrosity that scuttled through the dark, he'd managed only two steps before his legs gave way underneath him. His face had gone scarlet, his chest had heaved like a bellows while his throat was as tight and white as a strangling ligature.

The other two had been less dramatic. One had tried to prise open a doorway and been struck on the head in the ensuring rockfall, the other had simply wandered off. They'd only noticed he was gone when they stopped for a rest, about to debate whether to return to their camp or not. The oppressive darkness had claimed him, Toil realised. It crowded her too, pushed and teased and prodded from all sides – testing her defences, seeking a way in. And last night they'd slept inside the ruin itself under weak lamplight, having followed ramps and rappelled rock faces so deep into the ground there was little value in returning for the night.

She tried to imagine how far down they were now. There was no clear way of working it out, no regularity to the levels that great square pit led to, but twenty of the houses she'd grown up in could have been stacked beside them on the descent. *And we still never found Oper's body.*

'Done,' came Kastelian's slightly muffled voice from above. 'Good luck.'

'Aye, we could do with some.'

Bade set off down the stairway, lamp held high and mage-gun prodding at the steps as he went. Chotel followed silently behind, keeping a careful distance, while up ahead he could hear the skitter of Bug's spear-like feet on the smooth stone racing back to whatever awaited them at the bottom.

Chapter 24

As dawn began to reveal the churned horror overlaying Jarrazir's broken wall, a bearded man emerged from a street to survey what remained. The crater dominated everything, looking nothing less than a gods-inflicted punishment on sinful man. Commander Vigilance Deshar scratched his cheek and lifted his head to look beyond the city to the fields outside. Truth be told there was no difference between the two now. Furrowed and cratered mud, darkened smears of ground where blood tinted it, crumpled bodies and tattered cloth.

Makeshift barricades had been raised between the two broken ends of city wall – piecemeal, staggered obstacles that served more as shooting platforms and targets than any great defence. Behind those huddled knots of men and two small catapults. The fighting had waxed and waned throughout the early part of the night, one renewed burst an hour earlier, but now they waited. As Vigilance watched, several companies of grey-coated troops hurried forward to relieve the shocked and battered defenders. Bands of brown-jackets roamed the wasteland like jackals, hauling away the dead or carrying food and water to the stations.

'Next wave won't be much fun,' commented the woman beside Vigilance.

He turned and frowned at his cadaverous lieutenant, a woman of grey hairs and hollow, lined cheeks called Ulith.

'Compared to this playground?'

Her pale cheeks crinkled into a ghastly grin. 'It'll get worse.'

Vigilance nodded. It would, he knew. For all this scene of utter devastation, it would get worse. The ruin was at its worst beyond the line of the walls, where the defenders had desperately fired everything they had at the advancing Charnelers.

'How many dead do you think?'

'Can never tell on a battlefield.' Ulith gave a wave of dismissal. 'They always look worse'n they are,' she added, ''cept for the times they ain't and the ordnance hasn't left enough bits o' the dead to count.'

'But you don't try to exploit *that* unless you throw hundreds into the breach,' Vigilance said, 'and I doubt many came back out of that.'

'That they didn't. When's our turn then?'

Ulith didn't sound daunted by the prospect of defending this patch of mud, but then Vigilance had rarely known her to be surprised by anything, let alone worried.

'I've had no word. Might be they don't want to trust recently hired mercs to their vital defence.'

'More fool them then.' She tugged on the faded red scarf around her neck that Vigilance also wore. 'Our reputation should be enough, but if the Monarch wants her own men to die in our place, I ain't complaining.'

'After the next wave, it'll change,' Vigilance said. 'The Red Scarves will be mustered and armed by then. They'll find a use for our guns quick enough.'

'What if the city don't last that long?'

'Then we have our orders.'

He let the words hang in the air for a little while, lingering like smoke on the breeze before the inevitable explosion from Ulith.

'Shitting gods, from *her*?! I ain't letting your mad bitch sister drag us inta the deepest black. Since when does she give orders to the Red Scarves? She ain't you, she ain't your dad – she's nothing to us.'

Vigilance raised a hand. 'Easy now, she *is* my sister, and she's as much my father's child as I am. Toil needs only speak one word and she'll get command of a regiment.'

'You'd have a damn revolt on your hands!' Ulith spat. 'She'd get her throat cut by the next morning.'

Vigilance laughed, the sound drawing startled looks from the soldiers nearby. 'That would be her problem to deal with,' he said softly, 'but anyone trying to cut Toil's throat might not have everything their own way.'

'You can only hang a killer if you catch one.'

'That wasn't the problem I was anticipating.' He shrugged. 'It's almost worth doing. Toil's got my father's temperament; it might be good to remind the men how nasty the company discipline could be.'

Ulith opened her mouth to reply then thought better of it. 'You mentioned orders?'

Vigilance nodded. The woman might be a cold-hearted, fearless monster of a mercenary and one who'd only soured as the years passed, but she was no fool. Family was family.

'Establish our principal camp in Prophet's Square,' he said. 'Have food and ammunition stored there, encompass the neighbouring buildings and make preparations to seal off the streets if the city falls.'

'Box ourselves in?' Ulith queried. 'Why there?'

'Because my sister has an excellent sense of direction underground and will need to come up for air sometime.'

'There's an entrance to the labyrinth there?'

'There is. Any entrance that sits on ground we need to concede gets an earthshaker dropped down it first. The poetry of that might prove lost on Sotorian Bade, but it'll cheer my sister up.'

'Then what? If the Charnelers push into the city, it's lost whatever defence we mount. They'll burn it down around us if they have to.'

'There'll be no heroic last stand for the Red Scarves,' Vigilance confirmed, 'but if the city falls, best we have Toil with us. She's a girl for surprises and those might come in handy.'

*

'You know? This really isn't what I was expecting.'

Lynx glanced back at Deern, who stood in the middle of a knot of mercenaries. There wasn't much of his expression visible in the weak light of a single lamp, but Deern's bored tone told enough.

'What were you expecting?'

'More labyrinth, less . . .' Deern waved around at his companions, all keeping tight together on the narrow strip of paved ground that had been marked as safe. 'Less shuffling around,' he said at last. 'An' trying not to fall through the floor. Glad I passed on Shadows Deep if it was like this.'

'We're all glad you passed on Shadows Deep,' Sitain muttered from Lynx's side. 'The maspid packs were great fun compared to your moaning.'

'Ah, I've barely got started on moaning,' Deern said, 'it's all been helpful observations up till now.'

'In that case,' broke in one of the Monarch's agents, Suth, 'when you get really going on it, I'm going to shoot you in the face.'

To reaffirm her point the woman flicked open her long coat to reveal holstered mage-guns strapped to each thigh and a pair at her belly. Lynx guessed there were one or two on her lower back, too, looking at the line of her coat. Mage-cartridges could explode if they were within a hand-span of one being fired so all mage-guns were one-shot weapons.

'Deern,' called Toil from the front. 'If you want to lead the way, you're welcome to it. Until then, shut up and remember rule one.'

She stood on the wide path they'd found running along the centre of the great upper chamber. In the dark she could only see that it ran in both directions and an identifying marker stood above the stone doorway they'd entered through.

Crouching, she steadied herself and again put her head and lamp beneath the line of illusion. It was disconcerting to watch, her face and arm just disappearing from view, but this time there came an exclamation of success and she soon popped back up again.

'Found it,' Toil declared as Lastani edged forward, her excitement immediately obvious despite the darkness.

'Are you sure?'

Toil ignored her and moved a bit further along the path before prodding down with her staff. It sank a little way into the illusion then stopped with a crisp clack. Toil probed around the edge for a while, testing out the size of hidden stone, then pulled a pot from her pocket and dabbed her finger in. Lynx had seen the stuff before, back in Shadows Deep. Toil had used it to make her finger glow in the Duegar lamp's light – mimicking the luminescent fingers of the Wisps as she spoke to them in their sign language.

Now Toil used the concoction to mark the limits of the stone, thin smears two yards apart that glowed bluish-white in her lamp's black light. With the safe ground marked, Toil stepped down on to the hidden step and probed again each side, quickly finding another lower down. She made swift progress now she knew what she was looking for and before long ducked down so that only the pack on her back was visible as she surveyed the path ahead.

Aben gestured for Sitain to go after Toil. The young woman stared as though he'd suggested she jump off a cliff, but she said nothing and eventually followed, Lynx close on her heel. The steps were long and shallow, each a couple of yards square, but as Lynx went and the white light of the oil lamps was left behind, he felt a familiar lurch of fear in his belly.

Toil's black lamp illuminated little to his eyes. He knew Sitain would be perfectly happy, being a night-mage, but to Lynx the darkness seemed to swallow him up – all the worse for knowing there was a great yawning drop just a few feet away.

'What can you see?' hissed Toil, barely visible two steps further down.

'Sod all,' Lynx growled. 'Mebbe this wasn't such a good idea.'

'I think she meant me,' Sitain said.

'Yeah, I know, but talking's good.'

Lynx fought the urge to flee and instead pressed his shoulders against the stone wall behind him. There was some sort of handhold there, a long groove in the bare rock face, and he grabbed it gladly, but still the fear trembled in his belly.

'Keep talking if you need to,' Toil said, 'just so long as Sitain does too.'

Lynx couldn't tell if that was kindness or pragmatism, but chose not to ask, knowing how fractious he was in the dark. Any chance to pick a fight and he'd grab it down here, but there was also a voice at the back of his head reminding him that they didn't have time for that. He took a long deep breath instead and focused on what Sitain was saying.

'Sorry to disappoint, but I don't see a whole lot. The steps lead a long way down. The path we were on is the top of a bloody big bridge-type of thing, supported by some sort of web of stone. They all extend further than I can see. In the dark there's just a faint suggestion of lines further away but nothing I can make out.

'On the other side of the upper chamber there's a . . . a column maybe? The far wall's curved anyway, it's huge but looks like it's not just the far side of a great hall. Gods in pieces! If that's a column then . . .'

'Then we're in far bigger chamber than we thought,' Toil finished.

'Deep too,' Lynx added for no real reason other than to torture himself. 'Really bloody deep.'

'Don't worry; it'll be far smaller than the great rift in Shadows Deep.'

'Given what you bloody stirred up from the bottom of that rift,' Lynx said slowly, 'that's not as comforting as you might think.'

'I doubt there's anything alive down here,' Toil replied. 'With the canal and Parthain, if this wasn't sealed off from the outside, it'd be full of water by now.'

'Or we just can't see the water – or when we open up whatever this leads to, we release the pressure and a million tons of blackness rises up to drown us!'

'Lynx, take a breath,' Toil advised. 'The Duegar made things to last and this place is dry – you can taste it on the air. Now come on.'

Before she could turn to continue down the steps a sound rang out across the entire upper chamber. Distant and echoing, it seemed to roll forward like thunder and for a moment of pure mind-numbing panic, Lynx thought he'd been right after all. In his mind's eye he pictured a tidal wave of water sweeping over the path, dragging all of them in its wake down into the great depths far beneath.

'Oh gods,' Lynx moaned, sinking down to the floor, back pressed against the stone behind and arms tight around his body.

His heart started to hammer away in his chest, blood roaring in his ears like the crash of waves on rock. Bursts of light started to flutter before his eyes as the sound built and washed past them, becoming the resonant echoes of an impossibly large bell's toll. He felt it in his bones, shuddering through his marrow as the bitter taste of bile filled his throat. His head became a jagged mess of thorns snagging his thoughts and making every breath exquisitely painful.

'Sitain, check on the others,' he heard distantly as rough hands took hold of him and the sound began to fade.

Lynx closed his eyes and tried to breathe properly. A familiar cord of panic was pulled tight around his chest and he could only manage shallow pants, but the effort itself gave him a focus.

'Lynx,' Toil said as smooth fingers slipped over his cheeks. 'Can you hear me?'

He made a garbled sound, still with his eyes closed.

'Lynx, we're safe,' Toil continued gently.

Lynx didn't answer her. The words made it as far as his ears, but 'safe' meant nothing to him right now. There was only the stink of sweat and stone dust, mud and blood. The clink of chains, the groan of wood and the clash of tools on rock. He pressed himself harder against the smoothed stone wall behind him, finding comfort in the fact it was nothing like a chipped-out tunnel.

Toil kept quiet for a while, cradling his face but saying nothing more as he fought the panic inside him. Her presence was a help all the same, as much of an anchor as the rock behind him. After a short time he heard a cough from somewhere nearby and light footsteps. He opened his eyes and squinted through the dark as someone crouched and whispered close to Lynx's face.

'Ah, Toil?' Kas said, glancing at Lynx before returning to business. 'Bit of a problem back here. The shitting door's just closed up behind us, we're shut in! What in the name of all that's shattered do we do now?'

'Oh hells, shut? Well, get those bloody mages working – get it open again!'

'They already tried, it ain't shifting.'

'We're shut in?' Lynx wheezed, dark humour and increasing fear clashing inside him. 'Oh screaming black hells.'

'Lynx, you just breathe, focus on that. This is no different to Shadows Deep, not really.'

'Not different? We're fucking locked in!'

'In a magical labyrinth with multiple entrances that some have suggested is a form of contest ground. That sound we heard. That wasn't something breaking – doubt it was a trap either. More likely it's a signal of some sort – maybe that the contest's begun. It wasn't triggered by us or Bade getting into the upper chamber but it must have been something. My money would be on Bade having just opened the labyrinth proper, he'll have needed magic to activate the door most likely and it sets off some sort of magical locking mechanism. But the Duegar wouldn't have built this to imprison their own, they didn't think that way. Locking everyone inside until someone survives to crack the secret of the place, however, that's more than just possible. So we're not in a tomb, it's just another big space underground we need to navigate, nothing like a mine. No shackles, no guards.'

'Just fucking relic hunters looking to kill us,' Lynx muttered, 'and some sort o' labyrinth full of all sorts of nasty surprises.' He scowled at her. 'Explain how this is better?'

'No maspids,' Toil said firmly, 'no gigantic magic-hungry monsters chasing us, no walking for days without sunlight. You can handle this, just like you did last time.'

'Barely managed it last time.'

'But you kept your grip all the same and that's what counts.'

Lynx raised his trembling hand. 'Not much grip left.'

Toil pulled his mage-gun from the sheath on his back and slapped it hard into his hand, closing his fingers around the forestock. She let go and leaned back. 'Grip looks good enough to me – now on your damn feet, soldier.'

Shakily, Lynx obeyed and allowed himself to be ushered back up the steps to where the rest of their party were waiting.

'Lastani, should we be worried?'

The young mage shook her head. 'It looks like our test of faith has begun,' she confirmed with a wan smile, failing to hide her anxiety. 'Mistress Ishienne speculated something like this.'

'Right,' Toil agreed. 'So the labyrinth is sealed until someone comes out the other side. Not the best news, what with most of our soldiers still outside, but this isn't a children's party and we're not helpless or clueless.'

'But we could be stuck down here for ever?' Deern blurted out.

Toil gave him a nasty grin. 'If you think that's the most dangerous thing about this place, you've not done this before.'

'No one's done this before,' he pointed out. 'Ain't that the point? No one in the whole o' bloody human history has opened it before this bint came along.'

'Who is he again?' Lastani asked, cocking her head at Toil.

'The company jester,' she explained. 'Either that or a malingering curse from the gods upon the rest, I'm not really sure which. I assume that they find him amusing in some way – either that or they like being reminded there are worse bastards than them alive today.'

'Oh you're funny fer a red-headed—' again Deern was cut off mid-sentence, but this time it was Teshen clouting him around the head.

'Enough, Deern,' the man growled. 'You can fall off this walkway pretty easily you know, ain't no Reft here to stop me. My head's still buzzin', doubt I could even feel bad about it if I tried.'

'If you're all finished now,' Kas snapped. 'Mebbe we can get back to work?'

Toil nodded. 'Listen to the woman,' she advised them all. 'Now – me and mine are going down this stairway to check

337

out what's below. You brave fighting types stay up here until I find us a way into the labyrinth itself – just in case that sound has told our friend Bade he's got company down here. Last thing we need is some shite doubling back and firing burners down these steps after us.'

When there was no dissent, Toil jabbed a thumb down the hidden steps. 'Right then, Paranil, Barra, Aben – come on. Lastani, you too.'

'And me?' asked Elei, Lastani's designated handler.

'Yeah, and you. You've got the Monarch's light in your pack there, right? Good. The rest of you, keep still and cover those oil lamps so Sitain's eyes give you an advantage. Once we find the bottom I'll send Barra back up.'

She gave them all a brief, incongruous grin and started down the stairs. 'Cheer up the lot of you, this is the fun bit!'

Chapter 25

'And what in the hairy holiest o' holes was that noise?'

No one replied. Bade watched the varying emotions play out on his comrades' faces. Chotel was looking up, as though expecting the great rumble to herald the roof falling, while Ulestim watched the stairs, one hand on his pistol. Torril had shrunk nervously back against the great door's jamb while, off to one side, Bug stood quivering with alertness – the runt maspid's eyeless head angled up as well.

The mages, Spade and Fork, both quailed, but they'd been pissing themselves over Bug for hours now so that was little change, while Sebaim, Bade's gnarled tracker, was as unruffled as ever.

'Thoughts, Ulestim?' Bade asked, hoping the most learned man in the group might have an idea.

'Very few, I'm afraid,' the bespectacled man said in a distracted tone.

'Even a few will do, old Sebaim here's shitting himself,' Bade joked, 'so give it a try.'

'Not ordnance, I'd say,' Ulestim said, to nods from several others, 'and nothing we did made any such sound.'

'Rock falls don't sound like that either,' Bade added. 'One single sound it was, echoing but clear and crisp for all o' that.'

'Indeed, so it was the labyrinth itself perhaps, something triggered by you touching the door.'

Bade turned to the stone door. It was . . . Well, for a relic hunter it was a thing of beauty, but right now it was just in his way. Anywhere else and he'd have put an earther through it by now, but this wasn't your usual city-ruin.

'Or we got company down here,' Bade said slowly, 'and the fun and games have started.'

They had descended no more than fifty yards before finding themselves on a half-moon platform set against a large stone block, two banks of Duegar script running all around it, while set into the centre was the doorway. The recessed arch was surrounded by more script, carved with an emphasis on beauty by Bade's estimation, even by the elegant standards of the Duegar language. The mages and Ulestim agreed that they were simply invocations of blessings and prayers that followed the familiar form. It was the black metal door itself that bore the secrets of its entry.

On the door were three stone circles set into the metal and marked with Duegar numbers, eight on each. In the very centre was a smaller disc, composed of silvery metal that shone faintly in the light and had the glyph for 'gift' inscribed on it.

'Sebaim,' Bade said, realising he had to make a decision. 'Back up the steps while we work on opening this, fetch down the rest in orderly fashion. If we're not alone down here I don't want to find a regiment of Bridge Watch stumbling across them so get 'em out of sight.'

The tracker gave a small nod and padded back up the steps as stealthily as a cat. He was a compact, ageless man who'd looked weather-beaten and greying when Bade had first met him, twenty years earlier. Even now Sebaim could run all day and spot a threat on the horizon before anyone thirty years his junior. He had no vices, expensive tastes or family to spend his money on. Bade had a strong suspicion that when he stopped bringing Sebaim to rare sights like this labyrinth, the man would just be gone one morning.

'Boss?' Chotel said, nudging Bade's elbow.

He nodded hurriedly, realising he'd been staring up after Sebaim as the man slipped away. 'Got an idea?' Bade said.

'Spade does.'

'Out with it then, we ain't got all day.'

'The prayers,' said the fire mage hesitantly, 'they contain numbers.'

'Eh?' Bade quickly scanned the writing around the door. His Duegar wasn't as good as the others, he knew, but still it didn't take him long to identify the words that could correspond to the Duegar numerals on the stone circles. 'Seems a bit obvious, don't it?'

'It's only the front door,' Torril remarked. 'Easy to get in, harder to get out?'

'Aye, true. Use numbers to keep the wildlife out, but if Hopper's got a nasty surprise for us, he'd probably want us trapped in a box first.'

'It don't sound so reassuring when you say it like that,' Chotel said with a snort.

'I'll hug you later, princess.' Bade gestured to the steps. 'Let's not take any chances, though, the rest of you back up on to the stair in case there is some tricksiness.'

'And you?'

He grinned. 'We're about to open the fucking Labyrinth of Jarrazir itself, I ain't hanging back from this! You all feel free to exercise caution, I'll edit it out o' the history books, don't you worry.'

With it put like that, none of the others made for the steps. From their faces, his enthusiasm was infectious – the pay was good, but Bade knew none of them did this job just for the money. Once the mage had pointed out the numbers, Bade quickly turned the stone circles until the correct numerals were at a marked point. The stone moved

341

easily despite its age and in no time he rested a hand on the mage's shoulder.

'Off you go then, Spade – gift.'

'Magic?'

Bade nodded. 'Bigger than the doors before I'd guess, a burst to kick-start ancient mechanisms. They'll draw in more themselves after that, but they need to be woken up first and you'd have noticed if that was going already.'

The nervous mage ducked his head in acknowledgement and placed his palm over the shining disc in the centre of the door. A brief flicker of orange flame washed over his fingers then was sucked down into the metal. The disc began to glow faintly with inner light and Spade grunted, his arm twitching as the disc began to draw hungrily. He left it a little longer then broke the flow of magic, jerking his arm away and stepping back.

He rubbed his fingers and frowned at the disc as it continued to glow for a few moments longer. Eventually the light dimmed and Bade was about to ask what had gone wrong when the disc was suddenly edged in crisp white light.

'It's drawing magic like you said,' Spade commented, the nervousness momentarily falling away from his face as he looked up in wonder.

'What's that?' Bade said. He cocked his ear to the door then looked around. 'Anyone else hear that, some sort of humming sound?'

'It's the mechanism,' the mage replied. 'Sucking in the latent energy in the air around it.'

'We in danger?'

'No, it's gentle. There's a slight pull on my own magic, but nothing that will leave me drained. It's simply gathering whatever is in the ground here, it'll take a while to build any great reserve.'

'In the meantime, how do—' Bade cut off as the door abruptly slid open to reveal a small room just a few yards across.

Inside there was another stairway, this one rather more elegant than the plain steps they'd descended thus far. It was all still mage-carved stone, but now the steps were delicately scalloped, the rail a twisting braid supported by tree-shaped banisters.

Bade took a cautious step inside. Nothing surged up out of the darkness to kill him so he clapped the mage on the shoulder.

'Good work, Spade. Ready for the real fun?'

Bade didn't wait for a reply. With his Duegar lamp held high, he slowly advanced inside and on to the first step. Still nothing bad happened, but the light of the lamp illuminated the stairway ahead – a long, regular spiral walkway with a grooved floor for grip. He'd seen enough of those before to walk a little faster. It was typical Duegar construction, bar the fact the stonework was far more carefully done and there was a clear swirling pattern to the mineral within the rock that caught the lamp's strange light.

Each side of the slope bore the blue glowing swirl while the path was speckled with the mineral. The mage drifted along behind Bade and gaped at the slope. The man might not have been a relic hunter, but he was highly educated within the field of magic if nothing else and the Duegar were a fundamental subject there.

The spiral sloping tunnel continued through a half-dozen turns then opened out abruptly on to a large black space. Bade lingered at the bottom, wary of stepping straight out before he'd got some sense of the room he was in. Fortunately, the usual Duegar illumination continued beyond the slope; a haze of faint, dark blue seams in the rock that looked more natural and haphazard. It offered enough for an experienced relic hunter to make out where he was, however. With the others close behind, Bade checked around as far as he could lean out before committing a foot.

There was little to see, just a wide and very high room that had to be the interior of one of those cubes they'd seen earlier. It was entirely featureless other than two doorways, one in the right-hand wall and one on the left-hand, similar to the one they'd entered by. They were made of the same metal, wider and taller than normal doors with a half-circle arch at the top. Neither bore the stone circles, but each had the shining centre plate with the glyph for 'gift' inscribed. The only difference between these two were the inscribed symbols above each – more numerals.

He realised he couldn't linger so, seeing nothing at all on the smooth walls, ceiling and floor, Bade walked out into the room with his heart hammering. Still no fiery death engulfed him so he started to breathe once more and moved around the sloped tunnel to see what else there was.

'Two doors?' Chotel remarked as he followed Bade out of the tunnel. Behind him came Bug, the maspid skittering down and out past him with her usual deceptive grace. The first time they'd tempted Bug out of the catacombs she lived in had been a dark night and clearly Bug had been wary and unsure. The feel of turf under her spear-blade limbs was not something Bug enjoyed, but still she'd been fast enough to chase down a deer. Underground, Bade guessed she was faster still.

'Aye – no, wait, there's another,' Bade replied as he skirted around behind the slanted shaft of the tunnel they'd entered by. The room was a cube just as they'd guessed, containing only the doors and the shaft running diagonally from the centre of the floor to the top of the rear wall. Behind that featureless projection was another block of stone with a third doorway set into it.

'And numbers,' Torril pointed out, 'hey, look, above where we came in, too.'

Bade did just that and, as Torril described, there was the Dueger numeral for 1 carved into the stone above where they'd come out of the tunnel.

'The others?' Ulestim said. 'Thirty-three and seventeen. How about round the back?'

'Twenty-five,' Bade said. 'They mean anything to you?'

'Not much,' he said as he went to see for himself. 'Door looks the same. We should light a proper lamp and inspect the room before we do anything else.'

'Aye, Spade and Fork – you keep away from the doors and don't do any magic until the rest have caught us up, understand? If the "gift" is a trigger for the doorway, it might shut the other one behind us.'

Chotel pulled an oil lamp from his pack and lit it with a sulphurous match rather than risking any further spark of magic. With the wick turned up it cast an acceptable light around the cube after the hours they'd spent in near darkness, but it only revealed the room was indeed plain other than the doors.

'Douse the lamp,' Ulestim said after a while, 'there's nothing to see and we don't want to turn the air bad.'

'Don't think that's a problem,' Bade replied as Chotel turned the wick down. 'The air's musty, but we're breathing fine. Must not be as sealed as it looks, otherwise the air'd be bad already in this box.'

A voice called cautiously down the slope and Torril went to answer it, cheerily bellowing up Kastelian's name to give the soldiers a fright. There was a slight clatter that sounded like someone dropping their gun but nothing else so, other than giving Torril a baleful look, Bade just waited for the soldiers. Bug attempted to clamber up one sheer stone wall, maspids being able to exploit the most unlikely of footholds, but was defeated and resorted to stalking the unoccupied area to the rear of the room.

'Should we be in a closed box with Bug?' Chotel asked softly as Kastelian's dragoons clattered into the room.

Bade turned to watch the maspid. Clearly she wasn't entirely happy, but was used to the company of humans to some degree at least. He hadn't paced out the room, but it was a good forty yards in each direction. Not vast but, at the same time, not small enough to force them all together. Even with a fat tunnel shaft in the centre, there was plenty of space.

'We'll manage,' Bade decided. 'I lead her back up, she's running free in the upper chamber but there's no certainty she gets back out again.'

Chotel lowered his voice further, not wanting the dragoons to hear him. 'Still, she could go for one of us. Strange smells, startled by traps . . . she ain't a dog you can put on a leash.'

'Yeah, but she ain't going for either of us first, if she does snap,' Bade pointed out. 'Unlikely any o' the crew. If we need to put her down, we do it. My biggest worry will be some grunt firing wildly, but one less soldier ain't going to lose me sleep.'

Chotel accepted Bade's point and stepped back, not wanting to draw any more attention to the matter.

'So which door then?' he said in a normal voice.

'Dunno. Ulestim, what do you reckon?'

'If there's a key, I can't see it,' the tall man declared, looking frustrated. 'There's no way of knowing what those numbers meant to the Duegar.'

'So we pick one at random? Sounds safe.'

Ulestim shrugged. 'You're the one who saw this place from the outside, got a preferred direction?'

Bade paused, hands out in front of him as he looked at the spiral slope and tried to work out how he'd been positioned. *We turned a few times. The steps ran that way, straight down to the platform which was at an angle. The labyrinth was positioned there, we came to it from there.*

He opened his eyes again. 'We're about halfway to the central column I'd guess, more towards the middle of the nearer side. But do we want to go in or straight down?'

'Down's no good,' Torril piped up, joining them. 'All the good stuff is at the bottom in Duegar cities, remember?'

'Surely going down's a good thing then?' Ulestim said.

'Aye, but a bit fucking obvious.'

'First step in a labyrinth isn't likely to be in the right direction,' Bade agreed. 'A double bluff works in the favour of idiots and anyone with the brains to construct all this probably wasn't on the side o' the stupid.'

'Thirty-three or seventeen then?'

Bade sighed. 'Shattered gods and little fishes, guesswork'll be the death of us.'

'Thirty-three,' Torril said. 'This is a cube, innit?'

None of the others spoke for a while as they exchanged looks, taking long enough that Torril started to look worried that he'd said something particularly stupid.

'I can see it,' Bade said eventually. 'Always thought Hopper had a sense of humour, could be it's one o' his little jokes even. Anyone got any other ideas?'

When no one spoke up Torril looked relieved and they all turned towards the doorway on the left-hand wall.

'Thirty-three it is. Fork – you're up this time.'

The woman timidly approached the door before pausing to glance back at them. 'Are you sure?'

''Course we are,' Bade snapped loudly, 'we're the fucking experts so stop arguing and open the bastard door!'

She reached out and placed her palm on the centre plate, closing her eyes and wincing as she let her magic surge out.

Chapter 26

Everyone held their breath. There was a moment of complete silence then the door swung open on its own and they all flinched. There was only dark in the chamber beyond, black enough that Toil could see nothing at all. For a horrible moment she imagined herself stepping through on to nothing and falling silently into the dark. Aside from Lastani and Sitain the rest hung well back, clustered around the mouth of the tunnel they'd walked down into this cube-shaped tomb. In the light of the Monarch's Duegar lamp, she could see that most were watching her with a strange grimace on their faces, clearly expecting something terrible to happen very soon.

Toil shook her head and beckoned Sitain forward.

'You're up, girly.'

Lastani, who had opened the door with a burst of magic, edged aside for Sitain who peered forward into the next chamber of the labyrinth. The night mage had described what she could see of the labyrinth below as they descended the stair, providing plenty of incentive for Toil and Lastani to get the above doors open in a matter of minutes. A massive cube-shaped room on the other side, empty but for three doorways, had been something of a disappointment, but Toil had taken it as a sign they really were in the labyrinth now and the game had properly begun.

'Well?' Toil demanded.

'It's dark,' Sitain replied after a few moments. 'Dark and empty.'

'Is that good?' someone behind asked. Lynx.

Toil turned to look at Lastani, who made a non-committal face. Toil shrugged. 'Of course it's good news, we're not dead, are we?'

'You ain't stepped through the door yet,' Lynx pointed out. 'I'm just saying.'

'Yeah, well, thought I gave you all instructions about saying too much.'

Toil hung the metal handle of her Duegar lamp from a notch on the end of her staff and held it out over the chamber threshold.

'It's empty,' Sitain confirmed. 'Just doorways— No, wait. There's something on the floor. A circle I think.'

Toil checked the floor was solid then took a breath and stepped through into the room. With her lamp held high she looked all around, pausing when she spotted something above the doorway she'd just entered through. 'There's another number here, a two,' she pointed out. 'That follows on nicely from the "one" above the tunnel we came out of. Mebbe we did choose the right door after all.'

'And the others?' Lastani followed her through, advancing a few steps further into the room.

There was one doorway on the far wall, a second on the right-hand wall and a trapdoor in the floor, identical to the other doors, bar its orientation, right down to the shining disc inscribed with a Duegar symbol. Just before the trapdoor there was indeed a circle – or rather, a ring of Duegar glyphs almost ten yards across. They were inscribed on small squares of stone raised up on the inner edge so each glyph was angled slightly outward.

'What is it? A test?'

'Paranil?' Toil called back, the man looking rather more assured in a long plain coat and tunic than he ever had in his Lighthouse Guard uniform. 'Thoughts?'

Paranil joined them ahead of the rest of the group. 'Fire,' he said.

'What? Where?' Sitain demanded, whirling in alarm.

'Written on the floor.'

'Ah. Oh.' Though there wasn't much light to see, by the set of her shoulders Toil was pretty certain Sitain was blushing.

'Don't worry, Sitain,' she said. 'Any mistake that doesn't kill you doesn't count and there're huge holes in every Duegar expert's knowledge.'

She approached the ring but stopped well short and held a hand out to make it clear she wanted the others to keep clear.

'What do you think, boss?' Aben asked, joining her.

Toil glanced back. 'Are we all through?'

He did a quick head count. 'Aye.'

'I think we might have made a mistake picking that door after all.'

'Shit, really? How do you know?'

'Looks like a firetrap to me, one they're not even trying to hide.'

'So mebbe it's another test?'

'Let's hope so.'

'You want to go back?'

'You can't!' Lastani broke in. 'I mean, you really shouldn't.'

'I know, I know.'

Aben blinked at her. 'Well I don't, why not?'

''Cos it's a test,' Lynx said from behind them. 'You make your choices and you take the consequences.'

Toil managed a small laugh at that and looked back at him. 'The labyrinth of your life, eh?'

He scowled at her. 'Oh, funny.'

350

'He's right,' Lastani insisted. 'It is a test – the riddle of the Fountain made that clear. The labyrinth is a test for the worthy. Deciding to backtrack could prove just as dangerous as a wrong choice.'

'That's comforting,' Aben said. 'Think I prefer Lynx's way of looking at it.'

'Either way, we press on.'

Toil held her lamp high and took a lap around the perimeter, looking for anything of note on the smooth, plain stone walls. Eventually she came back to where the rest were waiting.

'Three exits, just like that first room.' She pointed to the door directly opposite where they'd entered. 'Twenty-two above that one, sixteen on the right-hand wall.'

'And thirty-nine on the floor,' Lastani finished, skirting the circle as she returned from looking.

The chamber was the same proportions as the one they had just left – forty yards in each direction. Toil realised it didn't echo as much as she would have expected. With stone on all sides and nothing to absorb the sound, to her ears it didn't sound quite right, as though the Duegar had done something to the rock to dull the sound.

Or maybe to stop you hearing the screams from your competitors, a treacherous voice at the back of her head added.

'None of those mean anything special to me,' Toil said. 'Right now I want to work out if we can keep that door open as we choose.'

'It's a risk,' Lastani said.

'I know,' she admitted. 'But how much of one? You're our expert on the riddle. Do you think this puzzle-box is one that'll allow us to learn its rules or expect us to know them from the start?'

'I, ah, I don't know. You mean some sort of cultural context?'

'I guess so. Who was this puzzle designed for? Other Duegar, right? I've never seen or heard of anything like the labyrinth before. We don't have much to compare it to, but it could be they all knew what they were getting into before they opened it up. Maybe some sort of priesthood on the surface to warn them they'll die if they make a mistake, die if they try to open one door without shutting the first or something.'

Toil pinched the bridge of her nose, feeling her thoughts turning full circle upon themselves and never nearing any part that looked like a conclusion.

'What sort o' dumbshit don't want the option?' Deern broke in. 'That glyph says fire, woman. If this whole box fills up with fire, we need a way out.'

'You really think leaving yourself a way out will help if this place wants to kill you?' Lynx replied scornfully. 'You think it'll just let you have another try?'

Deern sneered. 'Poor convict Lynx. No matter how far you run or how much you eat, you'll always be that broken little prisoner, eh?'

Lynx made to storm forward, but Teshen grabbed him. 'Hey, stow it! You too, Deern!'

'I ain't startin' nothin',' Deern said, pistol drawn and levelled. 'But if fat-boy does, I'll finish it.'

'And I'll finish you,' Teshen snapped. 'Either o' you. One of you pulls a weapon without cause again while I'm stuck inside a stone box with you, I'll kill you before you even fucking see me coming.'

'Sure, sure,' Deern said, a small smile on his lips. With a deliberate movement he turned his mage-pistol aside and made the hammer safe. 'Mebbe you can keep hefty o' Tempest on a leash since Toil clearly won't.'

'Merciful gods,' Lastani gasped. 'I'm stuck in here with madmen. You're going to get us all killed!'

'No they're not,' Toil said firmly. She took a few steps forward and laid a hand on Lynx's shoulder as Teshen released him.

'Lynx, keep it together. I know you're scratchy in the dark, but we can't keep having this conversation. You're right, though. We're not going back and there's no point not playing the game sensibly. Either the first door needs to be shut or it doesn't matter – either way, leaving it open does us no good.'

Lynx grunted and reluctantly unpeeled his fingers from around his sword hilt. He went to shut the door, giving Deern the evil eye as he passed. The door itself took little effort to shut and with a soft grind of stone, it closed behind them.

'There's a panel on the back of this door too,' he reported, pointing at the shining disc with the glyph 'gift' inscribed.

'Maybe there is some going back after all,' Toil said, looking at Lastani. 'But we're not for the moment, so let's move on. Which door do you fancy?'

'What about the circle?' Sitain pointed out. 'We can't just ignore that, can we?'

'Another offering?'

From the back of the group, Atieno cleared his throat. The ageing mage stepped stiffly forward, a glass ball tinted faintly orange between finger and thumb. 'Perhaps another gift?' he suggested.

'Seems a bit big for that,' Toil pointed out. 'How many have you got?'

'Of fire? Two.'

'Go on then, might as well give it a try.'

They all stepped well back before Atieno tossed the glass ball into the centre of the ring. It broke as it landed and a gout of flame washed over the stone floor. It spread like a pail of spilled water before winking out again – starved of fuel once the modest spark of magic had been consumed. The glass balls were far less powerful than burners, having been created without a God Fragment to focus the magic, but the fire extended far enough for Toil to see something important.

'It stopped at the glyphs,' she exclaimed, pointing. 'Look, the flame went up to the edge but never crossed it.'

'How does that help us?' Lynx said.

'It's more information than we had before. Now we just need to work out what it means.'

She walked around the circle once more, checking all the glyphs were the same. That done, Toil reached out with one end of her staff and pushed it through the boundary. She felt no resistance and nothing happened, but a sixth sense made her set it down on the floor rather than pull it out again.

'Two choices,' she announced. 'We pick a door and try it. Or we all get in the circle and then one of us leaves it to pick a door.'

'Why?'

'Magic didn't get past the circle,' she explained, 'but pushing something in was no effort, so it's not a physical barrier. I think it's like a test of faith – you have to step inside before you go any further.'

'And then what happens? You step out and get burned, or only when you try a door?'

'Doesn't a little mystery add spice to your life, Lynx?'

'Reckon I've got enough to be going on with,' he replied grumpily.

Teshen stepped forward, clearly having reminded himself that he was the senior Card there alongside Safir, Toil's unusual appointment notwithstanding.

'Vote on it then, mages and relic hunters. What's your best bet?'

'Vote?' Toil said. 'I don't think so.'

'Vote,' Teshen said firmly. 'Let's see how everyone who matters thinks before we talk about whether this is a democracy.'

To add weight to his words, Safir took a small pace forward to stand beside Teshen. The easterner said nothing, but he didn't need to. Toil didn't bother trying to glare them down. She'd browbeaten lords and hard-bitten veterans in her time, but she knew Teshen was a stone-cold killer, trained and tempered in the Mage Islands if her guess was correct. It was rare she came up against someone like that and she wasn't going to risk wasting her breath or life starting a confrontation.

'You heard the Knight of Tempest,' she said, inclining her head very slightly to the man. 'Cast your votes. After that we can have a lively discussion about democracy in Anatin's Mercenary Deck.'

She heard Kas give a snort, but ignored her as she looked to the mages for comment.

'Circle,' Atieno said first. 'It's there for a reason.'

'One of us tries the door,' Sitain countered. 'Either it works or it doesn't. A mage is harder to kill with magic anyway, you've all seen that, and we don't know the circle isn't a trap either.'

'I would prefer to test every option,' Lastani said cautiously. 'The gift to enter the room was modest; to channel it into a weapon and kill the mage it came from is unlikely.'

'Paranil?' Toil asked. 'Aben, Barra?'

'I agree with Atieno,' Paranil said with a nervous cough. 'Perhaps it's a ruse, perhaps it's a lure, but there is *nothing* else in this room. I would expect some sort of indication if the circle was anything other than integral.'

'I'm with you, boss,' Aben added loyally, Barra just grunting in agreement.

'I'm for the circle,' Toil confirmed. 'Anyone – anyone other than Deern – got an opinion I might be interested in?'

No one spoke up.

'How about you, Teshen?'

The burly man grinned and swept back a lock of hair that had escaped his topknot. 'Not me, Princess, you're in command here.'

'Oh, you remembered that, eh?' she said and patted the badge sewn on to her jacket. 'Thought I'd lost this for a while there.'

'So which door?'

'Buggered if I know.'

*

General Derjain Faril of the Knights-Charnel of the Long Dusk stood on the top deck of her command barge and surveyed the camp around her with one lip caught under her front teeth. It was an old habit dating back to her childhood, one she hated but somehow could not shake when she was lost in thought.

'Casualties?'

'Ah, unclear at present, general. Limited, I'm led to believe.'

'Because they were after the supplies?'

'Yes, sir.'

Faril was quiet a long moment. The east flank of her camp still burned, and she could see that the supplies were gone from there. The pickets had been taken unawares. Sloppy, that. Someone would be punished, but right now she had more important things to deal with.

'How many horsemen?'

The captain hesitated, standing a little more stiffly to attention as though regulation order would improve matters. 'Reports are unclear also,' he said, 'or rather, wildly mixed. I would expect it to be between four and five hundred cavalry given what the survivors claimed.'

'Five hundred cavalry,' she repeated slowly. 'Under Crown-Prince Tylom's banner? I thought the man was supposed to be a weakling whose wife ruled him? No soldier.'

'That was the intelligence we received.'

'And yet he leads slash and burn raids on our lines like an experienced campaigner. Raids we cannot easily counter given our lack of horse.'

'Yes, sir.'

They had only just broken the city line an hour or so before. All had been going to plan; a precise, efficient drive into the city. The breach had been consolidated, the great artillery unable to strike targets on the corridor her regiments had marched down. The fight at the crater had been surprisingly fierce it was true, mostly for the determination of the city's response.

But her superior troops and numbers had taken their toll and the Jarraziran soldiers were in full retreat – fighting street to street but only buying time. They had withdrawn all the way to the palace, Faril had been informed, and she knew they wouldn't stop there. The only question had been how long they could delay, how slow they could make the fight. How much blood they were willing to shed.

How much are they willing to bear? she thought. *They must know our resolve; they must know we will endure horrors in the service of our god. Will they see the whole city burn to resist, or salvage what they can?*

'Bring the camp closer to the walls; make it harder for them to raid. Dig fixed positions there, there and there – force him into the heavy ground if he wants to attack further. I will write orders for the regiment colonels, have runners ready.'

'Yes, sir.'

'Dismissed.'

Left alone she turned to the fires of the city, a more satisfactory sight in the dull afternoon light. Somewhere beneath all that was a prize the likes of which no living Knight-Charnel had ever secured. She had not long since visited the Charnel Vault of Highkeep sanctuary. The air was different there, the gods-touched members of the Order more animated than she had ever seen before – and Faril had been a member of the Key-Circle of the Vaults, highest council of the Knights-Charnel, for more than a decade.

If this is a cache as the writings say, it might change everything. It might change the face of the world for ever. We cannot fail.

*

'Everyone into the circle,' Toil said, having stepped gingerly over the threshold. 'Sitain, here at the front. Keep your eyes on the doors, the rest of you too, just in case we get a wink or something. Lastani, Atieno – be ready to do whatever you can in case this is a trap, okay?'

With a slightly comedic amount of huddling, the group all stepped inside the circle and kept close to each other. Once she'd confirmed they were all inside, Toil turned to Sitain.

'Anything?'

'Not that I saw.'

'Damn. Your eyes are probably most like a Duegar's.'

'So our conclusion is that there's nothing to see,' Lastani said. 'Pick a number, Toil.'

'Twenty-two, sixteen, thirty-nine, and the two behind us. What was the first room's? Paranil, tell me you wrote them down.'

'Of course. A one above where we entered, as there is a two above this door. Our choices in the first room were the four on our left as we entered, which was the one we took, a seven ahead and twelve down.'

Toil shook her head. 'Anyone seeing anything like a pattern?'

'Why did you pick four, just out of interest?'

'We're in a cube and a square has four sides, I couldn't think of much else that seemed to fit in any way and we don't

358

have the luxury of thinking for days. I did wonder about the gods, though; how scholars used to say that our gods were once Duegar, that they *became* gods and at first there were only four of them.'

'Banesh was said to have come later, it's true, though we don't know when in their history the labyrinth was built,' Lastani said. 'If the Militant Orders had built this, you'd probably have been right, but I don't think the logic extends.'

'Yeah, I know, it was mostly the square thing because that's all I had.'

'Glad we're doing this all scientific-like,' Lynx muttered.

'Welcome to the exciting life of the relic hunter, my friend,' Toil replied. 'Now enough talk. We've got a choice to make.'

'Perhaps the numbers don't matter, perhaps it's simply direction,' Lastani said after a short while.

'But we don't know what direction we need to go in. There's nothing I remember from anywhere that would suggest a certain path, not even the patterns on the Fountain.'

Lastani shook her head. 'Nor I,' she admitted. 'But we need to pick one.'

'Fine. Twenty-two,' Toil decided. 'There are worse things than moving forward when you don't know what to do.'

'We're all gonna die,' moaned someone from the back.

'Shut it, all of you. Lastani, you ready?'

The young woman nodded. 'Everyone move away from me, it's about to get very cold in here.'

They all edged away as far as they could as Lastani held her palms out, like she was pushing her way through the circle. The temperature dropped almost immediately, the Duegar lamplight flaring white and blue on a bubble of cold magic surrounding her. Lastani stepped forward and the room exploded around her. Lynx howled and threw his hands up to cover his eyes from the blinding flash of orange light.

A wall of fire erupted around them, pouring out from the glyphs in one expanding pulse of power. It lasted only a moment but in the next there was a shriek from someone behind him. Lynx blinked and turned, seeing only a blur of movement at first until he made out the flailing shape ahead.

'Hold still!' shouted someone.

'Fuck – I'm on fire!' the flailing figure shrieked back. It was Haphori, a hirsute man from somewhere so far away even Safir just described it as 'bloody miles east'. He'd lived most of his life on the shore of Whitesea Sound, however, so he swore like a local.

Brols pounced on the man, using his body to smother any flames while Haphori howled in renewed pain at the man now lying on his burned arm.

'Sitain,' Teshen snapped, rubbing his head and wincing, 'shut him up or I will.'

The young mage picked her way past the rest and reached out to Haphori as he kicked Brols off him. The darker man saw Sitain advancing and wriggled backwards but was pinned down by his comrades long enough for her to grab his hand and dull the pain to a point where he stopped screaming.

Lastani, in the meantime, had walked towards the next door and pressed her hand against the gift disc. With her magic up as a barrier the flames hadn't harmed her and she looked unruffled by the torrent of flame. With a second, smaller, burst of magic she triggered the door – again throwing up a shield of magic, but all that happened was the door silently opening into the next room.

Once Haphori's arm was wrapped, Toil led the company through into the next room and ordered the door closed behind them again. This one was empty but for the doorways ahead, on the right-hand wall and in the floor, so she told the company to pause and eat while the scholarly members thought about the new set of numbers. The entrance had a 3 above it this time, the exits displaying 55 ahead, 42 down and 33 right.

'Thirty-three comes up again. There must be a message in that.'

Paranil nodded as he added the new set to his record. 'I believe so, though the pattern still eludes me. Perhaps the repetition is the key or a sign that one awaits us.'

'How about we look at it a different way?' Toil said, feeling suddenly very tired. She dug a small honey-cake out of her pack, jamming the sweet treat into her mouth before continuing in a slightly muffled manner. 'If we made a mistake in the first room, getting that fire-trap, that means we're should've taken what?'

'Ah, twelve or seven.'

'Right. Then twenty-two gets us to an empty room. What's the link?'

No one answered and Toil felt her head sink. She was well used to taking risks in a city-ruin, but she had instinct to rely on there. Sometimes a jump wasn't worth taking, sometimes her gut told her to just walk away and she'd learned to listen to it. Right now it was grumbling uneasily and not out of hunger. There was something amiss, something she'd not noticed perhaps.

Or maybe I'm just feeling like I've used up enough luck for the time being.

'Come on, anyone?'

Paranil looked around at the others before replying for them. 'We need another room.'

Toil sighed and licked the last of the honeyed crumbs from her fingers. 'One more door, go on then. Your turn, Sitain.'

Chapter 27

'Two dead? Deepest black, we're only just started down here!'

Chotel rubbed at the icer burn on his cheek and hissed. 'Two,' he repeated before pointing to a dragoon being helped to the far wall by one of his comrades. 'Another who's not gonna last the day.'

'And this'll be the easy bit,' Bade added. *At least none of my crew was killed. It might teach the dragoons to step a bit more carefully.*

'Let's just hope this door is the right one,' Kastelian said, joining them. 'We don't need many more traps.'

'Hopper's just warming us up. Teaching us the rules of his game. A few more chambers in and mistakes'll get properly punished, I reckon.'

Kastelian looked back across the room they'd just crossed. There were bulbous studs jutting from the side walls and ceiling, while a chaotic spread of tiles occupied a ten-yard stretch of the chamber up to the door on the right-hand wall. Each tile had the glyph for 'ice' carved into it and putting the slightest pressure on any part activated a burst of ice magic from one of the studs. The bursts hadn't had the power of a properly charged ice-bolt, but they were lethal enough. Two bodies on the floor attested to that, and several others carried injuries from glancing blows.

Bade and his crew had moved carefully, ahead of the dragoons, one by one and with few mistakes. But when a mistake was made, it was hard not to fall – hard not to trip others and trigger a barrage. One of the dead had seven or eight wounds in him, his chest torn apart and half-frozen by the ice magic. His body had proved a useful waypoint for the rest, however, covering several glyphs as it did.

'Is your man going ta make it?' Bade asked Kastelian.

'Do I look like a doctor to you?'

Bade lowered his voice. 'He can't hold us up an' he can't be carried for long.'

'I'm aware.'

'Might be you need to step in then, they won't like me doing it.'

Kastelian's face hardened. 'Don't tell me my job, Bade, I'm the ranking officer here, remember? You do what you're paid to do and leave command decisions to me, understand?'

He received a lop-sided smirk. 'Oh aye, sure. Whatever you say, sir. I'll get back to work. Just tell me which door you want me to open, sir.'

'Don't give me the dumb soldier routine,' Kastelian snapped, 'you've known me too long for that.'

'Thought I did, but now you're pulling rank?'

'Oh don't start getting precious on me. You're giving me advice about *my* command and you complain I remind you about rank?'

Chotel stepped between the two of them. 'The pair of you, shut it,' he growled, using his greater size to present a physical barrier. 'Cock-measuring is over for the day – ain't neither of you going to win on that front anyway.'

Bade forced a laugh. 'Don't gimme that shit, I've seen you naked more often than's good for my stomach. You ain't winning nothing.'

'Aye, but Torril's wife has something of the poet about her on the subject o' her man's tackle. Don't give that horny ferret any excuse to pull it out and show the ladies here again. I dunno what Sonna would do but Gull gets an appraising look that worries me.'

'He's got a point,' Bade conceded. 'Gull does go all thoughtful and intense at the sight.'

'Damn right I have, now kiss and make up the pair o' you.'

'Don't be disgusting,' Kastelian said primly, just the hint of a smile on his face.

'Oh go on, pucker up!' Bade pleaded.

'Get the right door and I'll think about it,' he replied and turned away to avoid laughing in the presence of his dead troops.

'Nothing like a bit of motivation, eh?' Bade rubbed his hands together. 'So what are our options?'

'Down is marked twenty-five, twelve there, nine ahead,' Ulestim said. 'Didn't we have a twenty-five already?'

'Aye, first room. Torril?'

'What?'

'You write all the numbers down so far?'

'Did you ask me to?'

'Oh for buggery's sake. Well, I'm asking now.'

Torril bobbed his head. 'Writing 'em down now, boss. I can remember the rest anyway.'

'What's it say on this side of the one we came through?'

Ulestim gave a grunt. 'That's worried me a shade, it's a five.'

'Why does that worry you?'

'There was no four. The room before this one had a three on the inside.'

'Think we missed something?'

'I think we might have taken a wrong turn.'

Bade shook his head. 'Course we did. Didn't the ice magic punching through flesh give you a hint on that front?'

'Certainly, I'm just concerned as to whether the missed four is significant in any other way.'

'Like what?'

'I've, ah, yet to quite fathom that part of the problem.'

Bade exchanged a look with Chotel. 'Well, you inform us when you've got around to it. In the meantime, we're taking twenty-five.'

'Any reason?'

'We've seen it before, mebbe it's Hopper's lucky number.'

'Really?'

'Don't be a shit-brained fool, course not. We came in at the door marked five an' twenty-five is five fives, no? That's a good enough reason for me.'

'You think the key is it's a multiple?' Ulestim said, eyes widening as though on the point of revelation.

'I think it's an idea when I've got few others from you lot.' He pointed to the door and raised his voice. 'Hoy, Spade, number twenty-five if you'd be so good.'

*

'Of course! I've been a fool!'

Toil stopped her investigation of the empty room and stalked over to where Paranil was waving his notes in Lastani's face.

'You're going to have to narrow it down for me there,' Toil said.

'The number code!'

'What? You've cracked it? How?'

'They all relate to the door you entered through, or rather the number above the inside of it. They're multiples – or rather the ones that matter are.'

'Wait, no, that doesn't make sense.' Toil grabbed his paper off him and studied the numbers a moment. 'There,' she said, pointing at the second set. 'We had a two on the inside of that first door we took and the options were twenty-two or sixteen, both multiples.'

Paranil smirked. 'The number informs the choice, you still need to recognise the right one. You took the right one this time round by the way, clever girl.'

'Enough of the patronising; short version?'

'Divide both of those by two. The choice you ended up with was between eleven and eight, since there was an odd number on the floor. In the first room the numbers get divided by one and don't change; we chose four and it was wrong, so either seven or twelve was correct. In the third room, after factoring in the three, you had a choice between eleven again and, well, nothing – the others don't divide by three.'

'Screaming firedrakes! A shorter version please?'

'Right, yes. Sorry. The important numbers are one, eleven, two, seven, three and eleven. They're all primes. I just didn't spot it until we came back to a "three" room, despite having no trap and therefore hadn't chosen wrongly.'

'So here, we . . .' Toil looked up. 'Which one? Fifty-seven?'

He nodded. 'Divided by three, becomes nineteen, yet another prime. It could be a coincidence, but it isn't – the deviser of this labyrinth was a lover of mathematics.'

'Ready to stake your life on that?'

'I . . .'

Toil raised an eyebrow. 'Ready to stake *my* life on it?'

'Oh, without a doubt.'

'You're lucky I enjoy this so much then.'

'Enjoy?' remarked Lynx from somewhere behind them. 'How can you enjoy all this?'

She turned. ''Cos I'm a gentle spirit whose nature is to be brimming with inquisitive joy, can't you tell?'

'And there was me thinking you're a madwoman who likes the smell of impending death on the wind.'

Toil snorted. 'I think we've both been around enough impending death to know the smell isn't a pretty one. But this is what I do, what I'm good at – and right here we've the ultimate challenge for a relic hunter. If Bade gets the prize ahead of me, maybe I'll give it all up and raise a brood of squealing babies – but until then I'm going to enjoy doing what I do.'

Lynx didn't say anything and Toil realised a few of the other mercenaries, the male ones at least, were looking at her strangely. She looked around, puzzled, as a hush descended.

'What happened?'

'Don't mind them,' Estal called, 'you just said the magic word, "babies".'

'Magic? Why?'

'Half are now stricken with terror at the word, the other half are picturing you makin' 'em.'

Toil pulled her mage-pistol. 'And which one of 'em is going to make a crass comment about it? Deern? Safir?'

No one spoke and slowly the male mercenaries averted their gaze.

'Damn right. Now let's get back to work. Lastani, door fifty-seven if you please.'

The young mage jumped to her task and opened the door, Sitain again peering through first before reporting that it looked empty. As Paranil gave a squeak of triumph, Toil led the mercenaries through and into another stone chamber, almost identical to the one before.

'Paranil, numbers.'

She checked behind her and saw there was a 1 inscribed above the door, almost like the labyrinth designer was confirming their theory. Of the other four exits, there was only one prime and it led down so they wasted no time in following. Again the room was empty and Toil felt a jolt of hope. Finally they were making some quicker progress. She just had to hope Bade had found an obstacle to slow himself up.

'Numbers,' Toil called. 'Which way now?'

Paranil gave a cough. 'Ah, yes.'

'What's wrong?'

'Ahem – nothing, per se. There's a three above our entrance – as for the rest. Five hundred and sixty-one, four hundred and seventeen, two hundred and seventy-three. This may take some time.'

'Bugger.'

*

Lynx watched Toil's cohort at its sums while he tried to ignore the growl at the back of his mind. This room, like all the others, was too much like a cell for his liking. A series of windowless cells that might contain something lethal behind every door.

And still they don't seem too worried. I might have my issues with the dark, but none of that lot act as worried as I'd expect – as I'd hope from people leading us through a maze of magic traps. Toil might be the only one actually enjoying herself, but even that girl, Lastani, seems more interested in the academic challenge.

He turned to the others. Kas was putting a brave face on it and Teshen was a closed book to the world around him, but of the others Lynx couldn't see one who seemed at ease with what was going on. The Monarch's lamp casting white light around the room improved matters, but still the enclosed spaces were grating on their nerves.

'What do you reckon our chances are?' Sitain whispered in Lynx's ear.

'They seem to think they know what they're doing,' he said.

'That's not what I asked.'

'Aye, I know.' Lynx found his hands tightening into fists, nails digging into his palms, and made an effort to release the tension in them before replying. 'I don't know about our chances,' he admitted, 'but given all we saw in Shadows Deep, what odds would you have given for us getting through that?'

'Poor odds,' Sitain agreed. 'Dunno if that's a comfort or not.'

'Me neither. Oh, here we go.'

Up ahead, the sums had been done and all but one door eliminated as a possibility. Atieno took a turn to open the door on the right-hand wall so the others weren't doing all the work and Lynx watched Sitain slope forward again to look. Soon they were all filing through and the door closed behind them. While the next set of numbers was being investigated, Lynx went to join Safir and Layir. The two easterners each offered him an inclined head and a slight smile, their actions and mannerisms strangely similar given Layir's formative years had been far from their homeland.

'Are you also getting the impression that we're far from useful?' Safir said, glancing towards the latest discussion.

'Yeah, but that also means there's nothing trying to kill us at present.'

'I hoped for a little more excitement down here,' Layir declared. 'This is the fabled Labyrinth of Jarrazir, after all.'

'We're in a giant puzzle-box, thousands of years old and hundreds of feet below ground,' Lynx pointed out. 'What more were you looking for?'

Layir shrugged. 'Riches for preference – statuary even? Great histories of the Duegar race inscribed on a hundred stone tablets? The secrets of life? Bloody *something* at least.'

'The youth of today,' Safir said in a mock-apologetic tone. 'Ever demanding. We, my dear Layir, are here as escort and, if we're very lucky, pack mules for whatever Toil finds. This is probably the good bit of our adventure.'

'Down we go,' Toil called across the room to the company at large.

Toil grinned. 'I don't, but I'm guessing the Knights-Charnel are pretty determined when they want to be. Either the city's fallen or there's still fighting going on. Either way, we can try to follow Bade out and hope we're not in the heart of the enemy, or pick our own path.'

'What about the paint?'

'It's dry so it likely takes us to the keep, which he blew up, or their safehouse, which he blew up. Either way, you've got a lot of digging on your hands and he won't be there once you're out.'

'So you know where you're going?'

'Of course!' She squinted at the map and nodded. 'Yup, I definitely know where we're going – just not so much where we are right now. Sometimes you've got to guess, eh?'

*

The journey to the surface proved quick by comparison to their descent, the looming emptiness of the upper chamber less intimidating to Lynx now he could see through magic-enhanced eyes. After the maspid attack on Teshen's party back in the lower labyrinth, they kept a keen eye open for more of the creatures but the long unbroken reaches of the chamber continued to be empty. It was less than an hour before Toil had found one exit and used the glyph marked above it to navigate to the one she was looking for. Sitain joined her at the front of the small column as they trudged up a winding path towards a wide circular cave. Toil assured them that above their heads would be Prophet's Square, but she stopped short of entering the cave itself despite the fact there was the faintest light creeping down the stairway – a sign the labyrinth was open again. Lynx had been trying to ignore the possibility that they would get all the way through the labyrinth only to discover the doors still closed, but it appeared the ancient Duegar had been cleverer than that.

'What is it?' Lynx whispered.

'I'm listening,' she replied. 'We don't know who's up there, remember?'

'And we don't know if they've got orders to shoot anything that comes out of these entrances,' Suth added. 'Might not have been told to be overly discerning.'

'So, what? We just stand here?' Lynx tried not to shift his feet as the agitation clawed at him again, so close to the surface he could smell the faint smoke on the air. 'Wait, do you smell that?'

'Smoke?'

He shook his head. 'Something else? Piss?'

They all sniffed hard and Toil gave a laugh.

'That settles it then,' she announced. 'Only mercenaries'd be dumb enough to piss anywhere near one of these labyrinth entrances!'

'We like to think of it as keeping to the traditions of martial boldness from bygone ages,' Safir commented from further back.

'Aye, well, half of those ancient warriors got drunk before battle so mebbe you're right.' Toil took a step into the room. 'HEY!' she yelled, causing her companions to flinch at the echoing shout. 'Who's up there?'

There was a pause. Eventually a tentative voice called back down. 'Who's down there?'

'Someone who wants to come up.'

'Come on then.'

'Someone who doesn't want to get shot.'

'Come up slow then!'

'Who's up there, first?'

'Someone who's going to drop a fucking grenade down this hole soon if you don't stop yapping! Get your shitstain arses up here and if you really fucking behave yerselves an' I like the look o' you, I won't shoot you. How's that for fucking assurances?'

Toil glanced back at the others. 'Varain?' she whispered.

Lynx shrugged. 'Sounds like his distinctive charm.'

'VARAIN?' Toil yelled up again.

There was another pause. 'Toil?'

She gave the others a relieved grin and set off. 'It's me!' she called. 'Give me a moment to stop the guardians here.'

She waved Lastani forward and pulled her last fire-charged glass ball, the pair of them casting fire and ice over the two glyphs on the wall. By the fading blue glow of their light, Toil checked around then set off for the open stairway, careful to have her hands up just in case as she neared the grainy light spilling down the steps. By unspoken agreement the others hung back a few paces. She realised this just as she started up the steps and cast them a half-amused glower before trotting up and greeting the Cards at the top.

Once clear it was safe, the rest quickly followed, blinking as they emerged into the grey of a predawn that was still brighter than underground. The plain stone steps led up into the centre of a large city square with apartment blocks atop arcades of shops on all sides. A stone statue lay fallen to one side – a figure Lynx didn't recognise that had been used to anchor a tent on the other side and a field canteen at the far end. Checking behind, Lynx saw the statue had once stood atop the stone block here, falling when one side dropped away to become steps when the labyrinth first opened.

The Cards were slow to wake despite Varain's yelling, the whole camp looking subdued, given their comrades were returning from an ancient wonder. Beyond them was a wide array of tents with a few flags scattered around – depicting an axe with a red scarf tied to its shaft. The buildings were dark, but presumably still occupied if the Red Scarves were camped in the square.

'You made it then?' Anatin said, pushing his way past sleepily rising mercenaries. 'Success?'

'Of a sort,' Toil replied.

'What the fuck's that?' Anatin demanded, blinking and pointing at her. 'What's that on your skin?'

'Long story. What's the situation here?'

'It's been busy for some,' he said, frowning in confusion. 'Us, not so much – though unlike you lot we didn't think of using the time to get new tattoos. When the labyrinth closed up behind you, the Monarch left a guard at the Fountain and sent us to the Red Scarves. Before we could be deployed to the fighting, the line collapsed and they were routed all the way down the canal.'

Toil cursed. 'The Charnelers have the city?'

'Not quite – Charnelers broke 'em in the afternoon,' Payl supplied, joining her commander. 'Messy rearguard work meant some major districts got chewed up in the process, but it was dusk by the time they passed the palace. Monarch didn't stay to defend that, had troops preparing the ground behind so they could make a stand at the Senate instead. Better ground for warding off attack, and she gambled they'd not be able to push through before nightfall.'

'Word is the Crown-Prince is harrying them hard. They pulled back on the main front once dark came because, well, you know what a confused shitstorm of fire and blood a night battle becomes.' Anatin grimaced at the idea as did several around him. 'They've dug in just out of catapult range and secured their lines, but we're separated from the Jarraziran troops so we've no idea what's left. Heard skirmishes all night, but your brother's made a deal with the Charnelers and we're all wrapped up tight. If I'd been in a position to object I might've not liked that, but . . .'

'Vigilance is doing as I've asked,' Toil clarified. 'I asked him to hold here, make sure we didn't come up in a Charneler camp.'

'Where is here again?' Lynx asked before anyone else could.

'Prophet's Square.' She nodded to the fallen statue. 'The prophet Otheq, for any scholars among you. We're in the north-east of the city, mebbe a mile from the palace. Far enough from the canal that I reckoned Bade wouldn't be aiming for this exit and the Charnelers wouldn't be so interested.'

Lynx eased his pack off his shoulders and wandered over to the disappointingly empty field kitchen. 'What's the plan now?'

'Now?' Anatin echoed. 'No rest for the wicked, eh?'

'Aye, kick the rest of these lazy shits out of their bedrolls. It's time for the Cards to earn their pay. And someone go fetch Vigilance.'

Reft pointed across the square. Heads turned and through the array of tents Lynx saw a party of Red Scarves was advancing towards them.

'Already on his way? Good, we don't want to waste any more time. Anatin, I want them ready to move out in five minutes.'

Lynx watched the group of Red Scarves march forward, the Cards only reluctantly making way as Toil's brother made a beeline for her. Clearly there hadn't been many friends made between the mercenary companies, but the Cards had more sense than to block his way and Vigilance walked like a man well aware of that. He was dressed ready for battle, a bulky jacket on his back, mage-gun over one shoulder and a dozen armed men and women on his heel. Beside him walked an older woman with a ghastly, skull-like face that made her look like some sort of demon in the weak light.

'Vigilance, old auntie Ul,' Toil said in greeting.

The Red Scarves' commander paused on the point of snapping a retort, looked at Toil's face then at the others around her too. *The tattoos,* Lynx realised.

'What the buggery happened to you lot?'

'It's a good question,' Toil said with a smile, 'but it's also a long story.'

'I don't care that much. Where are we?'

'Bade's grabbed a haul of God Fragments I think, we need to stop him getting them out of the city.'

He nodded and turned to the terrifying woman, apparently his lieutenant, then one of the others behind. 'Ulith, see to our nannies. Sathra, start getting the troops awake quietly.'

'Nannies?' Toil asked as the two broke off in different directions.

'A squad of Torquen dragoons and some officers, supposedly making sure I keep to the terms of my agreement. You've put me in not the finest position, little sister. I don't like breaking contracts, even if it ends up only being in pretence.'

'Reckon I can find something to distract our religious friends. Once I've got a proper sense of the situation we'll be moving.'

'The situation is that the city's been roughly romanced most o' the way down her canal!' Vigilance snapped. 'And a lot of it's down to you.'

'Yet if I'd said that, you'd just have called me arrogant.'

'Aye, you're that too. So you better give me a damn good reason why the Red Scarves broke their contract and sat on their arses here for a day and night while the bloody Charnelers tore the guts out of this city!'

'Had word of the Monarch?'

He threw up his hands. 'Fucked if I know. We've got a few squads of Torquen watching us and sentry posts outside the camp so getting intel isn't proving easy. I assume she's still alive and free but that's all I've got. The deal I made with the Charnelers means unless you've found something pretty gods-howling wonderful down there, there's a decent chance my captains will string you an' me up before they bugger off out of Jarrazir.'

454

'We found . . .' For a moment Toil seemed at a loss. 'Like I said, it's a long story. We found enough, the Monarch won't object about you breaking a contract unless she loses the city. Those Torquen troops . . .'

'Are getting a metal breakfast,' Vigilance finished angrily. 'Which I ain't happy about anyway, but at least they're Torquen scum and don't count as real people. We've been allowed to sit here all quiet and meek because they don't need the distraction while they take the city, but sooner or later today we'll end up co-opted or disarmed. The Monarch's troops won't last beyond midday from what I've seen. Either she surrenders or someone does it for her and puts her head on a plate to welcome their new fanatical overlords.'

'We've no time to lose, then,' Toil declared.

'So you *do* have a plan?'

'Don't I always?'

'Aye. I remember some of your plans when we were growing up, though,' Vigilance said darkly. 'More'n a few lacked any sort of sense.'

'Don't worry, I've learned from my mistakes.'

'What, then?'

She grinned. 'They'll be getting ready for a final push? Best time for an all-out attack, then. Get your men ready, it's time to cut the head off the snake.'

Chapter 35

There was little time for reunions for the Cards and little appetite for back-slapping and cheers. The past day and night had seen bloody and brutal conflict in Jarrazir. While they had been spared the worst of the fighting, the wholesale destruction that had torn through the ancient city like a rampaging elemental had lowered every spirit.

Only the strange new tattoos seemed to garner much more than gruff acknowledgement, and even then, in the growing predawn light, their faint sheen was barely perceptible. The design was obvious enough, especially once Deern cheerfully stripped to the waist to show it off, but the ethereal, magical quality seemed to have been left in the darkness.

Just as well, Lynx reminded himself, *given what Toil's planning. If we live through the day, we can bother with worrying what it all means.*

Even in the privacy of his own head, it sounded a hollow ideal, but Lynx could only grit his teeth and set about getting ready. He replenished his cartridge case and ate a scrap of gritty bread, shedding the pack he'd carried through the labyrinth so it didn't slow him down further.

A thin spread of cloud seemed to suspend the encroaching dawn, snaring its light and holding it ransomed in the heavens rather than permitting it to illuminate the broken streets below. The Skyriver had faded from a dull smear to almost invisible by the time the Cards slunk through the gloom to the western picket where the biggest barricade stood. Lynx had to fight the urge to just stand there with his arms stretched wide, staring up at the beautiful open sky and breathing in the clean fresh air of outside, as a weight lifted from his shoulders. Had he been on his own and somewhere else, he might have, but there was a hard day ahead of them all and it was no time for celebrating.

The barricade was a ragged affair, four yards high but flimsy all the same. Tables and chairs, carts, barrels and crates, even roof beams and a stone statue had been incorporated and strung together by a tangled mesh of wire. Few defences would stand up to an earther so few tried. This flimsy obstacle would be shot through in moments, but with a dozen cables looped through it all, it would at least remain an obstacle to invasion even if it offered little actual protection.

A small tunnel had been built into the design on the left-hand side, currently plugged by a large dining table. As Anatin led his Mercenary Deck to the barricade, they heard raised voices from the other side. The sentry sitting atop the barricade seemed unconcerned by what was being said, keeping his eyes on the street beyond and clearly only half-listening. At the arrival of the Cards, however, the man looked back and gave them a small nod.

'Officer's here,' he announced in a bored tone, 'you can come in if you want 'im.'

'Open the damn way then!' barked a man on the other side. 'You've as long as it takes me to load my gun.'

'Whoah!' Anatin said, hurrying forward as the mercenaries on the ground started to drag the obstacles out of the way. 'No need for shooting, certainly not this early.'

A Knights-Charnel officer with a puffy face and thin moustache appeared from behind the table. 'Have that sentry whipped for insubordination,' he snarled. 'Man's been refusing to admit us for five minutes. Unless you've forgotten your company's terms of surrender—' He broke off and looked around at the Cards. 'You're not Red Scarves? Why are you armed?'

Anatin gave him a friendly grin and pulled a pistol, pointing it at the man's face. 'Like I said, there's no need for shooting this early, so don't force my hand, eh? Call your men in. Any of 'em tries to run and you all end up dead, understand?'

The blood drained from the man's face, but as he was hauled forward he began to splutter in fury. 'You've signed the death warrant for every man and woman here, you know that?'

'We all got to go sometime.'

The man drew himself up to his full height. His uniform markings declared him an infantry captain, a narrow scar on his cheek worn like a medal in an army where commissions were bought more often than earned.

'When I do not escort Commander Deshar to the general, she will assume you've reneged on our agreement. You'll be wiped out. Drop your guns and get to your knees right now or every person here is as good as dead.'

'We'll go see her ourselves if you like, where is she?'

The captain paused. 'Gods on high, you're insane.'

'That's what my men say,' Anatin said amiably. 'Now, where?'

'Her command post.' The captain's lip curled. 'Enjoy finding it yourself, I'll not help you.'

'Thought as much, but I had to ask. Mebbe someone here will beat it out of you, mebbe not. I ain't going to bother.'

Three mercenaries started stripping the Charnelers of their weapons as the last of the captain's small command were pulled through the gate. There were only six in the end, not even a full squad, and the regular soldiers looked as resigned as their captain was furious. The man had the sense not to put up a fight or shout for help, though – the threat of having your throat slit tended to have that effect on a man. His loyalty to his Order might be undimmed, but he saw the writing on the wall and complied meekly enough when his turn to be bound and gagged came.

'What have we got out here then?' Anatin commented, peering through the makeshift sally port with Payl and Toil, while Teshen and Kas scrambled up to join the sentry.

'Looks pretty quiet.'

'There's a regiment barracked in that building there, with the lights,' supplied the sentry. 'Pickets at every major cross-road. I saw a column move south not long ago, towards the university district.'

'Do we know where the general's stationed?'

'We've sent out some scouts. Only one's got back so far, but he said they're keeping to the canal avenues and her barge is inside the city.' The sentry sucked his teeth for a moment. 'Your friend came straight down this road,' he said after a while, pointing. 'Came from the right around that corner there, not the quickest route but likely they've only secured the main roads.'

Lynx glanced behind them and saw the Red Scarves were forming into their units. Other, smaller, groups had been dispatched on distraction missions and they would be slipping out through surrounding buildings right now. Speed was their only advantage – there were thousands of Charneler troops in the city and together the Cards and Scarves had no more than five hundred in total.

'The barracks is our target,' Toil reminded Anatin. 'We take that out and cut north, try to skirt behind the main body of troops as Vigilance's skirmishers create a distraction and the Red Scarves tie up the centre.'

'Sitain,' Lynx murmured, turning to the young woman beside him. 'How strong are you right now?'

She raised an eyebrow. 'Still buzzing after that water, why?'

'Could you put out a whole regiment?'

'What?' Sitain coughed. 'Shattered gods, how should I know?'

'If they're all in that building still,' Lynx clarified. 'All nice and close.'

'Ah, maybe?'

'Good enough. Anatin!'

The commander turned with a scowl. 'What now?'

'Let me and Sitain go ahead. She's full to bursting, all the mages are. Might be she can take out all the barracks there without us drawing too much attention to ourselves.'

'What?' Anatin opened his mouth to berate Lynx but, before he could, Toil laid a hand on his arm.

'If she can,' Toil said quietly, 'it's a huge advantage. Lastani – where are you? Could it be done?'

The other mage stepped forward. 'I . . . I don't know. I've never felt so strong, though, so maybe she has a chance.'

'All I needed to hear. Lynx, grab some coats off our friends there. Might give you cover enough. If anyone comes to challenge you, we start shooting, okay?'

Lynx ducked his head in acknowledgement and in moments two black-and-white greatcoats were passed over. He and Sitain put them on and slipped out into the deserted grey streets, glancing back once at the barricade before heading down the street to the building that had been pointed out.

The road was covered in debris – broken bricks and tiles along with the detritus of a fleeing population. They had a hundred yards to walk and, despite the chill morning air, Lynx's neck was tacky with sweat as they tried to act like part of a conquering army. The building was a large block five floors high with a smaller wing jutting off the side and a warehouse nestled in its lee. It seemed to be a consortium office of some sort, but the flags of its companies had been pulled down and a heap of goods had been pulled from the warehouse and set alight in the street.

They approached from the rear, holding back until a patrol had rounded the corner then hurrying to the stable gate while they assessed the problem. There was a face at one top window, but he was watching another approach. No doubt he saw Lynx and Sitain, but he'd have seen the delegation arrive at the barricade so would have no reason to be suspicious. Lynx could hear Sitain gasping short, nervous puffs of breath as she hugged her plundered coat close. They wouldn't stand up to close scrutiny, that much was obvious.

'How close do you need to be?'

'I don't know.'

'Is the wall going to be a problem?'

'I've never done this before, remember? Just hurry up – I can feel the magic seeping out of me.'

'What?'

She hissed in irritation, not at him Lynx realised, but at a lack of words to explain herself properly.

'Whatever happened underground, if felt like I was filled to bursting with magic. Like a wineskin.'

'So?'

'So I'm no trained mage. I can't keep it all in, the power's slowly draining out of me. Might be no human was ever meant to hold that magic, but every moment I don't concentrate on holding the seams together, more trickles out.'

'We probably should have planned this better, right?'

'Shut up and go.'

Lynx nodded and drew his sword, hiding it behind his back before he tried the ring latch of the stable gate. It turned and opened easily enough, revealing a small courtyard.

'Hey, who goes there?'

'Easy friend,' Lynx said, advancing towards the challenging voice. A man appeared from one of the stables, mage-gun in hand. 'Got some girls, I couldn't bring 'em in round the front, could I?'

461

'Girls?'

Lynx beckoned and pointed at Sitain, lurking in the gloom of the gate. 'Whores, Sergeant Ulain sent me out for 'em.'

On instinct the guard stepped forward to see Sitain better. 'What company is—'

Lynx lunged forward, closing the ground between them with one pace and driving his sword into the man's gut. The impact drove him back, and as Lynx yanked the gun out of his hands he almost ended up on top of the guard as he fell to the ground. He could smell the man's breath as he gasped his last – the stink of peppered meat washing across Lynx's face as he abandoned his sword and pulled his dagger. The man hardly moved, impaled by the sword and pinned by shock and agony, so it was a simple job to drive the dagger up into his brain and end his pain.

Lynx withdrew his weapons and quickly wiped the blades on the dead man's uniform. Sheathing both, he dragged the guard into one corner of the stable and waved Sitain forward. The young woman peered at him dumbly from the gate, face white, as Lynx hissed and beckoned – for a moment not realising why she was holding back. Then he looked down at the blood on his hands, the body at his feet and felt a pang of shame.

He'd killed the man without a second thought, it was an instinct etched into his bones and Lynx was under no illusions about himself, but Sitain . . . She'd seen her mercenary comrades kill before, but usually it was using a mage-gun or amid complete chaos. She might have even killed someone herself, by accident most likely given how poor a shot she was, but it would have been different. Here, Lynx had pounced on a man and stabbed him to death. He could see in Sitain's eyes that the awful truth of their chosen profession had never been clearer to her.

'Sitain!' Lynx said a fraction louder. 'Look at me, remember what we're here to do! They *all* die if you can't put them out before the rest reach us.'

That seemed to break the spell as Sitain flinched and swallowed hard, nodding. Eyes averted from the dark pool of smeared blood, she scampered forward and joined him in the shadows.

'Can you do this?'

'I . . . I'm going to have to try.'

Lynx caught her by the arm and saw the resolve in her eyes. She might not like it, but she was a stronger soul than she realised, and Lynx stepped back, satisfied.

She looked up at the large building. It was bigger than any of the inns the company had taken since she'd joined them – most likely there were more than a hundred soldiers camped there while they awaited orders. Clearly the Charnelers were confident that Toil's brother was as good as his word, happy to leave their flank largely undefended when there was no safe route around behind wherever the front line was.

Normally they'd be right to, Lynx reminded himself. *I doubt even Toil alone would have been able to persuade the Red Scarves to try something like this. They know the damage a breach of the line can cause once the burners start to fly, but they also know the casualties you'll take if you try anything more than a quick raid.*

He looked down at the back of his hand. The tattoo was clear on his skin there but not shining any longer. It just looked like a thin coating of pearly paint – hardly impressive, but perhaps enough to tip Vigilance over the edge. There was no doubting that they had found something in the labyrinth, something magical, and had three mages in their midst. Perhaps that would prove the key to success and, if not, it was the Cards out front. No doubt if they got obliterated Vigilance would shed a tear for his sister as he ordered his men to flee.

Just as well there was no time to explain what we found. The man might be less confident after hearing 'we've piss-all clue what this is, but it was all shiny earlier'.

'The main part of the building is there,' Sitain muttered to herself. 'So I need to . . .'

'Sure you can do this through a wall?'

'We better hope so, unless you want to try every room individually.'

'Good point.' Lynx stepped back. 'Any time you want then.'

She gave him a sharp look but didn't bother replying, just placed one hand against the wall and the other past the corner, directed towards the other part of the block. Eyes closed, Sitain bowed her head and took a few long breaths. In moments the air began to faintly shudder and distort around her, shadows turning in on themselves as the night magic surged out of her.

Lynx felt his breath catch as the shadows took on sharp edges, twisting and flittering like the wings of a butterfly. He'd seen this before not long after meeting Sitain – an elemental, night magic made incarnate. Shadowshard, that's what Lastani had called it.

The black shards seemed to radiate out from Sitain as the flow of magic increased, unfurling like wings from all parts of her torso and disappearing through the wall ahead. He felt a furious itch crawl across his skin, scratching once at his hand then catching himself. The sensation slipped like oil all over his body, but after that first moment it was strangely pleasant, not a maddening irritation.

As he looked. the tattoo on his hand suddenly glowed again with the cold shine of starlight. Quickly, Lynx pulled up his jacket to look at his stomach where the tattoos ran down it – those too were now bright again.

He opened his mouth to say something to Sitain before realising that, though half her body was now hidden by knapped fragments of darkness, she was also glowing. Her tattoos shone even through her shirt and were inscribed on the shadow shards of her magic, white lines traced clearly on the deepest black.

Then he felt her reach out, summoning her strength to drag yet more magic into her saturated body. This was no grand working, that much Lynx could tell, just a tidal wave of power about to be cast forward at the building and the soldiers inside it. His own tattoos seemed to jolt on his skin as Sitain reached higher, tugging him towards her and suddenly he felt . . . something flow out of his skin, as though he was a mage himself. Lynx gasped but could find no words for anything more. He simply stood there, astonished and enraptured as a power he'd never guessed at flowed through his body.

All of a sudden Lynx found himself able to feel Sitain's presence on his skin, like they were connected by a thousand spider-threads – the shape of her body, mind and thoughts. Nothing clear, but the strongest sense of 'her' as though they had grown up twins. Before he could do anything or make sense of it all, his body was ablaze with awareness of the others too. Lastani an icy sculpture in his mind, elegant and intricate, while Atieno was a roiling, shifting figure of smoke. Then those who weren't mages too – Toil's sharp edges and iron will, Teshen's cold heart and raptor focus, Safir's grace and the kernel of bitterness hidden deep inside . . .

He could feel them all, their minds crashing into his like the weight of some ancient shield wall, sweeping him up in their momentum and charging on towards Sitain. She embraced their power as it struck and added it to her own, blackness threatening to overwhelm Lynx's mind for an instant before it was all hurled away. The world seemed to be split in two – that wave of shadowy power bursting forth to engulf everything in its path even as Lynx was hurled backwards to his own body.

He staggered as though physically punched and found himself blinking and gasping for air. Ahead of him the night mage crashed to her knees. As for the building, there was no change, but Lynx could sense the power move like a fireball scorching the night. The power had been immense, so many more times more powerful than any magic he'd ever witnessed. He felt his hands shake at what it might mean – at how they'd been changed – but right now Sitain needed him again. He took a few unsteady steps, driven mostly by will, before recovering himself and sweeping Sitain up just before she flopped to the ground.

'Shattered gods,' she croaked, looking up at Lynx with unfocused eyes.

'Let's hope they didn't notice,' he said, only half-joking. 'Best they don't think they've got a rival on their hands.'

Her tattoos were still glowing and he could feel the ebbing magic tremble through her bones. It waxed briefly as his skin touched hers, but then continued to fade as the light of their skin dimmed.

Lynx headed back out of the gate, Sitain in his arms, and he saw the Cards closing fast – the shine of several tattoos clearly visible in the dawn light. Before he'd even reached them a volley of barely hushed voices rang out.

'What did she do?'

'Gods, did you feel it?'

'I'm bloody shining again, how do I make it do that?'

Lynx set Sitain down as they reached their comrades and held her steady until the young mage found her feet.

'Is it done?' Toil demanded over the voices of the others.

'Reckon so, aye,' Lynx said.

'You're sure?' Anatin asked.

'Didn't you see?'

'I saw nothing,' their commander said, jabbing a thumb at the tattooed mercenaries at his side. 'All of a sudden, this lot starting whimpering and moaning – then they started to bloody twinkle like pretty little forest fairies. What the hairy fuck's she done to you?'

'It wasn't her,' Toil answered for Lynx, 'and we don't have time to explain. Aben, go back and tell the Scarves what's happened. They'll be waiting for a fireball or something as a signal.'

'And the rest of us?'

'We move as fast as we can. Word is the Crown-Prince is still alive, harrying the Charnelers with his cavalry group. Most likely that's why the general moved her headquarters closer in, where Tylom can't threaten her. It also means if we stir the pot here, he might notice and hit the rear again.'

'So which way?'

'Suth?'

The scowling agent of the Monarch pointed, saying nothing.

'What's up her arse?' Lynx asked Toil.

Toil grinned wolfishly but it was Suth herself who answered. 'I just started to fucking glow like a Skyriver festival lantern when *she* did her thing. If that keeps happening, I'm either marked as some magic-touched freak the Charnelers will want to put in a sanctuary, or I have to resign my commission 'cos I'm stuck with you deranged idiots.'

'Now that's a worrying thought,' Atieno said.

Sitain laughed weakly. 'Join the shitting club,' she croaked. 'I'll get us all badges saying "I'm with those drunken madmen".'

'I think we're being impugned!' Safir declared with mock outrage. 'Permission to shoot them, commander?'

'Mebbe later,' Anatin said darkly. 'Meantimes, let's go and go fast. Suth, you're leading. Shoot anyone who gets in our way.'

Chapter 36

The Cards advanced a few more blocks, keeping as quiet and unobserved as possible. Somewhere behind them the Red Scarves were moving up – taking a more direct route to the canal that ran straight to the Bridge Palace. The Monarch had retreated from her palace, not wanting to see it obliterated and drawing the Charnelers deeper into the city. The Senate was as defensible as anywhere else in the city and forced the Charnelers to stretch their lines much further.

'Here,' Suth said, stopping at the corner of one street.

The dawn light illuminated their path and, though the sky was overcast, there was no hiding in the cover of shadows now. The stink of burned buildings was stronger here, carrying on the breeze across the city. Thin trails of smoke rose up into the sky, melting away before they reached the cloud cover. They stood like memorials to the dead, pyres arrayed across Lynx's view of the sky above the rooftops.

'This'll take us all the way?' Toil asked, peering around the corner.

'It's pretty much a straight run down this street and the ones beyond it.'

The nearby buildings were mostly intact, marked by a few stray shots but without the flame-scarring of burners or earther holes. It could almost be a normal street view but for the deserted road scattered with debris dropped by fleeing citizens.

Fortunately for the Cards, this was a poorer district with winding narrow streets and few vantage points. Against the background rumble of gunshots there came from somewhere closer the distinctive crack of icers over the rooftops, single shots rather than a skirmish.

'Hear that?' Safir said. 'Snipers.'

Toil nodded. 'They'll be watching the flanks of their supply line. Lastani, how strong are you feeling?'

'I'll not be outdone by Sitain,' the young woman replied with forced bravado. Her pale face betrayed her real feelings, but clearly she had them under control for the moment.

This is her home they've torn the guts out of, Lynx reminded himself. *Never underestimate what folk will do to stop someone destroying their home.*

'Good, we'll need the cover.'

Toil gestured to the air in front of them all and Lastani nodded. A shield of magic could hold back mage-shot sure enough – but it was a gamble whether they'd get the shield up in time. Normally no mage would be strong enough to maintain one for any length of time. If they could, mages would be co-opted into every army across the continent. After what Sitain had just done, though, and the link existing between them all, Lynx realised the Cards might now be unique.

'First we wait.'

'For what?'

'The signal.'

It didn't take long to come. The Cards had hunkered down as best they could in the street, not seeing troops of either side as they waited, then a boom rolled across the sky. Lynx looked back the way they'd come and realised it was probably the barracks even before the smoke began to rise.

Shit. Poor bastards, he thought as guilt stabbed at his gut. But how to persuade hardened mercenaries to leave a regiment of enemies alive at their backs, trusting in magic they'd never seen? He knew it was a faint hope even as his heart burned with shame. He chanced a look at Sitain but the young woman didn't seem to have connected the sound and he looked away, not wanting to be the bearer of those tidings.

The roar of fire followed soon after as orange flames and dirty black smoke rose high in the sky above the lesser pyres of the city – a vast obelisk amid a field of memorials. Enough of a signal to the entire city that the fighting had begun again. If the Monarch and Crown-Prince had any troops left, they'd know this was their last chance.

'Vigilance will be past the barracks, ready to ambush troops drawn by the fire,' Toil announced as she patted Suth on the shoulder and directed her forward. 'With luck it'll clear a path for us.'

'Here's hoping,' Anatin said as they filed out. The narrow street left little space for the Cards to spread out so the suits advanced in tight knots, guns raised. They saw no one as they followed the first section then came to a bend in the road where Suth hesitated.

'Tavern,' she whispered back. 'Thirty yards up.'

Lynx felt the tattoos on his skin renew their glow as Lastani drew on her reserves of magic. A haze appeared above them, a faint cloud of mist that caught the morning light. With her arm outstretched, fingers splayed, Lastani drove forward with the cloud ahead of her and the Cards trotted alongside. Around the corner they saw the tavern through the haze, three storeys of stone and timber that looked as dark as the rest of the district it towered over. They had barely gone a few paces when a gunshot rang out and a white streak arrowed into the shield of ice-magic Lastani had raised.

The Cards faltered, then a second shot rang out – this time the roar of a burner, but the flames also burst fruitlessly over the shield.

'Now, drop it!' Toil shouted over the crackle of fire.

The shield vanished and in the next instant Toil fired an earther into the upper floor of the tavern. The faint trails of their shots had betrayed the snipers' location and she hit it dead on – smashing clean through the wall and tearing the entire window frame out with it. Payl followed it up with a burner and fire exploded through the gap, sweeping the top floor and cutting off the brief scream they'd heard from inside.

'Faster,' Toil demanded as she reloaded. 'We've announced ourselves.'

The Cards jumped to obey. Rounding the burning tavern they came to an alley mouth. Suth glanced down it and jerked back as an icer flashed straight past her face. Before the others could do anything the Jarraziran soldier had dropped to one knee and pulled two guns from her collection. She fired in rapid succession while three Cards stepped past her for a better shot. The whipcrack of icers echoed down the tight alley and then all was still.

'Patrol,' Suth reported back, reloading as she went. 'Dead now.'

Ahead of them was a right turn so she upped the pace to the corner, pausing at the side to check around it again.

'We need to cross this square and bear left,' she called to Anatin. 'Couple of squads by the looks of it.'

'Sun takes the lead with Lastani,' he said. 'We advance until I call the halt, then cover Stars as they come. Blood and Snow to follow us, Tempest watches our rear.'

Not waiting for any acknowledgement, Anatin pulled his pistol with his one remaining hand and started forward. Payl, Karra and Varain moved ahead of him, guns ready. There was a shout from somewhere and they fired immediately, three crisp shots ringing out as Darm and Foren moved ahead. Once the last of Sun had gone, Estal led Stars out at a crouch, and then they were all following. More gunshots came. The bursts and echoes off the surrounding buildings had merged into one great jagged sound by the time Lynx turned the corner.

The flash of icers was everywhere, the jagged tongues of sparkers lashing a building on the far side. As they moved into the square, a burner roared out from their right and spilled flame across the ground. Two Cards were caught in the fire but Lynx didn't have time to see who as the whole of Tempest charged, firing. The lead suits jerked left, towards the open street leading off the square, but Blood and Tempest continued to hammer earthers and icers into the surrounding buildings.

'Move!' Teshen called.

Payl and Suth were already at the next street, firing on more Charnelers there, while Lynx reloaded frantically and continued to scan the shattered house fronts of the square. Teshen hurried forward to a blackened, writhing figure in the middle of the square, slamming the butt of his gun hard into their head. Lynx didn't know if it was one of theirs or not, but it was a mercy any soldier would offer if they could.

You lived your life fearing that – not the sparkers or earthers, but burning alive and every moment feeling like an age. The power of burners was undeniable and unavoidable, but Lynx wasn't the only soldier to feel sick every time he fired one.

'Reft!' yelled someone from up front.

The mercenaries of Blood hurried forward, adding their guns to the volley the lead troops were laying down. They edged forward every few seconds, a pace or two only but moving, constantly moving. Lynx saw Flinth shot through the head, but there was no time to pause. The Charnelers retreated under a steady hail of shots, the Cards' firepower and numbers overwhelming each small group they came across.

As the morning brightened, the sound of gunshots began to boom from somewhere south of them and they found their progress quickening. The number of patrols dwindled – some even fleeing from their path. They'd broken the flank lines, it appeared, and the Red Scarves were drawing most of the fire from the reserve troops in this part of the city. The bulk of the Charneler army was on the front line by the Senate buildings, too far to recall in time, but Lynx was well aware they had no idea what was being kept in reserve.

Press on, drive deep. The words kept running through his brain; at every pause and hesitation his old training screamed them. This was the commando way, the Hanese way. Heavily armed troops pushing hard and fast through enemy lines – wreaking mayhem and slaughter in those minutes when the enemy were unable to react.

The crack of icers started to fade from his awareness – the grey and ochre of the city became green and brown as he found his mind returning to the close, frantic battles of the Greensea a decade earlier. The unprepared armies of each city-state and principality. The dawn raids from the forests, sweeping inexorably and ruthlessly over camps and villages – killing everything in their path. Hand-to-hand fighting when they were too close to waste time reloading, axes and swords chopping a path through young men and women too stunned to fight back.

It all settled like a dark shadow over his mind, eclipsing everything but for the part that recoiled at that side of him returning.

But this is the part I need now, Lynx realised in one moment of quiet, when they paused at a demolished building and listened to the sounds of fighting somewhere to the south. *This is also me. Right now it's all I have.*

The Cards came to another square – larger this time, with a well and shrines occupying the centre. Around that were pitched tents and a ragged barricade so the mercenaries charged straight on. Earthers and sparkers smashed into the barricade and tore chunks from it. The surprised Charnelers were thrown back, some not even armed as the Cards pushed on through. They split left and right around the shrines, while Estal led her suit through the centre to clear it of defenders. Lynx saw Kas's deadly skills as he glanced across, three men shot down even as Lynx reloaded his own gun.

A flash of movement through a doorway caught his eye and Lynx turned, bringing his gun up. A glimpsed uniform was enough for him to pull the trigger and the Charneler was thrown back down the hallway. Nearby, Foren and Sitain were scavenging cartridge boxes from the dead, neither being much of a shot.

Lynx popped the breech of his gun open and yanked the spent cartridge out, hissing at the deep cold that stung his fingers. He loaded another icer but slung the gun on to his shoulder, drawing his pistol instead. The shorter range wouldn't matter here and he didn't want to freeze the barrel of his mage-gun in the middle of a fight. It could happen, firing too many icers in rapid succession could turn the metal brittle. Lynx had seen a man swap to a burner after a long fight at distance – the cold barrel hadn't been able to cope with sudden heat and it had exploded, killing him and everyone beside him too.

'Dragoons!' someone yelled from the far side, followed by streaks of flame overhead.

Icers hammered back across the square, tearing through a squad who'd run to support the defenders. Their bravery was their undoing as the others fled and they found themselves exposed, cut down in moments.

'Get their cases!' Anatin roared, knowing the dragoons would carry burners and grenades too.

All of a sudden the gunfire tailed off, the last of the Charnelers abandoning their positions. Lynx knew it wouldn't last, that it meant the next fight might be all the harder, but a pause for breath was necessary. He was almost out of cartridges and the rest would be the same. Not waiting for Sitain to distribute some he grabbed the nearest corpse and rifled through their cartridge case. Nine or ten icers went into his own, along with a couple from the next corpse before he handed them to the woman next to him. That was Braqe, the Jester of Tempest who despised Lynx for the actions of his people during the Hanese conquest. She grunted her thanks, enmity put aside for the fight.

'Sitain!' yelled a voice from the far side. 'I need you!'

The young mage blinked dumbly for a moment before realising it was Himbel, the company surgeon. She shrugged her plundered cases off her shoulders and scampered through the shattered mess of barricade as a wail of panicked pain cut the air.

'Catch your breath, get ready to move,' Teshen said, checking over his troops.

Lynx looked around. Other than Flinth, Tempest hadn't lost anyone, but he could see the bodies of several Cards lying still behind them. A burly, taciturn man called Sandath lay on his back, arms outstretched as though welcoming the icer that had torn open his chest. Another, Hald – a sandy-haired, grinning monkey of a man – lay crumpled in a ball further back, never to laugh again judging by the blood on his head.

'We're coming out on the canal,' Suth called, advancing towards the far end of the square. 'One last push and we're there.'

In the distance, the battle intensified, the snaps of icers and rolling booms of earthers followed by the thunder and shake of collapsing buildings. Lynx looked around once more, this time seeing more scars of battle on the once-beautiful city. There were faces at the windows too – scared, pale citizens peeking out only to shrink back as Lynx turned towards them.

The lower floors were most damaged, but nothing looked ready to fall so there was little to be done. A grenade had ripped away one corner of a building, some stone-built townhouse, while the packed earth and cultivated shrubbery was furrowed and torn – mostly by the Cards in their savage assault. Glass shards were scattered across the street, a dull glitter amid the dust and splinters.

'Burners!' called Aben, who'd gone to inspect the dead dragoons after first checking the street behind.

He checked inside one case then swung it by the strap and flung it back to the mercenaries. Lynx wasn't the only one to catch his breath at that, but Toil plucked the case from the air with ease and brought it down gently. She'd been wounded, he realised – jacket ripped open at the point of one shoulder and blood showing underneath, but not badly given she was still using the arm.

Teshen went to gather another case and handed out what few cartridges he could to each of the named cards of his suit, Llaith, Lynx and Braqe. Only two burners, but better than nothing when firepower was the only thing keeping them alive. Llaith was also injured, his jacket open and showing a bloody bandage covering a flesh wound in his side.

'Himbel, ready to go?' Anatin yelled, striding after Suth.

'Almost!'

Lynx followed Teshen round and saw it was Darm, wounded in his shoulder given the attentions he was receiving. He lay on his back, pawing feebly at Sitain as she pressed her hands to the wound – but he stopped screaming after her magic had done its work. His coat was slashed apart, exposing black spiderweb tattoos half-obscured by smeared blood.

'It's time,' Toil declared. 'You've done all you can. Either the locals help him or he waits until this fight is over, that's all there is.'

Himbel nodded, face grim but he'd seen enough battlefields to know that. You could patch up some injuries, give your friends a chance at least, but the fight waited for no one. Sitain looked more conflicted about abandoning Darm, but Himbel took her by the elbow and she was so drained already she didn't have the strength to resist.

The Cards all moved forward to the far side of the square. A short street no more than twenty yards long met another running across, tall expensive houses rising all around. Somewhere to the north there were explosions, presumably Vigilance's additional distractions. A small number of troops could make a lot of noise and confusion, slowing any response to the main threat. And given the main threat was the Red Scarves, who in turn were serving as distraction to let the Cards drive deep behind Charneler lines, it would likely confuse them enough to work.

Up to the point some fucker decides to tear the city apart with burners, Lynx reminded himself. *The Charnelers have done it before – lost patience when on the back foot, so they've destroyed everything in sight as they retreated.*

'That street runs parallel to the canal,' Suth said. 'The boulevard is just the other side. If we skirt right we'll be not too far from—'

'Or we go through,' Anatin pointed out, glancing at his sergeants while he spoke. 'People always forget the value of a straight line.'

'Through?'

'Aye – not civilised I grant you, but it's fucking war. Likely they'll be waiting for us at the side streets, but houses tend to back on to alleys and other houses. A few hefty kicks from our own man-mountain and most doors open. We can blow any that don't and break down walls in between.'

'Getting off the streets would be good,' Payl agreed. 'If there's a reserve force somewhere, we'll be badly outnumbered.'

'Reft,' Safir said, 'I believe this is your department.'

With one look around the corner, Reft crossed the street at a run. The far side was a row of near-identical townhouses, four storeys tall with ochre roof tiles and wide windows. Reft ran up three steps to the nearest and slammed a boot into the front door. It shuddered and there was a splintering sound, but it resisted the huge man's strength. A second kick burst the door open and Reft marched straight on to shouts of alarm from inside. A white-haired man was shoved aside as he rushed towards Reft, seemingly trying to push him back out the door.

'Health inspectors!' Deern called cheerfully, following close behind the big mercenary. 'Oh shut it, you old sod – the city's infested with Charnel-rats, ain't you noticed?'

Teshen led his suit down the side of the house and kicked in a heavy side gate. Lynx saw Varain do the same further down, the Cards spreading out so they wouldn't be bunched through one entrance. It was a narrow passage Teshen led Tempest into, but they came out into the rear yard a few seconds ahead of Reft. Vegetable plots and raised herb beds flanked a chicken coop, a paved path leading down the middle of the yard to a rear gate.

That came off its hinges easily enough and then they were in a dark central alley between houses. Lynx caught a glimpse of Lastani as he passed through to the yard that backed on to the other side. Her tattoos seemed to shine in the dull light of an overcast morning and his own tingled in response.

Teshen checked before heading through the gate on the far side. He slipped the bolts open but only peered through the gap, trying to get a sense of what they were emerging on to. Lynx found himself craning up to try and see past the man, but all he could make out was the exposed bone-white trunk of a tree that had shed its bark.

'How's it look?'

'Not bad,' Teshen whispered back, 'not great.'

'What's the plan anyway?'

'The general.'

'Aye, but kill or capture?'

Teshen gave him a blank look. 'Whatever we can manage.'

'Does it look like we'll manage either?'

'Think I'm going through this gate if we can't?'

'You ain't gone through yet,' Llaith pointed out, 'you're hiding behind it.'

'Shut up.'

In the distance, the sounds of battle took on a new intensity, rolling like a thunderstorm up from the south. Lynx paused to listen. It sounded more distant and punctuated – catapults hurling mage-spheres. The clatter of gunshots remained but that was the Red Scarves and the Charnelers, this sound was new and the Scarves didn't have that sort of artillery. It had to be the Jarraziran regiments renewing the fight.

'Sounds like the Monarch's seen our signal,' Lynx commented with a lightening heart.

'Just as well. If this lot get reinforcements we're screwed.'

That cut the conversation short and the handful of soldiers simply stood and waited a few more minutes until at last Lynx heard a muffled shout of 'Cards!' from one of the buildings off to their left. Teshen wasted no time in yanking open the gate and they trotted out towards the canal. The boulevards flanking it were open and largely deserted – a handful of uniformed soldiers escorting grey-liveried auxiliaries with laden carts. They didn't stop to fight – as soon as the Cards emerged en masse, both auxiliaries and soldiers abandoned the carts and ran like mice.

Lynx looked left and right. The boulevard was chewed up pretty badly, both banks bearing the wreckage of the previous day's fighting retreat with most of the buildings in one stretch completely destroyed. There was a fight happening half a mile away given the flames and movement he could see – that had to be the Red Scarves. What he couldn't see was a relief force being held in reserve anywhere nearby. There were knots of black-and-white Charnelers scattered up and down the canal, but those who'd spotted the Cards clearly weren't keen to fight.

'Where's the general?' Teshen demanded of the city at large as he prowled back and forth. The trees ran in a line down each side of the boulevard, punctuated by broken or burned stumps but affording a certain amount of cover from snipers.

'There!' called Kas from further down the boulevard. 'Far shore, there's a barge.'

Suth ran forward to the canal-side trees. 'Berthed at the amphitheatre,' she announced, suddenly animated.

Lynx was one of several who headed forward to get a better view. The barge was a large, low-slung affair with a crest of canvas running down the top which he guessed was a pair of small, folded masts. It bore typical Knights-Charnel markings, the spear-and-setting-sun repeated down its side, the hull was black with white hatches. It was a few hundred yards away, but hardly a hub of activity so far as Lynx could see.

'Shit, where is she?' Toil said.

'The amphitheatre,' Suth replied. 'She must be using it as a command post. But why isn't she moving out? Bade must have reached her by now – unless he's double-crossed her?'

Toil shook her head. 'He won't, the man cares more for his hide than any profit he'd make off those God Fragments. It must be the Crown-Prince – if he's raiding their camp, she can't easily escape without an escort.'

'Better to withdraw the whole army,' Anatin agreed, joining them. 'If they've got what they want, why bother taking the city? It's not like the Charnelers would be able to hold it easily.

If I was the Monarch, before I got forced out I'd blow the sea defences – leave any conqueror open to the rest of Parthain. If anything can bring the Parthain states together it'll be the threat of piecemeal conquest.'

Toil snorted. 'Why else do you think we're here?'

Lynx inspected the amphitheatre. It was a massive oval building that towered over those around it, two hundred yards long and six storeys high at the north end, sweeping down to only two at the south to embrace the afternoon sun. Each storey had great arched apertures around the outside, perfect vantage points for the general's guards.

'We're not getting in there,' he said, looking from the vantage points to the wide, open plaza around it. 'Not unless Lastani's as powerful as the gods.'

'We don't need to,' Suth said, flashing a brief, mirthless grin. There was a hunger for revenge on her face now, the chance to find her partner's killer. 'We just need to make it as far as there.'

Across the open ground at the north end was a square building with a sharp spire. At first glance it could have been some sort of shrine, but it lacked any of the details a shrine would possess.

'What is it?'

'The players' entrance – I'm guessing none of the Charnelers know about it, but that's how the players go in. They can't be allowed to see the labyrinth before the game starts.'

'Another damn labyrinth?' Deern moaned. 'What's with you people?'

Suth shrugged. 'Jarrazir's always been known for the labyrinth beneath it, so one Monarch a few hundred years back made one the people could actually enter. The amphitheatre floor can be cleared for other entertainments, but it was built for the games – played through a maze that's changed for each match.'

Lynx charted the route in his head. They would first need to cross the canal, the nearest bridge being two hundred yards north and guarded by a handful of Charnelers at each end. If they met any serious opposition they would be horribly exposed, it was probably only their numbers that had prevented the bridge guards from picking a fight as soon as they saw them.

'Move out,' Anatin barked to the company, clearly of the same mind. 'Spread groups, hold your shots until they fire. We don't want to draw any more attention than necessary and I'm betting those guards will run as soon as we close.'

'Yeah,' Lynx muttered darkly, 'what with them having an army nearby, they don't need to fight. Letting us run straight into trouble will be easy enough.'

'You got a better idea?'

'Depends,' Deern laughed. 'Is it too late to join the Knights-Charnel?'

'For you, I reckon so,' Anatin said gravely. 'I seem to remember a priest of Insar in some town on the shore of Whitesea.'

'Ah, yeah. Well I'm sure he saw the funny side eventually.'

'I really doubt that.' The mercenary commander gave a weary shake of the head. 'And you wonder why I don't let you have tattoo needles any more.'

'Enough chat,' Toil growled. 'Let's end this.'

'Aye, time to be heroes I suppose.'

Toil looked around at the arrayed faces of the company. 'Let's not go overboard,' she muttered as she set off.

Chapter 37

Staggered runs took them to the bridge, Blood and Stars taking one side of the boulevard, Tempest and Sun taking the other, while Safir's suit of Snow was rearguard. The guards on the bridge were alert to the danger, but weren't keen for a protracted fight. With two hundred yards of ground to cover, the Charnelers opened fire as soon as they had a clear shot, but the Cards continued their steady progress. At least one suit returned fire while the others advanced behind the patchy cover of abandoned market cabins and stalls.

The bridge was a high-sided stone affair – easily defended up to a point, but near useless beyond that, given it was built for carts to pass easily. A hundred yards out, Teshen led his suit at a crabbed sprint while the others kept the enemy's heads down. One sparker and they'd probably all be dead so they didn't wait to test the theory, having no such firepower themselves. It didn't take the Charnelers long to realise the danger and they retreated.

They were long gone by the time Teshen had secured the far bank and signalled for the rest to follow, though the gun battle had drawn more attention that anyone was comfortable with.

'Into the back streets,' Suth called as the main group caught up with Tempest. 'Leave them guessing which way we're coming at them.'

'Aye – give 'em a good reason to hold back and let us run at their guns,' Anatin agreed. 'That way then.'

The Cards ran in a disordered group down the nearest street, cutting left into a covered arcade of hastily abandoned carts and worktables. Anything of value had been plundered already so even Deern didn't linger long as they made their way to an alley and Suth checked the road ahead.

'We all going?' Teshen asked in a voice that made his opinion clear.

'Why not?' Anatin said.

The long-haired Knight shrugged. 'We're trying to take the general, a small group can do that just as well as all of us.'

'Volunteering, are you?'

'We need the mages,' Teshen pointed out, 'then just a few others good in close quarters. The rest spreads out, distracts the guards and buys us the space. Hells, might be Sitain can end this all herself?'

The young mage looked startled as she was brought into the debate, but didn't waste much time in shaking her head. Lynx could see the bags under her eyes, the weariness that hadn't been there before she'd quietened the barracks.

'Something that big? No chance.'

'But Lastani can shield you, while I watch the rear,' Atieno said confidently. 'It might give you enough time to take her or give your terms.'

'Let's do that then,' Anatin said. 'All you tattooed freaks come with me. Payl, Reft, Estal, take your suits and make some noise out that way. Estal, take the leftovers of Tempest, Reft you get Snow. Take a few potshots at the guards up around the amphitheatre walls. Don't get caught in a fight, but get 'em looking long enough for us to get in place.'

The three mercenaries nodded and beckoned to their respective suits, creeping back the way they'd come to skirt another way round. Up ahead, the streets all led to the open plaza that the amphitheatre looked out over.

There was only one safe path, a narrow alley which took the Cards to the large, odd building housing the players' tunnel. It was a block significantly larger than a normal house with an imposing gate on the nearer side, bulky enough to obscure the view from the amphitheatre's arches. Lynx followed the rest until they were stood right outside the gate, shoulders hunched against the anticipation of a gunshot, but none came. Suth was about to break the lock on the gate open when Atieno stepped forward and placed his hands over the metal instead. The tattoos on his dark skin pulsed briefly white, a tingle of the magic echoing through Lynx's own skin, and when Atieno removed his hands the iron had corroded, flakes of rust falling away under the breeze brushing past.

Suth's eyes widened, but she wasted little time in pulling the lock apart and easing the gate open. It was dark inside and smelled of smoke and sweat. The lower floor was a plain single chamber with four racks of wooden sticks, presumably required for the game played, and two clusters of benches. Stairs led up on the left and right, flags bearing team colours hung from each banister and the landing above. What light there was crept through narrow slatted windows on the upper level.

In the centre was a wooden staircase leading down – wide enough for four people to walk abreast, worn and old, without decoration. There were sconces for oil lamps lining the staircase, but they were all empty and the tunnel beyond was just a semi-circle of black that began before the steps had even finished.

Suth and Teshen each took a side stairway, stalking up almost silently before confirming the rooms up there were empty. That done, Sitain crept down the tunnel steps and peered into the darkness beyond a second gate at the foot of the stair. She spent a few moments looking for guards in the tunnel, but quickly waved the rest forward and they shuffled into the pitch-black tunnel as Suth fumbled at her pack.

'Wasn't expecting to be glad I was still lugging this around,' she commented as the Monarch's lamp illuminated a chequer-board of white and red glazed tiles covering the tunnel.

'Just hold back with it,' Teshen ordered, nudging Sitain ahead so the two of them were clear of the rest.

The tunnel ran straight and clear, a damp smell the only obstacle as they slunk beneath the plaza and under the walls of the amphitheatre. At the far end was a half-open door. Sitain held up a hand to stop the rest of the Cards following, then crept inside with Teshen. Lynx heard nothing other than the slight scuff of a foot, but his tattoos tingled faintly before they were eventually beckoned forward.

Beyond the door was a very large, low room perhaps fifty yards by thirty. It was broken into three sections by fat brick pillars with dozens of smaller wooden posts between them, all supporting a wooden roof. At the base of one pillar were two Charnelers, presumably out cold. Lynx noticed both Toil and Deern giving them a calculating look before moving on.

In the centre of the room was a wooden platform with some sort of mechanism set to the side and a trapdoor above. A large lever stood next to it and Suth patted Anatin on the shoulder as she pointed at it, then the various narrow tunnels that led off the room in all directions.

'Three groups on platforms here, down there and there, a mage in each,' Suth whispered. 'Pull the lever and you'll ascend – fast, so don't let the jolt throw your aim off. There were no games scheduled this week, so the labyrinth walls will be down and the floor should be clear. We'll have to bet she's on the floor with her prize, ready to head through the canal gate and board once the army's moving up.'

Anatin nodded and divided his troops up. Before they headed off to their assigned platforms Toil caught their attention and turned full circle as she addressed them all in a hushed voice.

'Burners and sparkers in each group – mine goes up first. Take out any guardposts or soldiers in the stands to win some space to breathe, mages get ready to shield. Lastani, we're first so you'll be taking the brunt most likely. Whoever's nearest the general takes her captive unless you've no choice, understand?'

They all did and hurried to their assigned positions. Lynx joined Lastani, Anatin, Toil, Aben and Suth on the central platform. They drew and loaded their guns, taking their time to allow the others to get ready.

'What if the walls aren't down?' Lastani whispered as her tattoos started to glow steadily brighter.

'Then we're about to look bloody stupid,' Suth said, rolling her shoulders with one mage-pistol raised and her free hand poised over the release lever. 'But we shoot into the stands anyway, see who we can kill – after that, I'll have a bit of a think.'

Toil chuckled quietly at that and nodded. There was a strange mix of tension and anticipation on her face. She had a mission that brooked no failure or distraction butting up against a vendetta that robbed her of reason – a need for a cool head grating against her reckless, savage spirit. A leaf shape blossomed into light on Suth's cheek and Lynx felt his own tingle awake as the mages summoned their power.

'Ready?' Suth said after what felt like an age.

There was no reply, but they all instinctively bent their knees, ready for the ascent, and Suth took that as her cue. She pulled the lever and whipped her hand back just in time as the platform under their feet seemed to buck like a mule. Lynx felt the weight of the world on his shoulders as the trapdoor dropped open above them and the light of the sky slammed down with a clatter and a crash.

Up and out through the hole in a flash, Lynx felt his feet leave the platform as it shot up then jerked to a sudden stop. For a moment he could see nothing, just a blur of lines that made no sense, before the shape of the amphitheatre unfurled before him. Great banks of benches stretched almost all the way round, broken only by a squarish block of enclosed seating in the centre of the high north side. Against the wooden benches it was simple to pick out the knots of Charnelers there, but his attention was drawn to a half-dozen uniforms twenty yards ahead of him staring open-mouthed at the mercenaries.

His gun was already raised. Lynx simply tightened it against his shoulder and slipped his finger down to the trigger. The mage-gun seemed to fire as soon as he touched it and a jagged stream of lightning spat out towards them. The sparker caught the soldiers dead on and exploded in a shower of sparks. Bodies fell away, screams cut through the dull morning air, but Lynx was already reloading as more gunshots crashed out.

Distantly he heard the rush and clatter of the other two platforms erupting up through the floor of the amphitheatre – the roar of burners and crackle of sparkers blotting out warcries and whoops from the other Cards.

Beside him, Suth threw down two of her mage-pistols and drew two more. Off to his right Lynx saw a group of a dozen or more Charnelers, standing between a number of tables and a stacked pile of crates. Two guards were falling as Lynx took aim at a pair in the stand behind them. The burner screamed through the air and exploded – the two vanished from sight as benches were smashed aside.

He loaded an icer and followed Toil's lead as the woman surged towards what had to be the general's group. Suth shot two more guards, her aim unerring, while Toil unleashed a sparker at the fringes of the group and downed a handful as the rest reeled away. Those were without uniforms, Lynx noticed as he put an icer through the first Charneler officer to reach for his mage-pistol.

'Lastani!' Toil yelled as she raced to reload.

For a moment, Lynx felt his heart in his mouth. They were in the open and reloading as the Charnelers caught their breath and pulled their guns. Just as he watched a black man raise his mage-gun, a haze of white filled the air. Lynx shrank down as a volley of detonations smashed into it. His hands pulsed with light as Lastani staggered under the impact of more shots than Lynx could count. The pull on whatever magic was inside him grew to painful levels, but then it was over and Lastani steadied herself as Lynx slotted another cartridge into his gun breech.

'Enough!' Anatin roared as they continued on. 'Hold your fire!'

For a moment nothing happened but then the shield of magic fell away and revealed the stunned faces of their enemy, frozen in the act of firing. Mages weren't allowed anywhere near a battlefield, they were simply too precious when they could only deflect a few shots at best. They'd never seen anything like what Lastani had just done, but out of the corner of his eye Lynx spotted a roiled curtain of flickering grey and blue obscure another group of Cards. It was perhaps enough to confirm for the general that this wasn't just some crazed suicide mission and the woman at the centre of the Charnelers holstered her gun and called, 'Hold!'

'Raise your guns and you get burned, that I fucking promise!' Anatin roared as he advanced on them.

Lynx looked around the group. There were five officers still standing beside Bade's handful of relic hunters, but no mistaking the general. By far the smallest there, she had grey hair and a look of stern puzzlement on her face – unruffled by this sudden assault, let alone frightened.

Oh, this one's a true fanatic, Lynx realised, *a monster o' the worst kind.*

He felt his finger twitch at the realisation. It was a soldier just like this one who'd caused his downfall – not the same race or gender, let alone army, but he knew a monster when he saw one. The sort who'd not flinch to order rape and murder, who'd not even see how it could be wrong in service of their cause. Such fanatics were rabid dogs in Lynx's eyes, to be put down as quickly and efficiently as possible before they caused more hurt in the world.

'Fanatic by another name', he recalled someone calling him once. It was an uncomfortable comparison, but one he couldn't deny entirely. *But at least I only* want *to kill her. I won't actually do so unless I have to.*

'So you found your way out o' the black again?' called a tall greying man with a narrow beard Lynx remembered from the Monarch's great hall.

Bade, at last. Keep your head, Toil, Lynx willed.

'I always do,' Toil replied, pistol pointing directly at him. 'Just remember that. I'll never stop hunting you down.'

'Aye, well, if you're still chasing me, you ain't caught me yet and ain't that the story o' your life? Always a step behind, always second best.'

'Bade,' interrupted the general. 'Engage in your little banter on your own time. Are these godless wretches the ones you mentioned?'

'Aye. That 'un's called Toil,' he said, pointing. 'Relic hunter like misself. The rest are her crew so far's I know.'

'And that's how it'll stay I reckon,' Anatin said. 'More important is the fact we've got burners pointing at you and precious little inclination to hold off firing. So shut yer holes and listen up.'

The small woman took a considered pace forward.

'My name is General Derjain Faril. I am a High-Exalted of the Knights-Charnel of the Long Dusk and not some yokel to be cowed by dick-waving relic hunters, so save your threats. Speak your piece and be quick about it before I get bored and order my men to shoot on general principle.'

To his credit, or perhaps as a sign of his crazed sense of humour, Anatin grinned and bowed to her.

'Fair enough, miss,' he said with a laugh. 'Here it is then – we want the God Fragments and we want 'em now. As you've seen, we've got mages who can shield us from gunfire so if it comes to a fight, we might be outnumbered but you're not coming off best. Half o' you at least never bothered to reload by my count.'

Behind them, Lynx heard running feet and glanced back to check it was the rest of the Cards. The mercs clattered up behind and pulled in close together – spreading out wasn't going to be much use when they were surrounded by soldiers on every tier of the amphitheatre. They were close to the centre of the open ground, a long damn way from escape and only the various stacks of crates around the place offered any sort of cover.

'You want the God Fragments?' Faril laughed. With a slow, deliberate movement she drew her mage-pistol again but didn't go so far as to point it at Anatin. Instead she gestured idly with it, as though this was some council debate rather than a stand-off.

'Well, of course you can have these sacred remains of my gods, these holy relics of my religion and cornerstone of the Order I've dedicated my life to. Would you like me to wrap them in a bow too?'

'That'd be lovely, aye.'

'Allow me to make a counter-proposal,' Faril said. 'Drop your guns and, solely because I'm a busy woman, I'll allow you all to walk away unharmed.'

'Bade, tell her how likely that is,' Toil said.

'Oh, I think I can work that out from the look on your face, young lady,' Faril replied gravely. 'But while I'm not afraid to die, it would seem prudent to offer a way to avoid it.'

'There's one way you get to not die here. You hand over the God Fragments and get the fuck out of this city.'

'Now why would I leave? Even if I did hand them over, my orders are to secure the prize of Jarrazir's labyrinth at all costs. I can't leave without doing everything in my power to do so. In case you hadn't noticed, my army's got the upper hand in this fight and if I have to raze the entire city to secure these relics, I shall.'

'Two can play at that game,' Lynx called out, almost surprising himself at the interjection.

'Excuse me?'

He scowled as he tried to quell the growling anger in his belly and took a long breath before answering. Toil and Anatin both looked back at him with eyebrows raised, also surprised by Lynx's contribution, but his thoughts were on the one God Fragment they had seen.

'Scorched earth,' Lynx said, 'it's how monsters like you think, but two can play at that game.'

'If I must die to secure the prize, I'm comfortable with that.'

'Oh aye, I bet you are, but you wouldn't get the prize either.'

That got her attention, her gaze turning from cruelly stern to light-stealing rage in a flicker. All she said was, 'A bold claim,' in a neutral voice.

'See these tattoos?' Lynx said, raising his hands. 'Atieno, get over here.'

The tall mage pushed through the handful of Cards and stood beside Lynx as he indicated the tattoos on Atieno's skin as well.

'Very pretty.'

Lynx grinned, warming to his task. 'More'n that,' he said. 'They link us all – he can draw on our strength for his magic.'

'And?'

He pointed at the crates. 'The fragments are in there, right?' When he didn't get a response Lynx just nodded. 'Toss one over, I'll show you what I mean.'

'I've just said I won't give them to you.'

'And I've just said that we can both scorch the earth behind us – Atieno and our other mages can destroy your relics if they choose. While you might kill us all, your precious relics will be gone in the process – that I guarantee. Give me one and I'll prove it.'

'Preposterous. In case you hadn't noticed over in So Han, the Knights-Charnel know a little something about mages. I believe I'd know if such a thing was possible.'

'It ain't for *your* mages, it is for ours. You've seen 'em stop a volley already. Want to take the risk or test it out with one small one? Do you even use Banesh's fragments in your factories?'

She thought for a long while, biting down on her bottom lip as she did so. 'Very well. Fail and you all die, I'll brook no further delay.'

She turned towards the crates and Lynx inwardly breathed a huge sigh of relief. He'd not known what he'd have done if she'd called his bluff and claimed they were elsewhere. Chances were everyone's bluff would be called and they'd all die in a huge conflagration of fire and lightning, leaving behind some charred corpses all feeling a bit foolish.

The general pulled a battered pack from the crate and opened it, reverentially unwrapping the long white cloth to reveal the fragment within. This she inspected before replacing it and taking a second. That one she deemed suitable and she tossed the glowing chunk of smoked crystal over to Atieno.

In the same moment she nodded to her officers and, before anyone could react, they raised their mage-pistols, Bade's crew swiftly following. The mercenaries snapped their own up in response, and Lastani threw up a hazy shield between them, but no one fired. Everyone held their breath and glared like dogs at their now-indistinct enemy, hackles raised but all too aware what it meant to take the first bite.

After a long pregnant pause, Lastani released the shield and all eyes turned to Atieno as he held the God Fragment up between finger and thumb. It seemed to shine a little brighter in the winter light. Just as Lynx felt his guts start to turn to water, he felt a shiver run through his tattoos and the shattered piece of a god's body abruptly crumbled to dust and fell away. Atieno brushed the remains from his hands and gave Faril a sharp look.

'And that was without really trying,' he advised the woman.

The look on his face showed Toil wasn't the only person to feel they had a grudge there. Atieno was a mage who'd likely been looking over his shoulder his entire life because of people like Faril. He'd be as glad to kill her as Lynx would, and he'd have a better reason for it too.

'Your point is made,' she said in a more subdued tone. 'However, it means your death still. Do you honestly expect me to believe you'll do it? You're mercenaries, you care about your own skin above all.'

Toil took a step forward. 'I'm no mercenary,' she growled, 'so take a look at my face. Do you really think I lack resolve?'

'I think you're a calculating agent, one who'll prefer to try to win another day.'

'Deern,' Toil snapped, 'Teshen, step forward.'

The two men did so and Toil gestured towards them. 'If you don't believe me, how about this – do you really think this lot aren't shitbag crazy enough to do it, just to see the gods burn with them? Resolved or crazy, I don't care which you believe, but how many turns of the cards do you think you've got before the Jester appears?'

Faril matched Toil's gaze for a long while before glancing at the two men summoned forward. Finally, she gave a reluctant nod. 'I see your resolve,' she said at last. 'It is a familiar thing and I recognise it for what it is, just as I recognise one of your friends wears a Jester card on his chest. Very well, take the bags.'

'What?' exclaimed Bade and one of her officers at the same moment. Faril silenced the objections with a raised hand and looked around at the Cards as though marking the face of each.

'Take the bags and go,' she repeated. 'Bade, have your men unpack the crates. Let them take the fragments to the Monarch – I rather suspect she'll be more of a mind to negotiate with me.'

'Eh?'

She shot him a look that made even Bade's permanent smirk waver. 'You heard me.'

'Aye, sure.'

With a nod the relic hunter set his crew about the task. They pulled the various packs from each crate and dumped them all in a pile together between the opposing groups. It looked like there were a little over a dozen and Toil checked each one, replacing the shards as she confirmed there was something inside while Lynx found himself doing likely the same rough calculations she was. Once they were finished and Bade's men upturned the crates to show there were no more, Toil distributed the packs among the mercenaries and then hesitated.

'One more thing,' she said to the general.

'Oh?' There was a flicker of amusement on the woman's face now, clearly expecting some sort of insult to injury.

'I want Bade too. He and I got some unfinished business.'

'A final reckoning between you, is it? Perhaps we should form a circle and give you each a knife?'

'Nope, I don't care if it's a fair fight. The only reason I don't shoot him right now is that I've got a burner in the pipe and any gunshot will set all this lot off.'

'Sorry to disappoint,' Bade broke in, 'but I ain't going nowhere with you, Toil.'

'Who the fuck said you were getting a choice?' Toil roared. 'I'm talking to the mistress, not the dog.'

Bade shook his head with mock sadness and raised a bag that had been slung over his shoulder. 'I don't give a damn, woman, you'll keep your trap shut and listen a while longer.'

He held up the bag and half opened it to reveal the contents. Despite everything, the soldiers and mercenaries all took a small step back at the same moment.

There was a mage-sphere in the bag – the size of a melon and wrapped in frayed twine so none of the glass inside was visible. There were no markings on it, just roughly stripped-back oakum and flecks of yellow paint from an outer surface that had clearly been removed. Spheres were made to resist being dropped given the catastrophic results of accidents, but Lynx felt his guts turn to ice at the thought of this one falling.

'See, I thought this might be useful,' Bade went on with a vengeful grin. 'Just in case the army didn't reach the right point in the city by the time we escaped the labyrinth.'

'You took it from the North Keep,' Suth said, eyes full of murder. 'Their ammunition was marked yellow.'

'That I did – local lass, are you? Anyhow, there were still a few bombardment spheres in there so this little thing wasn't needed to breach the wall. Seemed silly to waste it.'

'Are you going somewhere with this, Bade?' Faril demanded, sounding about as impressed as she was intimidated.

'Aye – I'm walking away from this. If missy here or anyone else tries anything, it'll fall. Can't say I'm certain what happens after that, with the outer layer cut away, but in my experience there's shitbag crazy and there's suicidal. Some glassy-eyed merc might well try to survive a stand-off, but blowing yerself up is another matter so I'm walking away now. I've delivered the goods as ordered and whatever happens now is your fucking problem.'

'Are you quite finished?' Toil asked scornfully.

He gave her a nasty grin. 'Oh, I'm sorry, in a rush are we? I'm not surprised – the main body o' the army is disengaging from the fight under a flag of truce. That order went out an hour or more back, they should be tramping their merry way up the canal boulevards pretty soon. Feel free to hang around and let 'em shoot you on sight. Not like any of them will know about your mages, they'll just see some fucks who deserve to get shot, so let's see how it goes for you with a few hundred icers to chew on.'

'Still in love with the sound of your own voice, then, I see.' Toil raised her mage-pistol to point it directly at his face. 'And still full of shit too. You're a coward, Bade, you always were. Saving that scabby old hide of yours has always been your first concern so you're not blowing yourself up here.'

'Perhaps not,' General Faril broke in, turning to also point her pistol at the startled relic hunter. 'But I could always do it for him.'

Lynx looked around. The two groups all had their guns levelled – how many on the Charneler side actually had anything more than an icer he couldn't tell, but there were two Torquen uniforms among them at least, and Bade's own crew looked as villainous as Lynx's.

Not that it matters a whole lot, Lynx reminded himself, *given we've got more soldiers appearing on the stands all around.*

Now that he had a moment's pause to look, Lynx realised the whole scene was haloed by small fires burning in a dozen places around them. The wooden benches and tiers of the amphitheatre were easy fuel for the burners they'd fired. It would take a while to set the whole place going, but the longer the guards watched them rather than the fires, the more chance of an inferno there was.

'Hand the bag over,' Faril ordered.

Bade blinked at her a short while then did so, quickly backing off once the attention was back on the general. He glanced at his crew and the rest of them edged back a little way, guns still trained on the Cards but looking more like running than fighting now. Only when Faril ordered them to stop did Bade grind to a halt, face betraying his tension as he watched the confrontation between Faril and Toil.

'Changed your tune, haven't you?' Toil asked the general coolly.

Faril gave her a slight smile that was in that moment as disconcerting as Reft's. 'The fragments remain my principal concern and Bade has changed the options. Perhaps a mage-sphere can destroy them, perhaps it's something special to your tattooed mages. The look on your faces shows you're not certain yourselves and it's *my* soldiers who pick up the pieces once we're all dead. *My* Order that retrieves the God Fragments.

'If Banesh himself could only shatter the gods into fragments, it's not a bad bet that a standard mage-sphere won't make them crumble to dust.' She cocked her head at Atieno. 'It will mean you struggle to do the job yourself and save your mercenary hide at the same time. Look me in the eye and tell me I'm wrong.'

No one spoke. No one knew what to say so far as Lynx could tell. It wasn't quite an admission, but it opened the door to certainty enough for a crowbar to be inserted.

'Well that's disappointing,' Toil said eventually.

'It is, isn't it?'

Toil turned to look at the mercenaries behind her. Lynx saw her catch the eye of Atieno, Lastani and Sitain, nodding slightly as she spoke to the rest. 'Drop the bags,' Toil ordered. 'She's won this one.'

'Eh?' Deern demanded, lowering his gun and turning to stare, incredulous, at Toil. Lynx felt a sudden tingle on his skin, building with terrifying speed.

'You heard me,' she said as the bags started to thump down on to the wooden floor.

'Kas?' Toil called to the dark-skinned scout who still held her bow fully drawn, arrow pointing at the general. 'You too – do it!'

The tingle became a torrent of fire on Lynx's skin and swirls of light and colour erupted around them. Kas fired even as a veil of ice magic descended over them. Lynx caught sight of the arrow slamming into the general's chest – unaffected by the surging currents of power that knitted themselves into a skein of white.

There was one final glimpse of the shock on the general's face, the pain and surprise as she was hurled backwards under the impact. Then the shield solidified between them and Lynx had just a moment to crouch and cringe, to feel fear at what was to come. After that, the world blinked away in an explosion that eclipsed everything.

Chapter 38

Toil blinked and tried to move. Her whole body hurt; sharp pains mingling with a bone-deep ache. An orchestra of discomfort playing a hundred individual notes accompanied each movement as her wits slowly returned and she could begin to take stock. Each injury combined and magnified those around it to echo through her very bones – not merely the sum of their parts but some grand symphony elevated to shake the very rafters.

'Shit,' Toil croaked, pawing feebly as she tried to make some sense of where she was.

The explosion. The blinding light and the force of impact. Even the mage-shields hadn't been able to fully withstand it. They'd been hammered backwards, thrown from their feet and then . . . She looked around. There was wood everywhere. Broken pieces; planks and splinters. And it was gloomy – not dark, not night, but something not quite like day.

'Ulfer's horn,' groaned someone nearby. 'Am I dead?'

Slowly, Toil pulled a piece of wood from across her chest and shoved it to one side. Her hand was a mass of tiny cuts and her little finger burned with pain as she moved the wood. Toil frowned at it for a moment then, jerkily, lifted her other hand and tried to pull her dislocated finger back into place. The action made her scream at first, prompting a flurry of panicked movement all around her, but Toil could see little until she was done.

When it was in place, she lay back, panting until the pink spots faded from her vision. In their place came clarity and she finally realised where they were. A halo of torn wood seemed to hover above her, penning the sky overhead. They were in the lower chamber – the explosion had shattered the artificial floor beneath their feet. Toil looked left and right. There were Cards slowly rising from the rubble like the hideous risen dead – caked in dust, bloody and battered, scowling at a world that had tried to kill them yet again.

'Anyone got a gun?' Toil asked hoarsely.

Abruptly, Lynx rose from the mess of shattered wood a few yards away. 'Sod my gun. Ain't counted my legs yet.'

'Who's shitting idea was that?' Anatin said. The man whimpered as he tried to get to his feet with only one hand and an uneven pile of wreckage underneath. He slipped once, twice, then managed to steady himself and flapped at the empty holster at his waist. The Prince of Sun frowned, then kicked at the broken pieces, scanning around for a while until he bent and pulled a mage-pistol from the mess.

'Aha, that's better. Now I can shoot whichever shit-brained excuse for a heifer made the world blow up.' He scouted around, wobbling slightly and squinting at the faces nearby. 'Kas, where are ya? Here, girl, time to get shot in the face.'

'Put it away,' Toil said, grabbing Lynx and using him as support to get up herself. 'Or watch above, in case the Charnelers come looking.'

'Ain't they all dead yet?'

Toil shook her head and dragged Lynx to his feet, then went to help Lastani. 'Not the guards in the stands, the bomb wasn't that big. Doubt there's any bits of the general left up there amid the mess, though. I'll just have to pray that Bade was close enough to get the same but right now we're probably still outnumbered so no time for checking. You okay?' she asked the young woman.

Lastani blinked up at her with a blank expression, too dazed to reply, but Toil couldn't see any serious injuries so she didn't press the issue.

'Guess we got lucky,' Lynx muttered, looking at the wreckage around them. Almost the entire roof of the room had been staved in; part of one tunnel at the far end ripped open. 'I'm fine too, by the way.'

'Lucky?' bellowed Deern, lurching towards them with a mad look in his eye. 'You call *that* lucky?'

'Aye.'

'An earther,' Toil said, catching on a moment later. 'Gods yes. If he'd grabbed a fire-bomb, we'd all be cooking right now.' She looked up at the sides of the room. There were some scrappy ends to grab on to, but nothing that looked strong enough to pull her up and out of the hole. If it had been a fire-bomb there'd be no escape. As it was, the earther had destroyed the artificial floor and ripped open a chunk of ground beyond, but there was only a great cloud of dust hanging over them rather than the smoke of burning planks.

'Sound off,' Anatin called, still waving his gun around like a confused drunk. 'Who's left?'

More Cards struggled from the piles, Haphori, Safir, then Layir. Toil scouted around and found Aben lying prone not far behind her. She pulled him up and checked the man over. There was a wound to his head bleeding everywhere, but it didn't look fatal.

'Well?' she said to Anatin as there came unintelligible grunts from different directions.

'Sitain? Ah, there ya are. Lynx, pick her up, she ain't looking good.'

Anatin fished another mage-gun from the debris and tossed it to Teshen as the man sat up with his face hidden by his long hair. Teshen caught the gun seemingly without looking and swept his hair out of his face to give Anatin a baleful look. Then he stood, hauling Atieno with him. The mage looked as unsteady as Sitain, but Toil was happy to forgive him that.

'Looks like we all owe the mages a drink or two,' Toil commented. She grabbed a pack that hopefully contained some God Fragments. 'Get your shit, anything you can see, and head back the way we came.'

She pointed in the vague direction as the Cards turned uncomprehending expressions her way. 'The tunnel, clear the entrance.'

Finally, they looked back and some of them started to wade towards the half-covered tunnel entrance, its tile-strengthened walls mostly intact despite the explosion. Others started grabbing at the canvas packs that were scattered all around, apparently as intact as the mercenaries themselves.

'Shift yourselves,' Toil announced, finding a gun at last and realising with slight surprise that it was her own. She opened it and slotted a fire-bolt in. 'Burner in the pipe!' she called loudly, prompting startled looks.

Those guards won't be too far long, let's not stay like rats in a pit. The general didn't think God Fragments will burn and I reckon she'll know more about it than me. The Monarch can dig through the ashes in a few days.

'What's the plan, Toil?' Anatin asked.

'The finest traditions of the mercenary craft,' she said, feeling a manic grin cross her face.

'We're running away?'

Toil nodded. 'Followed swiftly by a good bit o' hiding too.'

'I like this plan.'

'How about this bit?' Toil aimed the gun down the far end of the shattered room and pulled the trigger. The burner hit the far side and exploded into flames, hurling fragments of burning wood high in the air.

'The fuck's this bit?' Anatin howled.

'Set the place on fire so no one follows,' she announced, sheathing her gun. 'Now get your shit and everyone into that tunnel!'

The flames spread quickly through what was now a huge firepit of sawdust and splintered wood. The Cards barely had time to grab their stunned comrades and all the bags they could see before the fire pursued them right to the tunnel mouth. Toil made sure she was last in, counting the heads once more to ensure only surviving Charnelers would burn. Half of them didn't have mage-guns and she guessed they were missing half the God Fragments too, but Toil didn't wait to search.

They scampered down the long tunnel, doing their best to ignore the sound of raging fire behind and glad the rush of wind in their faces showed it was drawing air in, not acting like a chimney for the smoke to escape. When they neared the far end Toil called a halt. They all sank to the ground, exhausted, while Toil arranged them to put Atieno and Sitain at one end, Lastani at the other.

'What now?' Lynx asked, settling the unconscious Aben down so his head was resting on one of the God Fragment bags. 'We just wait here?'

'We wait,' Toil confirmed. 'We sit and hide like quiet little mice unless it starts to fill with smoke. If anyone comes after us, the mages keep us alive while we use up whatever cartridges we've got left.'

'I don't think I can do much more,' Lastani said, her voice slurring with weariness and dyed white hair hanging limp over her face.

'Sit and rest for now. We've got an army out there with no leaders, the amphitheatre's probably on fire by now. They ain't getting the God Fragments in a hurry and no one in charge likely knows much about 'em. It might take a while to organise, but I reckon they'll withdraw and leave us to it.'

'Sit and wait,' Lynx said, nodding slightly drunkenly. 'Reckon I can do that.' He lay down beside Aben and stretched his legs out. 'Wake me if an army comes to kill us.' He paused. 'Mebbe don't, actually, not sure I'll want to know.'

*

The Cards sat in the dark of the tunnel for two hours or more. It was hard to gauge the time passing. They heard distant gunfire, shouts and the tramp of many feet, but didn't venture out to investigate. Toil kept awake and didn't say a thing as she saw others drift off – not even when the mages slumped and started to snore. Her hearing was sharp and she was confident of being able to wake them before a burner got fired down the tunnel, so until then she let them recover their strength.

When someone came, despite everything, Toil was so startled and jumpy she almost shot them on first sight. It was just a dark figure in the tunnel and the echo of boots, but then came a blessed sound – a voice even her exhausted, half-scrambled brain recognised. Her brother, Vigilance, advanced down the tunnel with a few of his lieutenants. After kicking the others awake Toil embraced her brother and happily allowed herself to be shepherded out into the grainy afternoon light.

Vigilance confirmed what she'd expected, that the Knights-Charnel had been harried out of the city in the confusion surrounding General Faril's death. Soon the mercenaries were reunited with the rest of the Cards and they were escorted as a group back to the palace while the amphitheatre continued to burn furiously. The city was a brutalised thing, whole streets shattered by earth and fire. Hiding in the shadows were frightened and bedraggled citizens shocked by the devastation and picking their way through the ruins.

Much of the fighting had taken place in the merchant district where they had lodged and those districts beyond it. Even from the palace Toil could see the damage done, the wreckage of a street battle. The great beasts of the city, the guild-houses and university, were holed and wounded amid the broken corpses of their lesser kin. And, among those, Toil saw bright robes of the dead, ordinary guildsmen in the uniforms of their trades alongside the mages of the city – selling their lives to defend it.

The palace itself was relatively untouched, one tower fallen and a lesser wing staved in down one side. Inside there was disorder and damage, but again it was minor. It seemed General Faril's control of her troops had extended to keeping them from looting, although Toil wondered if that would have continued after the battle was won. In the throne room, however, the white Duegar lamps were gone, recognised for what they were and plundered along with silver and gold ornaments. As Crown-Princess Stilanna formally received the tattooed group and all except Paranil, who was beaming from a stretcher, knelt to her, Suth pulled the one remaining white glass oval from her pack. Its light spread around the room and the Monarch gave a weary smile. The sight seemed to diminish the gloom in more ways than one.

'Not all plundered,' Stilanna said, gesturing to a servant to relieve Suth of the burden. 'Thank you, Suth.' She paused and looked again around at the faces. 'Elei?'

'No, Majesty,' Suth said, eyes downcast. 'Dead in your service.'

'As so many others.' She reached out and touched the arm of the Crown-Prince beside her, as though reminding herself that he was still there. Tylom was pale and still spattered in mud and blood, one arm in a sling. 'My husband tells me his life was saved more than once by those who gave their own for him. The sacrifices will not be forgotten.'

The Monarch took a deep breath and straightened. 'And yet, by most other measures we are victorious – thanks in great part to you, Mistress Toil. Your employer's faith in you was well founded.'

The packs they'd managed to recover were brought forward by more servants and unpacked on the floor in front of the throne. It was an incongruous sight; an untidy pile of plain canvas and white cloth before the great throne inlaid with jet and gold, then glinting shards of the gods themselves slowly appearing, to gasps from the watching court.

The servants were painstaking in their investigation of each pack, eight in all, and checked every fold of cloth before setting anything aside. The largest, a fist-sized chunk with jagged striations down one side that shone with a yellow light, was passed up to the Monarch. She cradled it in both hands and stared like a child, Tylom crouching down beside her despite the discomfort it brought.

'There are more,' Toil said, 'you just might have to wait for your amphitheatre to cool down a bit before you go collect them.'

The Monarch nodded slowly, reluctant to tear her gaze from the God Fragment. 'Yes, you do seem to have caused a fair amount of destruction in your wake,' she said with the hint of a smile, wonder eclipsing fatigue and shock. 'Perhaps we should not discuss a reward and I'll just hold back from billing you for a new amphitheatre?'

Toil gave a hollow laugh. 'Pretty sure I didn't cause most of the damage to the city,' she said, 'but I'll waive my usual fee as a gesture of goodwill.'

Crown-Princess Stilanna's face turned serious. 'Then goodwill you have, for you and your employer. Might he have something to request of me?'

'No doubt a whole list of 'em,' Toil confirmed. 'With your permission, can we leave the details for another day when I'm not hurting and exhausted? It was mostly goodwill I was sent here to build. The Militant Orders are growing bolder, as you're now only too painfully aware, and divided we will fall. The Archelect proposes a League of Parthain – an alliance between states that have all too often been enemies. He hopes you will agree to meet him and discuss the foundation.'

'A League of Parthain?' The Monarch was quiet a long while before nodding. 'I will meet the Archelect. Goodwill wins you at least a discussion and the hope for more.'

'And the God Fragments,' Crown-Prince Tylom added, 'might serve to expand that – gifts for the other states to bring us all together?'

Stilanna looked startled one moment, then laughed the next. 'How very selfless of me that would be, to offer gifts no state would think of refusing and ensure we were all equal targets, should the Knights-Charnel ever come looking for the God Fragments again.'

'What about the labyrinth? What else is down there?' Tylom asked. 'Does it pose a threat to the city? Are there artefacts to be removed?'

Toil managed another weary smile. 'That's a question for the scholars, I think. I'll gladly guide a party back down. There are lamps to make your halls famous, but not much in the way of gold and jewels I'm afraid. I'm sure closing the Fountain is a lot easier than opening it so, once Lastani has recovered her strength, I think we'll manage it.'

'We shall have to be content with the treasure you recovered from your competitors, then. What about the saboteurs – Sotorian Bade and his crew? Did they die with General Faril?'

Toil shook her head. 'I wish I could say for sure. They were backing away but it was a big bloody explosion.' She paused.

'But Bade's the sort of rat who might survive. Right now we can only hope not. If anyone heard our conversation with the general the Charnelers aren't done with the Cards, not by a long shot. For the time being, however . . . with your leave, Monarch, I'm going to fall over very soon. I'd like it to be into a vat of wine.'

The Crown-Princess stood and nodded to them all. 'Such a thing of course is not permitted within the boundaries of Jarrazir, but I'm sure one damned foreigner or another has managed to pollute the city with its corrupting presence. If wine can be found, you're welcome to ensure as little as possible remains to drag our gods-fearing citizenry down the path of iniquity. In the spirit of goodwill, that is.'

She paused and gave the merest of bows to Toil, despite the fact she was a Monarch standing before her throne. There were no intakes of breath among the Jarrazirans watching, but Lynx saw a few note the gesture and all the seriousness it implied.

'You have my thanks, all of you – Mistress Lastani and Master Atieno too. For all that you were party to the start of all this, I have no stomach for retribution and the city has seen enough death. Should I have need of your services in the future, however, you will remember this generosity, I trust. Mistress Toil, we will speak again when you have rested. In the meantime I've got a city to rebuild.'

Epilogue

Lynx opened his eyes and smiled. A faint glimmer of dawn crept through the curtains, the smell of peppery sweat hung in the small room. Below the window was a disordered pile of clothing atop a travel chest, on the floor a jumble of discarded clothes and boots. In the far corner stood a chair, cartridge cases hanging from its back and the muzzles of mage-guns visible behind, propped against the wall.

He turned his head slightly. A holstered pistol hung on the bedpost, within easy reach, but when he stretched his arm out it was to luxuriate in the quiet comfort of early morning and slide it over smooth bare skin. A distant thump echoed at the back of his head and the edges of his vision were blurry, but he could not tell whether it was the after-effects of the explosion or something more self-inflicted. For the present Lynx didn't care. He was content just to listen to the soft sounds of breathing beside him, surrounded by the fug of unwashed clothes, sweat and sex.

Somewhere in the building he heard movement and faint snatches of song breaking the quiet. Lynx tried to make sense of it, but they'd been drinking until late so it remained a jumble in his mind. The events of the last few days began to play again in his mind, the frantic fighting and those damned explosions. The injuries he still carried, the protesting muscles and dozen scabbed-over cuts. Somehow, the fatigue and aching felt welcome, though, the lingering sense of hard-earned victory.

It's been three days and I bet I'll be pulling more damn splinters out of my backside, Lynx thought as the various pains announced themselves once more. *Still woozy after that explosion, reckon we all are. The drink's helped there, after a fashion. Always good when an appreciative population find a way ta thank their saviours.*

The singing grew loud, the unsteady footsteps echoing up the narrow wooden stairwell.

Someone's just back from celebrating. Lynx smiled. *That'll be their bonus spent, then – not that I've been saving like a miser, o' course.*

He glanced over at the chair where the cartridge cases hung. The Monarch had given a bonus to each of the Cards who'd ventured underground, after more God Fragments were unearthed from the smoking pit at the heart of the half-ruined amphitheatre. A leather-bound book sat on the chair, half covered by a stained shirt. *Tales of the Last Days*, it was called – one Lastani had recommended as a seminal collection of Duegar tales, or those that had escaped acquisitive eyes during the Revival anyway.

Unlike most books he'd owned, this one was in near-perfect condition, the green leather embossed with a spiral of ancient Duegar symbols. Lastani had told him the willow tree was sacred to the Duegar and he'd resolved to read every such book he found until he understood what their new tattoos meant for them all.

Lynx looked down at his naked body. The pale shapes of leaves were barely visible on the skin of his belly, legs and arms, and hardly more noticeable even on the darker-skinned Cards. The marks had faded quickly over that first day along with the power Atieno, Lastani and Sitain could employ, but a brief test had shown they would still glow when the mages used their magic. And that magic itself remained greater than before – not the vast amounts available in the hours after the labyrinth, but more than any other mage Atieno or Lastani had ever met.

And we're all a reservoir for more, Lynx reminded himself, *even if we're no nearer to working out what it all means.*

Without warning the door burst open and a dark figure in a long leather coat charged in. 'City watch!' the figure bellowed. 'Where's the contraband?'

Toil was up in an instant, moving from sleeping to action in the time it had taken Lynx to blink stupidly. The figure swung towards the bed and Toil twisted to avoid its onrush, grabbing one reaching arm and using it to add force to her knee. Connecting hard, Toil hauled the intruder around and slid one arm underneath theirs, drawing it up behind their back as she slammed them face first into the cheap plaster of the wall. The whole room seem to shake with the impact and the figure howled with pain.

'I win!' roared a voice from the doorway. 'Hand it over, ya squint-eyed turds!'

Lynx sat up, frozen in the act of drawing the mage-pistol, and frowned at the figure in the doorway. He couldn't focus very well, but there was something familiar about the voice.

'Aben?' he said groggily.

'What the fuck?' Toil roared.

She released the intruder and spun them around to look at their face. It was Himbel. The company surgeon gave her an unsteady grin, white teeth gleaming in the dim light, as he looked her up and down.

'Hey, look, you were right, she's nekked!' the surgeon declared, puckering up. 'Give us a kiss then.'

Toil gave a growl of irritation and hurled Himbel back towards the now-crowded doorway.

'Ah, boss,' Aben said, 'yer, ah, well . . .'

Toil's growl deepened. 'What is it with you fucks and walking in on me naked?' she demanded, whipping the sheet off the bed.

Lynx flinched, now exposed himself, and flapped wildly around.

'Oh put it away, big fella,' Llaith called from behind Aben. 'No one wants to see that.'

Lynx finally succeeded in yanking one of the pillows from the end of the bed to cover himself. Just as he did so, Toil hooked something white on the end of her toe and flicked it towards Lynx. He caught it and held the undergarment up.

'Mebbe a bit small,' he hazarded, putting it on the bed and fishing his braies off the floor. He had to flop like a landed fish to haul them on, but in a short time he was sat on the edge of the bed, not quite as on show as he had been.

'Fancy explaining, Aben?'

The big man's grin wavered. Lynx could see he was still drunk; perhaps not quite so bad as Himbel, though, and better acquainted with Toil's nasty side.

'I ah, well . . . we were talking, about you, and someone mentioned a bet. I . . .'

He turned to those behind him, letting go of the door handle in the process. That made him stagger under the weight of mercenaries pressing forward and they all spilled inside. Llaith almost ended up in Lynx's lap, Suth and Layir stumbled over Himbel, while Ylor, a blonde woman who wore the Seven of Snow, seemed to take the opportunity to drape herself over Aben.

'A bet?'

Suth coughed and straightened up with the theatrical care of someone drunker than they realised.

'It's all Llaith's fault,' the woman declared. 'Apparently he thinks I ain't drunk alcohol before. An' stupid too.'

'Not stupid!' Llaith protested. 'Just hoping you were a bit gullible and we could get some hazing in.'

Lynx blinked at the Jarraziran for a moment then realised she was wearing her new badge on her jacket – the Knight of Tempest. So it was official now, she'd been released from the

Monarch's service, or at least on indefinite leave. Teshen had been made Knight of Stars, the more senior of the sergeant positions and responsible for more mercenaries, while Suth got the misfits of Tempest.

There had been little choice for Suth or the Monarch really, the tattoos marked her as one of them and once word got out, they'd need each other to protect themselves. She was a tough and capable agent as well as a Bridge Watch soldier. No doubt all sides – Cards, Jarrazir and Su Dregir – would benefit by the new arrangement.

She wasn't the only new recruit either. Lastani now wore the Jester of Stars, being an ice mage and as bad a shot as Sitain, while Atieno had the Prince of Tempest on his jacket. The man had impressed Anatin but showed no interest in command, so he'd been given the same honorary position as Toil, which seemed to suit everyone.

True to Vagrim form, Atieno wasn't happy at finding himself tied to the Mercenary Deck, but he recognised there was little he could do about it for the time being. It was more of a wrench for Lastani, Lynx knew. Vagrim were wanderers by nature, but she was a city girl with a family to say goodbye to. The tattoos left her with no real choice in the end and with Toil's assurance that understanding them was a priority for the whole company, she'd signed up.

'Fortunately for us,' Llaith continued, 'Himbel's exactly stupid enough after a few drinks. My money was on you shootin' him, though.'

'I said you'd put him down before he got halfway in,' Suth added helpfully. 'Himbel reckoned you'd see the funny side and give him a kiss.'

At that Aben seemed to collapse into somewhat hysterical laughter, dropping Ylor in the process, and Llaith swaggered forward to haul the dazed Himbel up off the floor.